# The Gospel Pedlar

JOHN BERRIDGE

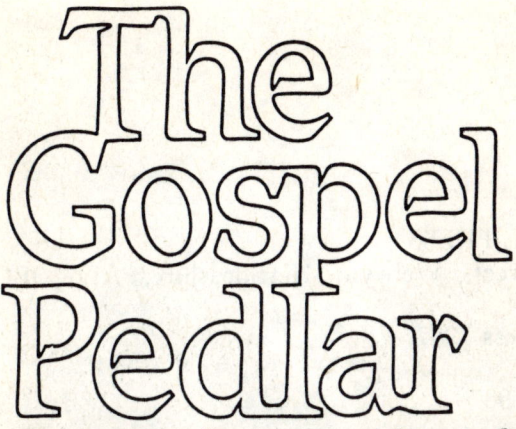

# The Gospel Pedlar

The Story of John Berridge and the
Eighteenth-Century Revival

Nigel R. Pibworth

 **EVANGELICAL PRESS**

EVANGELICAL PRESS
16/18 High Street, Welwyn, Hertfordshire, AL6 9EQ,
England
© Evangelical Press 1987

First published 1987

**British Library Cataloguing in Publication Data**

Pibworth, N.R.
 The gospel pedlar : John Berridge of Everton
 (1716–1793).—(Welwyn biographies).
 1. Berridge, John   2. Evangelists—Great
 Britain—Biography
 I. Title   II. Series
 269'.2'0924     BV3785.B4/

 ISBN 0-85234-236-5

Cover photograph by R M Rixon

Typeset by Alan Sutton Publishing Limited, Gloucester
Printed and bound in Great Britain by The Bath Press, Avon

# Contents

Part II   Evaluation

*Part I*
*The life of Berridge*

# 1.
# John Berridge: the need for reassessment

There have been several interesting accounts of Berridge's life. J.C. Ryle wrote about him in the context of other eighteenth-century evangelical leaders, acknowledging his unconventionality but concluding by appealing to his Victorian readers to 'reform our judgement of the good man, and cast our prejudices aside'.[1] Marcus Loane has written a warm and appreciative biographical chapter in his studies of Cambridge men who served the evangelical cause.[2] Charles Smyth has produced by far the most solid and detailed scholarship in his study of the origins of the evangelical revival in Cambridge in the eighteenth century.[3]

Although most historians have generally recognized the importance of Berridge in the evangelical awakening of the eighteenth century, few have evaluated the usual qualifying adjectives of 'quaint', 'eccentric', 'peculiar' and 'odd' that have been applied to him. Many mention his eccentricity without giving a clear idea of what they mean by it. Further confusion is caused by the gradual change in the use of this word since the eighteenth century. The word today has emotional overtones which hinder rather than help in our understanding of Berridge. We are not talking about peculiar idiosyncratic and personal habits, but about Berridge's willingness to break the accepted rules of normal behaviour in order to fulfil his mission and communicate with those around him.

Perhaps nineteenth-century historians, with their Victorian ideas, found Berridge's directness and frankness questionable and saw these qualities as evidence of his eccentricity rather than of his ability to communicate in an age when ordinary people were not used to packaging things

3

attractively or mincing words. J. Overton speaks of him being 'eccentric, in his words at least if not in his deeds'.[4] Whittingham, Berridge's curate, who compiled his works after his death, writes that Berridge's hymns could give offence to 'fastidious readers'.[5] Abbey and Overton questioned the propriety of saying 'that nature lost her legs in paradise, and has not found them since'.[6] Indeed, some of Berridge's remarks made in private correspondence could be classed as very unusual, as for example, when he writes to Lady Huntingdon declining a persistent request to go to preach at Brighton with the comment that 'his instructions must come from the Lamb and not the Lamb's wife'.[7] His letters are untypical of the age. 'In the correspondence of the time, so heavily weighed with solemn, stereotyped language, his letters stand out in their spontaneity and raciness, and call for a smile even when they deal with the most serious subjects.'[8]

Berridge was indeed an unusual man, but a fuller account and analysis of his life will qualify glib and superficial judgements of him. 'Berridge is a man much underrated, his eccentricities survive his excellencies; men think of him as the "Everton ass", as he styled himself, rather than as the polished scholar and man of letters.'[9]

Berridge was regarded by the majority of the clergy of his day with suspicion and downright hostility. Towards the end of his life, John Byng the diarist comments that Berridge 'is generally term'd a Methodist, and is held out by the clergy as a stumbling-block and a dangerous character'.[10] Berridge's evangelical friends saw him in another light. John Wesley, soon after getting to know him, writes to Lady Huntingdon that 'Mr Berridge appears to be one of the most simple as well as one of the most sensible men whom it has pleased God to employ in reviving primitive Christianity.'[11] A friend of John Sutcliff, the Baptist leader from Olney, speaks of Berridge's prayers as 'such sweet solemnity, such holy familiarity with God and such ardent love to Christ'.[12] Henry Venn, who came to Yelling, a few miles from Everton, after leading a prominent work at Huddersfield, says, 'His life is a pattern to us all, and an incitement to love and serve the Lord with all our strength.'[13] John Fletcher of Madeley spent much time and study in criticizing Berridge's Calvinistic views, but he warmly acknowledged that 'Few, very few, of our elders equal him in devotedness to Christ, zeal, diligence and ministerial success. His indefatigable labours in the Word and doctrine entitle him to a double share of honour.'[14] Cornelius Winter, the young companion of Whitefield, speaks of 'the affection with which Mr Whitefield always mentioned his name, and the honour in which he held his services'.[15] To Winter he was that 'truly apostolic man'.[16] His biographer and curate, Whittingham, wrote of Berridge's 'unaffected humility'[17] and 'exemplary piety'.[18]

Berridge would not have seen himself as a suitable subject for Christian biography. He had a poor view of himself, a self-image that deteriorated as he grew older. His letters and hymns speak of his consciousness of the fight between the old and new man:

> What a motley wretch am I,
> Full of inconsistency?
> Sure the plague is in my heart,
> Else I could not act this part.[19]

He writes to his friend John Thornton, 'I am growing, as I should, more small and loathsome in my own sight, and Christ is growing more precious and lovely; but I cannot walk in his strength, as I ought, nor feast on his fulness, as I might. Here I am an infant still but am praying daily for larger stature of faith, faith to remove mole hills at least, if not mountains.'[20] Three years before his death he writes that he is 'very sick of self, and of a daggling world'.[21] A man who considered himself

> Very foolish, very base,
> Notwithstanding Jesus' grace!
> Murmuring oft for gospel bread,
> Growing wanton when full fed!
>
> Brisk and dull in half an hour,
> Hot and cold, and sweet and sour,
> Sometimes grave at Jesus' school,
> Sometimes light and play the fool![22]

was not concerned with historians attempting to study his life.

Yet although he did not write an autobiography or prepare his papers for posterity, he was concerned to tell his own story in so far as it glorified the Saviour. He composed his own epitaph in his own inimitable style. Placed on his tomb in the area reserved for criminals and suicides, its message still speaks to those who visit Everton churchyard:

> Here lay the earthly Remains of JOHN BERRIDGE
> late Vicar of Everton and an itinerant Servant
> of JESUS CHRIST, who loved his Master and his Work
> and after running on his Errands many Years was called
> up to wait on Him above. Reader art thou born again?
> No salvation without new birth.
> I was born in sin Feb. 1716
> Remained ignorant of my fallen State till 1730
> Lived proudly on Faith and Works for Salvation till 1754
> Admitted to Everton Vicarage, 1755
> Fled to JESUS alone for Refuge, 1756
> Fell asleep in Christ Jan. 22nd, 1793

L. Tyerman comments on this epitaph: 'This is a truthful outline of the history of this remarkable man. To fill it up would require a volume.'[23]

How is it that such an outstanding Christian leader, communicator and shepherd has been comparatively neglected in the light of the recognition that he was 'the central figure in East Anglia, so far as the evangelical witness is concerned'?[24] David Marshall calls him the 'forgotten apostle of Bedfordshire' and considers it a mystery that 'so bright a light is well nigh universally ignored amidst the present darkness'.[25]

There are perhaps several reasons why this zealous and self-denying Christian leader with a remarkable ministry should have been neglected. The written sources are limited. Berridge did not keep a journal. He did not collect his letters, nor did he write much. He wrote hymns[26] (many of which contain autobiographical material and portray the inner man) and a small book discussing the Calvinism controversy of his day,[27] and towards the end of his life helped to edit a book of devotional readings.[28] Five letters were published before his death.[29] However, it was left to his curate and biographer to search for letters amongst the descendants of his friends and correspondents. In fact Whittingham apologizes for the long delay that this search caused in the publication of the *Memoir and Works*.[30] As more letters have come to light they have been published in various magazines. A book made from his marginal comments in his Bible was published in 1882,[31] and this, with some sermon outlines, his farewell sermon and an early tract complete his known written work. The materials are not as full as one would like, but his memorials were people rather than books.

The reason for the lack of materials is simple. Berridge had neither leisure nor inclination to write. He describes himself as a 'very tardy correspondent'.[32] He asks for forgiveness from his friend John Newton: 'During my latter years I have been continually making apologies for slack returns to my corresponding friends, and am not one jot better yet. No one can be ashamed more, or grieved more, or repent more, or resolve more, than I have done, yet no reformation ensues.'[33] Illness and his disinclination for writing were contributory factors, but more often he did not have the leisure or the emotional reserves on account of his itinerant preaching.

Berridge has also suffered neglect because of his churchmanship. His attitude to the future of his own church and to churches generally was pessimistic and this did not endear him to the next generation of churchmen. This pessimism, coupled with his lack of conscience in keeping to the rules of the Church of England and his founding congregations which naturally developed into nonconformist bodies, surely proved difficult for nineteenth-century Church of England leaders to accept. His plainly expressed views about infant baptism, the problem of evangelical succession in a parish and his opinion that most real Christians were forced to leave their local parish church in order to survive spiritually could not have endeared him to the generation of evangelicals who followed, for they were involved in an attempt to influence the national church from within.

Another reason for the neglect of Berridge, particularly amongst evangelical scholars, is that there is a complexity about his character which is difficult to unravel. J.C. Ryle puts him 'in a class by himself'.[34] There is an openness and honesty which is disarming; a 'quaint mixture of wit, sense and bluntness'.[35] Although his nineteenth-century biographer pleads for genuine biography which 'does not allow of partiality or any deviation from the reality of character',[36] Berridge was a difficult subject for nineteenth-century writers. He was deeply pessimistic regarding matters about which nineteenth-century evangelicals were confident. He strove for simplicity and directness in communication and turned his back on scholarship, order and polish. He was humble, generous and sensitive to the needs of the poor, and yet he could be outspoken and seemingly cutting in his remarks. He preached the need for personal dealings with God, and yet was sympathetic and encouraging to those who wrote to him doubting and troubled by their own lack of experience. He obviously found intellectual enjoyment in evaluating ideas, but he thought controversy unprofitable and preferred to seek communion with Christ as the prime aim of his life. Berridge's own personality, with its unusual combination of seriousness and humour, has posed a problem for the biographer.

A study of Berridge's life and work will, I hope, show that in spiritual matters the issues for the Christian remain the same whatever the age in which we live or whatever our circumstances. Berridge's own Christian pathway, his willingness to break conventions and change his mind, his seeking after spiritual reality and truthfulness rather than forms and ceremony and his living as an itinerant servant of Jesus Christ should challenge the state and genuineness of our own Christian profession. A reassessment of Berridge, if it is to be profitable, will lead to a reassessment of our own lives.

# 2.
# Berridge and his times

Berridge's life spans most of the eighteenth century – a transitional period as seen from the perspective of the twentieth century. When he was born in 1716 the religious and political upheavals of the previous century were still relatively fresh in the national mind. By the time he died, in 1793, the French Revolution was well under way. The century was one of social, economic and industrial change. The population almost doubled during that period and the shift from a mainly rural setting to urban dominance started apace. Changes in the organization and methods of farming were linked with the beginnings of an industrial economy.

These changes brought and accentuated problems. There was much rural poverty, particularly towards the end of the century, and the Poor Laws became more and more unworkable. The national church was not responsive to changes in the distribution of population and its organizational structure, with many plural livings and poor curates, did not forebode well for the future. Infant mortality was high and medicine, although improving, was rudimentary. The universities were run for the benefit of college fellows rather than dedicated to the aims of scholarship. Society was dominated by a rigid class system.

However, the eighteenth century was not altogether dissimilar from our own. The villages that were familiar to Berridge in his travels exist today. Eighteenth-century houses and cottages are still lived in. Despite the two-hundred-years time gap the language is basically the same. Even the clothes are not too different from those worn today. The fundamental differences existed in the presuppositions of the thinking of ordinary people. The squire and vicar were often the only educated people in a village. Villages were relatively isolated and, before the days of mass literacy, radio and television, the religious institutions often supplied the sole relief from the domestic scene.

However, travel was possible, even though roads could be very difficult in winter. Throughout the period improvements were being made to the main roads and in many places these were quite good. But away from main roads bad weather could reduce the poorer roads to quagmire. Towards the end of his life John Wesley records travelling from Hinxworth to Wrestlingworth, a village a short distance from Everton, 'through such roads as no chaise could pass. So we had the pleasure of riding on a farmer's cart.'[1] Henry Venn noticed the comparative isolation of village life after the bustle and contact of Huddersfield when he came to Yelling, a few miles from Everton, as a supposedly dying man in 1771. Because the winter was bad he wrote, 'I have not been on horseback once these seven weeks.'[2] Venn sent his furniture from Huddersfield to Yelling by water, coming up the Ouse through Kings Lynn to Paxton, just three miles from Yelling. Perhaps it was because of the difficulties of travel in winter that Berridge consistently preached in London for three months after December. During the early years especially, people travelled for miles for the Sunday meetings at Everton. 'People came to hear him from the distance of twenty miles, and were at Everton by seven o'clock in the morning, having set out from home soon after midnight.'[3]

The agricultural worker and cottager would normally have seen no printed matter except for the Bible, the Prayer Book and perhaps some ballads. Books were expensive and the average countryman would have a predominately oral culture, not a literate one. In the first full year of Berridge's work at Everton, out of four marriages all the couples had to put their mark. In 1757 out of three marriages there is one signature. The following year one couple, James Peck and Ann Bulter, signed their names. In fact, from 1756 to 1793, the period of Berridge's work at Everton, there were only forty-nine signatures in the register out of 188 persons married. In all probability there was not the need to read as there is today. However, those who responded to Berridge's message cried out for the Scriptures and Berridge, through the generous giving of John Thornton, one of the wealthiest men of his day, was able to help supply this need. Berridge writes to Thornton, 'My hearers are of a sound gospel class, very poor and simple-hearted, and cry out for the Bible.'[4] Berridge also used literature in evangelism, especially Alleine's *Alarm to the Unconverted*. Literally thousands of copies of this book were distributed by Berridge.

The physical landscape during the time of Berridge was radically different from that of today. The agricultural land in his area was still mainly unenclosed and walls and hedges were rare. Meadows were wild and undrained and woods and trees abounded, providing free fuel, as well as game, to the peasants. Great tracts around Cambridge were waste and uncultivated and while Berridge was at the university it was common for the undergraduates to return to their colleges with duck, snipe, partridges and bitterns from these shooting grounds. Most people lived in small towns or villages and life was dominated by rural concerns. This domestic economy of the whole village was to be altered radically by the enclosing of land. Berridge's world was an agricultural world on the verge of dramatic and painful transformation.

What was the state of institutional religion in the eighteenth century? Evangelical historians have stressed the 'before-and-after' picture, with the evangelical revival saving the nation from moral disintegration. They have quoted the nineteenth-century historian Lecky with approval: 'A religious languor fell over England.'[5] C.R. Balleine calls it the Glacial Epoch in our church history and illustrates this by referring to a drift into rationalism in polemics and into unitarianism by nonconformity, and the evils of pluralities and non-residence. A. Dallimore's book on George Whitefield was written to show that God can work mightily in the darkest of times. Abbey and Overton, the two historians who did much to stress the positive contributions of the eighteenth-century institutional church, still accepted that the clergy caught 'the spiritual inertia which clung over the face of the country'.[6] The early eighteenth-century religious scene can be regarded as a reaction to the excessive religious disputes of the previous century. It was a time when moderation ruled and extremism was problematic. The result was that the religion which prevailed emphasized observances and forms rather than the meaning of the symbols. It was institutional rather than personal.

How did Berridge view the institutional church of his day? Although he had evident signs of God's blessing on his work and few men met with greater success as preachers, he took a very pessimistic view of the state of what he regarded as true religion. In fact he seems unaware of the evangelical revival influencing the institutional church to any extent. He paints a black picture: 'God has promised a reformation when his Word is truly preached; but no reformation is produced by the modern preaching. Things are visibly declining from bad to worse. Therefore we must conclude, either the word of a faithful God is fallen to the ground, or his work has not been preached faithfully. If God is not in blame, the preachers are and must be so. For a long season the good old church doctrines have been much forsaken; by some they are derided and by many are deserted. Yet no doctrines can build the church of Christ up but those which planted it. We may labour much in lopping off loose branches of immorality and infidelity, yet nothing will be done effectually till the axe is laid to the tree's root.'[7]

Preaching was missing the mark because there was a 'need of regeneration as well as outward reformation . . . the want of a new nature as well as new conduct'.[8] Soon after his conversion he was clearly convinced that the gospel of his time which he had been preaching was not the true gospel, for he says that during the last one hundred years the 'clergy have been gradually departing more and more from our doctrines, articles, and homilies; so that at length there was scarce a clergyman to be found, but who preached contrary to the articles he subscribed. And almost all the sermons that have been published in the last century both by bishops and curates are full of that soul-destroying doctrine that we are to be justified partly by our own works, and partly by Christ's merits.'[9]

Berridge described this false gospel as the 'parish way of paying sinful debts',[10] a mixture of human effort and Christ's merits. There were few true gospel ministers and those who existed were 'thinly scattered about the country'.[11] He came to believe that 'The doctrines of grace are a common offence to the clergy, and the Bible itself a fulsome nuisance to the great vulgar . . . powerful efforts have been made to eject the gospel doctrines out of the church.'[12]

Berridge classed himself with a very despised minority: 'All that wear the gospel cloak of faith, full and deep, are thought enthusiasts or impostors – men who have lost their wits, or lost their honesty, and only fit for Bedlam or for Newgate.'[13] He had few friends amongst the local clergy and was generally disliked to the end of his life. Thomas Scott expressed the normal bias against such people as Berridge: 'I joined in the prevailing sentiment; held them in sovereign contempt, spoke of them with derision; declaimed against them from the pulpit, as persons full of bigotry, enthusiasm and spiritual pride.'[14] One of Berridge's few clergy friends in the area, Henry Venn at Yelling, writes of seeing no other clergymen in the neighbourhood as his name was sufficient to disgust them.

The existence of institutional forms did not mean there was spiritual life. 'Establishments may keep up forms, but Christ alone can give power.'[15] Berridge felt there was an emphasis on externals instead of internal realities:

> With solemn weekly state
> The worldling treads thy court,
> Content to see thy gate,
> And such as there resort;
> But, oh, what is the house to me,
> Unless the Master I can see?
>
> Whilst formalists admire
> The pillars, walls, and roof,
> Which bring no heavenly fire,
> And are but weather-proof;
> I seek a man more choice than gold,
> That lovely man whom Judas sold.[16]

Berridge saw most parish services as respectable but dead. The patient in *The Christian World Unmasked* says, 'Indeed, doctor, we have nothing to trouble us in our parish, besides family cares and bodily infirmities. The vicar's chief complaint is about his large family and scanty income, and the old clerk's weekly moan is about his rusty voice, which cannot rear a psalm without a woeful outcry. On Sundays we march to church in our best clothes, and are decently seated in pews, which are swept every Christmas. Aged people look grave enough, but the young ones stare about them and are peeping at everyone who steps into the church; for we keep dropping in all prayer-time. And during the sermon, which is soon dispatched, some listen, others giggle; and when the weather waxes warm, a few are half awake, and the rest are dropped asleep; which proves they have no burden. This is our parish way of going unto Jesus Christ.'[17] The gatherings were 'a dead scene of worship, conducted like an undertaker's funeral, with very cloudy face, and yawning entertainment'.[18]

What was the effect on society? 'Can any good thing keep its head above water in the present age . . . the Word of God despised . . . the house of God deserted . . . the name of God blasphemed everywhere? The Bible, like an old almanack, is either cast out of doors or cast upon a solitary shelf, to be buried there in dust and covered with a winding-sheet, weaved by a spider.'[19]

What were the results of this 'modern gospel' of grace plus works? 'A century is time sufficient to give us full experience of it. Do we find more praying families, more crowded churches and more empty jails? Are ropes pulled oftener in a chiming steeple and stretched seldomer at Tyburn? Can we travel roads with more safety and sleep with fewer bolts upon our doors? Are play-houses and gaming-houses become exceeding rare, and their owners grown very meagre, quite abashed at their occupation? Have we more preaching bishops and painstaking clergy, more staunch patriots and upright lawyers, more gentle masters and faithful servants, and more fair dealing practised in buying and selling? Alas, . . . I know the contrary. Gluttony and drunkenness, cursing and swearing, gaming and gambling, diversion and dissipation are become so common as to make the fashion; and sodomy, the last scum of a filthy land, is bubbling in the pot apace and boiling over. Wickedness wears no mask and fears no censure. Ever since the new gospel showed its face, profaneness and infidelity have been pouring in, like a sweeping rain, and overflowed the land. God has lost his worship, Christ has lost his office, Scripture lost its credit and morality has lost its carcass. It has become a pageant, held up in a pulpit, but seldom noticed out of it; and as for holiness, it is the land's abhorrence.'[20]

In spite of all the legions of discourses published on morality, the Word was not being faithfully preached: 'For a long season the good old church doctrines have been much forsaken; by some they are derided and by many are deserted.'[21]

The so-called 'age of reason' was far different seen from the perspective of God: 'The present age would fain be called a learned age, and the giddy people think themselves a wise people – wise to do evil, but to do good have no knowledge. Reason flirts at revelation, merit spurns the thought of grace, tapers would outblaze the sun, and human fancies far outweigh the truth of God.'[22]

This was how Berridge came to see the desperate spiritual condition of his age. However, this understanding came only after his own enlightenment, in his own conversion. Up until then his life and beliefs were similar to those of many other sincere vicars in the national church.

# 3.
# Early days and Cambridge

John Berridge was born on 1 March 1716 in the village of Kingston-on-Soar, near Kegworth, a few miles from Nottingham. His father was a well-known and prosperous farmer who had married a Miss Sarah Hathwait two years before. There were to be four sons in the family, John being the eldest. John seems to have spent much of his youth staying with his aunt in Nottingham. It was here that 'he received all the education which was necessary to qualify him for business'.[1] Before he was fourteen, and while he was still at Nottingham, Whittingham tells a story of a youth inviting him into a neighbour's home on his return from school in order to read the Scriptures. Although he felt a secret aversion to this pious activity, John must already have had some serious thoughts as he was soon reading the Scriptures with other boys.

At fourteen Berridge left his aunt and returned to his father with the intention of undertaking the practical side of the family business. It was at this age, according to his epitaph, that he became convinced that he was a sinner. He was fond of visiting a local tailor in order to discuss religious subjects and to pray. His parents were worried about where such conversations would lead and discouraged this relationship. Obviously religious contacts like these were of some importance in his spiritual development. From fourteen through to eighteen Berridge seemed incapable of picking up the practicalities of pricing cattle. His parents failed to stop his visits to his religious companion and 'finding this their scheme unsuccessful, and conceiving that his predilection for reading and religion would entirely unfit him for business, they resolved, though reluctantly, to send

16

him to university. In this determination, which was perfectly congenial with his own inclinations, he most readily concurred.'[2]

After some private preparation Berridge went to Clare College, Cambridge in 1734 or 1735. His college records him as matriculating in 1735 while Wilks, Whittingham and Berridge himself in the flyleaf of his Bible all say that he entered Clare Hall on 24 October 1734. Cambridge in the middle of the eighteenth century 'was a small market town of less than 10,000 people, bounded by the river and the King's Ditch and approached by execrable roads more or less infested by robbers'.[3] It was dominated by the university which, with roughly a thousand students, had declined radically in numbers from the previous century. Eighteenth-century universities did not perform like modern-day institutions of higher learning. Many tutors and undergraduates did little work. However, Berridge was a hard worker. He says, 'When I first came to the university, I applied myself diligently to my studies, thinking human learning to be a necessary qualification for the divine, and that no one ought to preach unless he had taken a degree in the university. Accordingly I studied the classics, mathematics, philosophy, logic, metaphysics and read the works of our most eminent divines; and this I did for twenty years.'[4]

There is no doubt that Berridge loved books and the learning and wisdom they brought. 'Being now in his element, he pursued his studies with uncommon avidity, and made such progress in every branch of literature as rendered him in no respect inferior to any of his contemporaries.'[5] So serious was Berridge in his quest for learning that 'From his entrance at Clare Hall, to his acceptance of the Vicarage of Everton, he regularly studied fifteen hours a day.'[6] Henry Venn, a friend of many years standing, said that Berridge was as familiar with the classical languages as he was with his own native tongue. His biographer declares that 'He possessed a strength of understanding, a quickness of perception, a depth of penetration, a brilliancy of fancy, and a fund of prompt wit, beyond most men.'[7] Natural ability and hard work brought him recognition as a 'senior fellow of Clare Hall, and moderator in the public schools, being a man of considerable learning, and condescension, as well as a great humorist'.[8] Soon after arriving at Cambridge, Berridge had become the Lord Exeter Scholar and remained as such until he obtained his degree in 1738. He became a fellow of the college in 1740, obtaining his Master's degree in 1742 and was 'an unusually studious fellow of his college'.[9]

Berridge had a reputation for wit as well as scholarship. His 'natural vein of humour'[10] made him a popular man. He seems to have had a wide circle of friends and, as the university was only producing about 100 graduates a year, he must have known some men who would rise to prominence. At social gatherings Berridge would entertain the company with quotations from favourite works, such as *Hudibras* by Samuel Butler, a poet who was extensively quoted in the past but whose reputation has suffered an almost complete reversal. Berridge would have had very mixed feelings indeed when from the vantage-point of a despised Methodist preacher he looked back to his Cambridge days and remembered the large sections of *Hudibras* he had committed to memory. However, at Cambridge he would have enjoyed this burlesque poem mocking the weaker aspects of the Puritan party of the previous century. To summarize, in C. Smyth's words, 'He was a studious, clever, fat and jolly don; the best company in the world.'[11]

What was happening to Berridge's religious life during these years? We saw how he came to Cambridge soon after he had received what appeared to be religious impressions. However, he soon caught the philosophy and spirit of the university of the time and discontinued 'private prayer for the space of ten years, a few intervals excepted'.[12] This quick reversal would seem to cast doubt on the strength of those original convictions.

Many leading theologians of the day appealed to reason rather than to revelation. Such a primary place assigned to reason and a fear of enthusiasm and extremism to which it was linked can be seen behind all the theological controversies of the period. The gospel of the time was a gospel of reasonableness. The scientific revolution led to a lack of interest in revelation, for truth was believed to be self-evident to the enquiring mind. Even those fighting against the general trend, such as Berkeley, Butler and Warburton, were basing their appeal more on reason than Scripture. It is hardly surprising that Berridge 'caught the contagion, and drank into the Socinian scheme to such a degree, as to lose all serious impressions'.[13]

During the period of ten years in which he discontinued private prayer there were times when he felt remorse concerning his state of mind compared with what it had been when he came to the university. Whittingham records how he wished, 'Oh, that it were with me as in years past!'[14]

Berridge was ordained deacon at Lincoln on 10 March 1745 and as priest in the Church of England on 9 June 1745. It appears that he began to take his religious duties and devotions more seriously from this time. Perhaps he felt that a clergyman could not be so free in his thinking as a young don with no public office in the national church. Whittingham adds that a short while before Berridge obtained a curacy 'he returned to the regular exercise of devotional religion, although it was but a small remove, if any, from pharisaical'.[15]

Berridge himself saw no fundamental change in his religious state while he was at Cambridge. For twenty years he was studying the whole range of human learning, 'and all the while was departing more and more from the truth as it is in Jesus; vainly hoping to receive that light and instruction from human wisdom, which could only be had from the Word of God and prayer'.[16] At Cambridge Berridge, as his epitaph says, was still living proudly on faith and works. Four years after ordination he obtained the curacy of Stapleford, a small village near Cambridge. Some have depicted this year as a time of religious awakening for Berridge. Marcus Loane speaks of a recovery of faith, and C. Smyth of a strong inclination to exercise the pastoral ministry. J.C. Ryle sees God as awakening 'his conscience once more'[17] and F.W. Bullock paints the same picture. There is no real evidence of this. A more likely date is 1754, when his tomb records that he stopped living on the mixed covenant of faith and works. As Berridge worked at his studies, so he seems to have worked at his preaching. Strong inclinations to preach and desires to help his parishioners do not add up to an awakening. At Stapleford, 'He took extraordinary pains, and pressed very earnestly upon them the necessity of sanctification: but had the mortification to find that they continued as unsanctified as before.'[18]

Back at his college, from which he served his church, he was thought to have Methodist leanings, much as did the Holy Club members at Oxford who were called by this name. Certainly he was serious and methodical in his religious duties. 'During this time I was thought a Methodist by some people, only because I was a little more grave, and took a little more pains in my ministry than some others of my brethren: but, in truth, I was no Methodist at all, for I had no sort of acquaintance with them, and could not abide their fundamental doctrine of justification by faith.'[19] Berridge's diligence as a preacher failed to produce changed lives. He was at this stage seeking to communicate in the language of the people, he lived in an upright manner, he was sincere, yet 'his ministry, throughout these six years, was entirely without fruit, to his own great annoyance and mortification'.[20]

Although Berridge had not yet reached a point of release he was, as it were, arriving at negative conclusions. Towards the end of his curacy at Stapleford he seems to have been in some degree aware of his own insufficiency and to have experienced serious doubts about an element of trusting in himself for acceptance with God. He 'lived proudly on faith and works for salvation till 1754'.[21] He may well have continued preaching and holding to the 'mixed covenant', as he was later to call faith and works, but his singling out of a date would suggest that whereas before this time he was supremely confident of the faith of his church and of the merit of his own works, afterwards he was questioning his whole approach to God.

There is a hint of this in Dyer's account of why Berridge went to Everton in 1755. It could have been a normal promotion, but Dyer suggests that 'He had too much the tone of a reformer to be enclosed in the university, and was now settled on a small college living.'[22] Berridge is described by Dyer as the first at the university to be influenced by Methodism and as a disturber of the peace, 'who occasionally preached in the pulpit of St Mary's and gave great offence to the university. He formed no party at the time, which openly countenanced him in the university; but he soon had many admirers in town and country. The Fellows of Clare Hall, it seems, disposed of him in a way creditable to themselves, and acceptable to Mr Berridge, by giving him a college living, which was Everton, in Bedfordshire.'[23] Dyer may, however, be confusing events at this time with those which occurred after the conversion of Berridge, by which time he had already been at Everton for two years.

The case against Dyer is that when Berridge came to Everton he still preached the same doctrines as at Stapleford. 'At length I removed to Everton . . . Here again I pressed sanctification and regeneration as vigorously as I could; but finding no success after two years preaching in this manner, I began to be discouraged, and now some secret misgivings arose in my mind, that I was not right myself.'[24] Were these secret misgivings completely new or were they, as the epitaph hints and Dyer suggests, acknowledged towards the end of his period at Stapleford? G.R. Balleine interprets as follows: 'Great had been the sensation at Cambridge, when it was known that the senior Fellow of Clare, the brilliant scholar and famous wit, had 'turned Methodist' and accepted a country living (1775). Greater still was the sensation in Bedfordshire, when, after a short period of groping in the dark, he grasped his message in its fulness, and began his work.'[25]

Whatever Berridge's state of mind at the time of his appointment, he did not take up residence at Everton immediately. According to the notes on the flyleaf in his Bible[26] he was admitted to the vicarage of Everton and Tetworth on 7 July 1755, but he did not take up residence until 25 March 1756, some nine months later. A John Jones was curate during these months, and is last referred to in the register in April 1756. Berridge was occasionally at Everton, for example, reading the banns for a marriage in November, although most of the work would probably have been carried out by the curate. The delay of nine months may have been due to the occupation of the vicarage by the curate, or Berridge may have been busy at college. His college had purchased the living of Everton in 1544 after the dissolution of the priory at St Neots.

Everton itself stands on the highest ground of the district

and commands a picturesque view of the Ouse valley.
Potton, two miles away, was the major market town in the
area. It is difficult to estimate the population of Everton,
although some historians multiply the average annual number of marriages by 120 to calculate this. From 1756 to 1786
there were seventy-six marriages, giving an average of 2.5
per year. On this basis the population of Everton and
district would probably be about 250. Everton was to be
Berridge's home for the next thirty-seven years. He was just
under forty years old when he became vicar and after a short
time he was to undergo a radical change.

# 4.
# Conversion

Berridge sums up his conversion in the short sentence: 'Fled to Jesus alone for refuge.'[1] Much power and experimental truth are concentrated in those lines of his epitaph. For Berridge the reliance on a 'mixed covenant' of faith and works was to break down with the dissatisfaction of his own spiritual life and the impotence of his preaching. Berridge's conversion was to put him in the category of 'twice-born men'. He came to see the absolute necessity of conversion. 'Till the heart is circumcised, we have no spiritual life. This spiritual circumcision is regeneration, a new spiritual birth, whereby we begin to love God.'[2] Commenting later on the blind man in John 9 Berridge says, 'How amazed he must have been when his eyes were first opened! How he would look and stare about him; everything was new to him, and would fill him with wonder. So is it when the eye is spiritually opened: so it was with me.'[3] Berridge's conversion is the story of a mature, educated and earnest vicar in the Church of England rejecting the combination of self-reformation and conventional theology as the way to God, and holding instead the need for 'a spiritual renovation of nature, a real but secret work of the Holy Spirit on the souls of men, producing a new and spiritual service'.[4]

The tension in Berridge's pre-conversion experience seems to have focused on the meaning of the doctrine of justification, or at least that is how he came to interpret the matter as he looked back. According to his epitaph, he became conscious of his state of alienation from God at the age of fourteen and then 'lived proudly on faith and works for salvation till 1754', that is, just before he left Stapleford to go to Everton. Intellectually he assented to the basic

Christian doctrines, except for a period of questioning the deity of Christ while at Cambridge, and viewed his Christian duties as of importance in obtaining salvation. However, he did not have peace with God. This inner tension can be seen in an autobiographical passage in *The Christian World Unmasked*: 'Formerly, when I had asked help in prayer, instead of looking for that help, and relying on it, I strove to help myself, and stripped to fight my adversary. Many of these battles I have fought, but never gained any credit by them. My foe would drop his head sometimes by a blow I gave him, and seemed to be expiring, but revived presently, and grew as pert as ever. I found he valued not an arm of flesh, but made a very scornful puff at human will and might. Often when a fire broke out in my bosom, the water I threw on to quench it only proved oil and made it burn the faster. The flame of anger would continue in my breast till its materials were consumed, or till another fire broke out. One wave of trouble e'er while passed off, because another rolled on, and took its place. One evil often drove another out, as lions drive out wolves; but in their turns, my bosom was a prey to every wild beast in the forest. Or if a quiet hour passed, it proved but a dead calm. My heart had no delight in God, a stranger yet to heavenly peace and joy. At length, after years of fruitless struggling, I was shown the gospel method of obtaining rest, not by working, but believing. A strange and foolish way it seems to nature, and so it seemed to me; but it is a most effectual way, because it is the Lord's appointed way.'[5]

It seems that much of the inner conflict within Berridge was due to his 'do-it-yourself' theory of salvation. This is not surprising, for theology at Cambridge was becoming dominated by an appeal to reason rather than revelation. Berridge himself struggled in the 1740s with an Arian view of Christ which reflected this approach. Writing to John Thornton in 1773, he confesses that 'Near thirty years I was an avowed enemy to Christ's divinity, and when God had given me some knowledge of his Christ, and sent me forth to preach his gospel, it was three years before I was fairly rescued from the quicksand.'[6]

If, as it seems likely, Berridge is referring to his ordination by being sent forth to preach, this would mean that it was not until about 1748-49 (the time when he became a curate) that he had regained orthodox views on Christ. Yet correct views on the nature of Christ did nothing to solve Berridge's basic problem of struggling with sin, lack of peace and joy, and the seeming lack of power in his ministry to change people's lives for good. It was this last aspect that increased his tension to such an extent that he concluded something must be wrong. He writes to a fellow clergyman six months after his conversion: 'At length I removed to Everton where I have lived altogether. Here again I pressed sanctification and regeneration as vigorously as I could; but finding no success, after two years preaching in this manner, I began to be discouraged, and now some secret misgivings arose in my mind, that I was not right myself (this happened about Christmas last). Those misgivings grew stronger and at last very painful. Being then under great doubts, I cried unto the Lord very earnestly. 'Lord, if I am right, keep me so; if I am not right, make me so. Lead me to the knowledge of the truth as it is in Jesus.'[7] In his struggle Berridge seems to have received no help from any individual. In a small village, separated from the physical and social environment of his college life, and probably after some years of intellectual, doctrinal and emotional turmoil, he reached the point of dramatic change. His years of unsettledness were to end.

There is some confusion over the exact time when, for about ten days, Berridge sought God in prayer for knowledge of the truth if he was wrong. His tomb says (in his own words) that he 'fled to Jesus alone for refuge, 1756'. In fact all the evidence clearly points to his entering this crisis in December 1757. Whittingham, his biographer, writes, 'Having continued for two years in this unsuccessful mode of preaching, and his inclinations to do good continually increasing, he began to be discouraged. A doubt now arose in his mind, whether he was right himself, and preached as he ought to do. This suggestion he rejected, for some time, with disdain, supposing the advantages of education, which he had improved to a high degree, could not leave him ignorant respecting the best method of instructing his people. This happened about Christmas 1757. But not being able to repel these secret misgivings though he strenuously opposed them, his mind was wrought to a degree of embarrassment and distress, to which he had hitherto been a stranger. This, however, had a happy effect, as it led him to cry mightily to God for direction.'[8] Writing in July 1758 of this distress, Berridge says, 'This happened about Christmas last.' John Green, vice-chancellor at the university, who wrote a serious criticism of his testimony, clearly understood 1757 to be the date: 'Your first secret misgivings, it seems, that you were not right yourself happened about Christmas 1757.'[9] Whittingham says that he started preaching outside his own parish on 22 June 1758, 'not more than six months after the change in his religious sentiments'.[10]

D. Marshall, noticing the discrepancies in the dates, has put forward a solution: 'If Berridge was right as to the year when he first exercised saving faith, and Whittingham was right as to the time this man of God first felt the power of the Spirit, then we have an interval of months between the completion of his conversion to Christ and his first experience of the fulness of the Spirit.'[11] However, the accounts of Whittingham, Green and Berridge all speak in terms of conversion and not of fulness of the Spirit. The evidence suggests Berridge made a mistake when he prepared his epitaph. Berridge relates how his prayers were answered: 'As I was sitting in my house one morning, and musing upon a text of Scripture, the following words were darted into my mind with wonderful power, and seemed like a voice from heaven, viz. "Cease from thine own works." Before I heard these words, my mind was in a very unusual calm; but as soon as I heard them, my soul was in a tempest directly, and the tears flowed from my eyes like a torrent. The scales fell from mine eyes immediately, and I now clearly saw the rock I had been splitting on for near thirty years.'[12]

Whittingham adds that immediately 'he began to think upon the words *Faith* and *Believe*, and looking into his concordance found them inserted in many successive columns'.[13] In his letter recounting his experience Berridge speaks of broken-heartedness for sin and of joy and peace in trusting Christ alone. He later was to see this work in the lives of many people and wrote of the Spirit's work:

If once the sun shines upon a soul clear
He reads the dark lines which sin has writ there:
Begins to discover his colour and make,
And cries, I'm all over as any fiend black.[14]

Berridge's joy and relief seemed to come by the discovery of a biblical way to God. His eyes were opened to the primacy of faith and he recognized with sorrow that his secret reliance on his own morality and good works had in practice negated the work of Christ. As he wrote later, 'Jesus Christ will admit no partner for our faith. He is worthy of full credit, and expects it, and we must either look to him alone, or look to be confounded. He will be all or nothing.'[15] Before this revelation of the primacy of faith he 'went to Jesus, like a coxcomb, and gave myself fine airs, fancying if he was something, so was I; if he had merit, so had I. And, Sir, I used him as a healthy man will use a walking staff, lean an ounce upon it, or vapour with it in the air. But now he is my whole crutch, no foot can stir a step without him. He is my all, as he ought to be, if he will become my Saviour.'[16]

Commenting on Leviticus, Berridge describes how the position and work of the high priest illustrate the supremacy of Christ in salvation: 'Aaron as the high priest was to have no associate in this work. So Jesus has no associate: he makes the whole atonement himself. Not his merit and ours jointly bring pardon; but his blood alone. He, and he alone is our peace. He treads the winepress of God's wrath, and treads it alone.'[17]

Berridge's understanding of the primacy of faith in Christ was soon expressed in the classic doctrine of justification by faith alone. Six months after his conversion he writes concerning his illumination, when he saw what had really been his problem for thirty years: 'Why, it was some secret reliance on my own works for salvation. I had hoped to be saved partly in my own name and partly in Christ's name, though I am told there is salvation in no other name, except in the name of Jesus Christ (Acts 4:12). I had hoped to be saved partly through my own works and partly through Christ's mercies, though I am told we are saved by grace through faith and not of works (Eph.2:7,8). I had hoped to make myself acceptable to God partly through my own good works, though we are told that we are accepted through the Beloved (Eph.1:6). I had hoped to make my peace with God partly through my own obedience to the law, though I am told that peace is only to be had by faith (Rom.5:1). I had hoped to make myself a child of God by sanctification, though we are told that we are made children of God by faith in Christ Jesus (Gal.3:26). I had thought that regeneration, the new birth, or new creature, consisted in sanctification, but now I know it consists in faith (1 John 5:1) . . .

'All that is previously needful to justification is this, that we are convinced, by the Spirit of God, of our own utter sinfulness (Isa.64:6), convinced that we are children of wrath by nature, on account of our birth-sin (Eph.2:3) and that we are under the curse of God, on account of actual sin (Gal.3:10). And under these convictions come to the Lord Jesus Christ, renouncing all righteousness of our own, and relying solely on him, who is appointed to be the Lord our righteousness (Jer.23:6) . . .

'And now, dear sir, hear what is the rise and progress of true religion in the soul of man. When the Spirit of God has convinced any person that he is a child of wrath, and under the curse of God (in which state everyone continues to be till he has received Jesus Christ into his heart by faith), then the heart of such an one becomes broken for sin; then, too, he feels what he never knew before, that he has no faith, and accordingly laments his evil heart of unbelief. In this state men continue, some a longer, some a less time, till God is pleased to work faith in them. Then they are justified and are at peace with God (Rom.5:1), i.e. have their sins forgiven them, for that is the meaning of the word *peace*. See Luke 7:48–50. When we have received faith from God (for it is his gift, Eph.2:8) to justify our persons, then we afterwards receive the Spirit to sanctify our natures (Eph.1:13; Gal.3:14). And now the work of sanctification goes forward; now his fruit is more and more unto holiness; now the love of God is shed abroad in his heart by the Holy Spirit (Rom.5:5). Now he walks in the comfort of the Holy Ghost (Acts 9:31). Now he is filled with joy and peace in believing (Rom.15:13). Now he rejoiceth with joy unspeakable, and full of glory (1 Peter 1:8). And now he hath the Spirit of God bearing witness with his own spirit that he is a child of God (Rom.8:16; 1 John 5:10). These are things that I was an utter stranger to before, notwithstanding all my reading, watching and praying; and these are things that everyone must be a stranger to, until he is made a child of God by faith in Christ Jesus . . .

'And now let me point out to you the grand delusion which had liked to have ruined my soul. I saw very early something of the unholiness of my nature, and the necessity of being born again. Accordingly I watched, prayed and fasted too, thinking to purify my heart by these means, whereas it can only be purified by faith (Acts 15:9). Watching, praying and fasting are necessary duties, but I, like many others, placed some secret reliances on them, thinking they were to do that for me, in part at least, which Christ only could. The truth is, though I saw myself to be a sinner, and a great sinner, yet I did not see myself an utter lost sinner and therefore I could not come to Jesus Christ alone to save me, despised the doctrine of justification by faith alone, looking on it as a foolish and a dangerous doctrine; I was not yet stript of all my righteousness, could not consider it all as filthy rags and therefore I went about to establish a righteousness of my own, and did not submit to the righteousness of God by faith (Rom.10:3). I did not seek after righteousness through faith, but as it were by the works of the law. Thus I stumbled and fell (Rom.9:31,32). In short, to use a homely similitude, I put the justice of God into one scale, and as many good works of my own as I could into the other; and when I found, as I always did, my own good works not to be a balance to the divine justice, I then threw in Christ as a makeweight. And this everyone really does, who hopes for salvation partly by doing what he can for himself, and then relying on Christ for the rest.'[18]

Thus Berridge's scholarship, reading, religiosity and works were all inadequate and God had answered his prayer by opening his eyes to the cardinal doctrine of being right before God by faith in Christ alone. Berridge's conversion was to prove the foundation of the rest of his spiritual life experimentally and doctrinally. He saw his new position as light from above, whereas his former life was:

> Full of vain and noisy strife,
> Making light of Jesus' blood.
> Rambling in a way not good.[19]

Or, again,

> In darkness born I went astray,
> And wander'd from the gospel way;
> And since the Saviour gave me sight;
> I cannot see without his light.[20]

Berridge's account in *Justification by Faith Alone* of the need of the Spirit's work and the powerful hand of God intervening in his life does not seem to fit the picture given by Whittingham of him as 'a very rigid Arminian'[21] in his early days as an evangelist. His own testimony shows clearly that the Calvinistic seeds were already present which were to develop in later life into a complete theology as a result of his experience of discipline from God. However, although he would later clarify his understanding of sanctification, election, perseverance and gospel presentation, he would never modify his basic understanding of justification by faith alone. It was this doctrine which provided him with a dynamic and adequate gospel to preach. As he said later, 'Effectual and final justification by faith is the capital doctrine of the gospel.'[22] The Christian was born and the evangelical preacher was to develop.

# 5.
# The new preacher

It is very easy to give a false picture of religious revivals in the past. Events occurring over many months and even years can be compressed into a page, resulting in a more sensational and dynamic account than was actually the case. Although Berridge was an outstanding Christian communicator and greatly blessed by God, he was under no illusion about the general appeal of the doctrines associated with justification by faith alone. 'It is but a little flock, a small remnant that are seeking the kingdom of God. The greater part are seeking after the world, and a poor seeking it is; seeking after that which will bury their bodies and ruin their souls.'[1] Writing a hymn during his serious illness in the early 1770s, he reflects on about fourteen years of gospel preaching:

> His blood, so freely spilt,
> Is loud proclaimed to all;
> Rich balm to heal the deepest guilt!
> Yet few regard the call.
>
> Sweet health his grace imparts,
> And grace divinely free;
> Rich grace to cleanse the foulest hearts;
> Yet few say, 'Give it me!'[2]

Yet there was a response that still challenges the Christian. However, the overall picture was as black as it is today.

Berridge's new faith soon found expression in his sermons. The people at Everton had already had time to accustom themselves to the man of high stature in the pulpit, to his remarkable natural gifts and jolly personality. 'His stature was tall, but not awkward – his make was lusty, but not corpulent – his voice deep, but not hoarse – strong, but not noisy - his pronunciation was distinct, but not broad.'[3] Although the congregation still saw the same man physically in the pulpit there was now something different about his preaching. Berridge himself says that 'As soon as God opened my eyes and showed me the true way to salvation, I began immediately to preach it. And now I dealt with my hearers in a very different way from what I had used to do. I told them very plainly that they were children of wrath, and under the curse of God, though they knew it not; and that none but Jesus Christ could deliver them from that curse. I asked them, if they had ever broken the law of God once in thought, word or deed? If they had, they were then under the curse; for it is written, cursed is every one that continueth not in all things that are written in the book of the law to do them. And again, he that keepeth the whole law, and yet offendeth in one part, is guilty of all. If indeed, we could keep the whole law, without offending in one point; if we had done, and could continue to do, all the things in God's law, then, indeed, we might lay claim to eternal life on the score of our own works. But who is sufficient for these things? If we break God's law we immediately fall under the curse of it, and none can deliver us from this curse but Jesus Christ. There is an end, for ever after, of any justification from our own works. No future good behaviour can make any atonement for past miscarriages. If I keep all God's laws today this is no amends for breaking them yesterday. If I behave peaceably to my neighbour this day, it is no satisfaction for having broken his head yesterday.

'If therefore, I am once under the curse of God, for having broken God's law, I can never after do anything, of myself, to deliver me from this curse. I may then cry out, "Oh, wretched man that I am! Who shall deliver me from this body of sin?" and find none able to deliver, but Jesus Christ (Rom.8:23–25). So that if I am once a sinner, nothing but the blood of Jesus Christ can cleanse me from sin. All my hopes are then in him; and I must fly to him as the only refuge set before me. In this manner, dear sir, I preached, and do preach to my flock, labouring to beat down self-righteousness, labouring to show them that they were all in a lost and perishing state, and that nothing could recover them out of this state, and make them children of God, but faith in the Lord Jesus Christ.

'And now see the consequence. This was strange doctrine to my hearers.. They were surprised, alarmed and vexed. The old man, the carnal nature, was stirred up and railed and opposed the truth. However, the minds of most were seized with some convictions, and the hearts of some were truly broken for sin, so that they came to me as those mentioned in the Acts, thoroughly pricked to the heart, and crying out with strong and bitter cries, "What must I do to be saved?" I then laid the promises before them, and told them, if they found themselves under the curse, Christ was ready to deliver them from it; if they were really weary and heavy laden, Christ would give them rest; if their hearts were broken for sin, and they would look up unto Christ, he would heal them. I exhorted them also to thank God for these convictions, assuring them it was a token of good to their souls. For God must smite the heart, before he can heal it (Isa.19:22). I generally found that they received comfort from the promises; and though they complained much of the burden of sin, and of an evil heart of unbelief, yet they always went away refreshed and comforted.'[4]

This account by Berridge of the substance and effect of his new message was written six months after conversion. It shows clearly the kind of message that Berridge was preaching, a message that he was to preach for the rest of his life. From the outset Berridge was to stress the reality of sin and the condemnation of God's law before bringing forward the healing of Christ. Berridge illustrated preaching the law by comparing it to a horse-dealer carefully inspecting a horse for blemishes. 'If my master guide my hand, I shall reach the quick, and hear you cry, as a perfect man of old did, "Behold I am vile" (Job 40:4).'[5] The law was no optional extra: 'The moral law must be preached in its utmost rigour to awaken every sort of sinners, and convince them of their lost estate. When the law is set home by the Holy Spirit, it becomes a schoolmaster, sharp indeed, and scourges sinners unto Christ.'[6]

This clear preaching of the doctrine of sin was to be a hallmark of Berridge's preaching: 'All men by nature are in spiritual darkness: they see not the spiritual misery and danger, nor the evil of their heart and life, nor the end of sin; nor the things that make for peace: nor the emptiness of worldly goods, nor the blessedness of having God for a present pardon.'[7] The Fall and the death of man spiritually constitute a fundamental element of his preaching. He applies the law that God may bring conviction and a heart-felt need of deliverance and new life. We also see the experimental note in the emphasis on the sufficiency of Christ for the sinner. In his own account of his preaching, which is echoed by his epitaph, all self-righteousness must be beaten down.

What kind of response did the message find? Some in the congregation at Everton were surprised and alarmed. Some were convicted concerning their sin. These would come to the vicarage seeking help for their troubled consciences. The memoir in the *Evangelical Magazine* after his death includes the first of these visits: 'After he had preached in this strain, two or three Sabbaths, and was ruminating whether he was yet right, as he had perceived no better effects from these, than his former discourses, one of his parishioners unexpectedly came to enquire for him. Being introduced, "Well Sarah," said he. She replied, "Well, not so well I fear." "Why, what is the matter, Sarah?" "Matter? I don't know what's the matter. These new sermons. I find we are all to be lost now. I can neither eat, drink nor sleep. I don't know what is to become of me." The same week came two or three more, on a like errand.'[8] Thus a month after Berridge's reorientation a few were experiencing conviction of sin.

At the end of April 1758 we have a fuller account by Berridge in a letter to a Mr Daw: 'God has been pleased to bless and prosper my labours in a very extraordinary manner, for these last three months. Since I preached the real gospel of Christ, seven people in my own parish have now received the gospel in the appointed way of repentance towards God, and faith towards our Lord Jesus Christ. Nine or ten from Potton are in a very hopeful way, two at Gamlingay and two at Eaton. There is now such a storm arising that I know not how it will end, or when.'[9]

At the beginning of June 1758 John Walsh, a Methodist of Bedford, was writing to Wesley that Berridge 'meets little companies of his converts from several towns and villages, at his own house. He was once ashamed of the word Methodist, but takes it to himself as freely as I do. The country seems to kindle round him.'[10] At the beginning of the next month Berridge writes of many who had come with burdened hearts and who had gained refreshment from God's promises. He adds that 'More are continually coming; and although some fall off from their first convictions, yet others cleave steadfastly unto the Lord. They begin to rejoice in him and to love him; they love his Word and meditate much upon it; they exercise themselves in prayer and adorn their profession by a suitable life and conversation.'[11]

Berridge writes that, as a result of preaching Christ and Christ alone, 'Believers were added to the church continually, then people flocked from all parts to hear the glorious sound of the gospel, some coming six miles, others eight, and others ten, and that constantly.'[12] From this time forward until Berridge's death Everton would be crowded on Sundays with people come to hear the gospel preaching. They would bring their meals and during the fine weather would eat in the open air. The vicarage was always available for the visitors, as was the meadow for horses. Septimus Sears, who was to be used of God in the nineteenth century at nearby Clifton, speaks of his grandmother coming all the way from Chatteris to hear Berridge: 'She has at times travelled the whole of Saturday and Sunday night in order to hear John Berridge at Everton.'[13] Of course, most people would come shorter distances. Whittingham says, 'People came to hear him from the distance of twenty miles, and were at Everton by seven o'clock in the morning, having set out from home soon after midnight. At that early hour he preached to very considerable congregations; also at half-past ten and half-past two, and again in the evening.'[14] Whittingham is probably describing the period of the actual awakening. However, the crowds that began to flock to Everton in the first year of Berridge's converted ministry became a regular feature of the religious scene.

Berridge was to find that his conventional method of preaching was to change as a result of new circumstances.

He had been brought up in a social milieu where sermons were carefully composed and were read and judged as literacy exercises. Both at Stapleford and Everton he had been accustomed to write his sermons out completely. During the early months of 1758 he was busily engaged in writing new sermons as he had decided to burn all those which he had previously preached. He was invited to preach on a Monday at another village what was called a 'club sermon'. He found that there was no time for preparation of this sermon because he had a busy week with the many who came to him for counsel and so he decided that he would preach one of the new sermons he had recently delivered at Everton, thinking that most of those present would be strangers. After the evening service on the Sunday one of the congregation informed Berridge that he was going to accompany him on the next day. This was, no doubt, a kind action and although Berridge sought to discourage him he would not be put off. Berridge arranged to start early in order to arrive in good time, thinking that he could prepare his sermon at the place of preaching. As he rode along he assumed that there would be a small congregation and that they would not expect a long discourse. When they arrived he was informed that all the clergy in the area and many people were coming to hear him. No doubt something of the news of Everton had travelled. Let Whittingham continue the story: 'This wrought up his mind to such a degree of agitation, as absolutely incapacitated him for study: and he therefore was obliged to ascend the pulpit and preach *bona fide* an extempore sermon. But here God wonderfully and most agreeably disappointed his fears, by affording him such extraordinary assistance as enabled him to rise superior to all his embarrassment and to command the most solemn attention from his numerous audience.'[15]

Berridge was now released from the burden of writing his sermons and except for very special occasions he preached without the aid of a manuscript. This, of course, gave him the opportunity to preach more frequently not only at Everton but in the surrounding area.

22 June 1758 was a significant day in Berridge's spiritual pilgrimage, for it was on this date that he started preaching outside his parish. He now started his life as a 'riding

pedlar', or as he calls himself on his epitaph 'an itinerant servant of Jesus Christ'. We know that he had been in some conflict of mind over this step because he wrote to friends asking for advice on account of all the opposition he was receiving. In a letter to David Simpson some twenty years later he says, 'As you are now doing, so did I, send letters to my friends, begging advice, but received unsatisfactory or discouraging answers. Then I saw, if I meant to itinerate, I must not confer with flesh and blood but cast myself wholly on the Lord. By his help, I did so, and made a surrender of myself to Jesus, expecting to be deprived, not only of my fellowship and vicarage, but also my liberty.'[16] He had already made contact by letter with John Wesley and George Whitefield and one wonders what advice he received from these itinerant preachers *par excellence*, although they were without responsibility for a particular parish. For Berridge this issue seems to have been a matter of obedience to Christ rather than obedience to the rules of his communion.

On 22 June he felt that the Lord himself encouraged him. In the flyleaf of his Bible he noted the date and that 1 Chronicles 17:1,2 had been given him 'when I began to itinerate, and when my squire and Potton vicar complained of me to the bishop'.[17] The words of this scripture, 'Do all that is in thine heart: for God is with thee', spoke to Berridge amidst all his conflicts. From this time he would preach in barns, cottages and farmhouses around his area because he viewed people as perishing. And so Berridge threw off the views on decency and order in which doubtless he had been cradled. Although the full step of preaching in the open air would not be taken till the following year, he had in a sense crossed his Rubicon. For the next thirty years he was an itinerant preacher.

The career that Berridge adopted immediately brought him into more open conflict with the established powers. 'When I began to itinerate a multitude of dangers surrounded me, and seemed ready to engulf me; my relations and friends were up in arms; my college was provoked; my bishop incensed; the clergy on fire; and the church canons pointing their ghastly mouths at me.'[18] It is clear, however, that Berridge was in difficulties before he started itinerant preaching in June. The above account was written some eighteen years later and perhaps by then Berridge had forgotten the trouble he was in even before he started itineration, or perhaps his itineration helped to form the open breach with the Establishment which would last until his death. In April 1758 Berridge writes, 'Some time ago I was told by several friends that twelve clergymen had combined together, in order to oppose and prosecute me, if they could. My squire swears he will do my business; and last Lord's day evening, when I came from church, he stopped me and called me the usual names of 'Enthusiast', etc., etc. Today, I hear the squire has sent for such of his tenants as are disposed to hear the Word of God and has given them warning to leave their farms directly.'[19]

In early June John Walsh writes, 'He had many great friends and admirers before, who now turned enemies and persecutors. They attempted to deprive him of his living, but failed.'[20] Perhaps Berridge's itinerant preaching brought more formal complaints. In his Bible flyleaf Berridge notes 24 July as the date his squire complained to his college. The scripture that encouraged him at this time was the message to the church in Philadelphia in Revelation: 'Behold I have set before thee an open door and no man can shut it.' Despite difficulties from his squire, local clergymen and masters, Berridge would not shrink from preaching the gospel. He would be from now on a 'stigmatized pilgrim'.[21]

It is hardly surprising that Berridge's views and actions upset the local fellow clergy as he now saw them to be blind guides, as he himself had been. The 'apostle of Clare Hall', as he was nicknamed, was ruffling clerical feathers by challenging the normal viewpoint. One clergyman, Samuel Hicks, at Wrestlingworth, a short distance from Everton, was so upset by Berridge's preaching that 'he denied the sacrament to those of his parish who went to hear Mr Berridge'.[22] This hostility gave way in the beginning of August 1758 to conviction of sin and it was on 17 September that Hicks was to preach for the first time the same gospel as Berridge. After this he was to be the only local clergyman for many years who was to help Berridge in his travels and preaching.

Berridge obtained his response mainly from the lower sections of society, the poor agricultural labourers in particular. Wesley's *Journal* a year later (May 1759) notes 'That few ancient people experience anything of this work of God; and scarce any of the rich. These generally show either an utter contempt of or enmity to it.'[23] One of the responses of masters who saw their labourers acquiring a taste for Berridge's gospel preaching was to impute the motive to laziness. This may well have been a talking-point as Berridge penned a poem at this time on this theme. It suggests that the eighteenth century is not too dissimilar from our own.

Ye are idle, ye are idle; therefore ye say, let us go and do sacrifice to the Lord (Exod.5:17).

To be read, but not sung.

1. When Israel's grieving tribes complain'd
   Of Pharaoh's hard oppressive hand;
   'Idle ye are,' the tyrant cries,
   'And therefore would go sacrifice.'

2. And now when sinners flock to hear,
   The tidings of salvation dear;
   'Idle ye are,' task-masters say,
   'And therefore would go sing and pray.'

3. Objections old are never stale,
   So long as flesh and hell prevail;
   What Pharaoh says to Israel's race,
   Is said to all who seek for grace.

4. The same objections still are found,
   And bandied round, and round, and round;
   In matter such, and language too,
   And always old, and always new.

5. But make the sons of slander know,
   That ye can hardship undergo;
   Then labour much, and don't repine,
   But look on laziness as sin.

6.  Enquire of some, what calls them out.
    To see a race or wrestling bout,
    What leads them to a wake or fair,
    And ask, if now they see you there.

7.  Enquire of others, why they spend
    Their evenings at an idle end,
    Why to an alehouse they repair,
    And ask if now they see you there.

8.  Enquire again, why others play
    Their time in cards and dice away.
    And ask, if this is right to do.
    And ask, if this they see in you.

9.  And when the sons of Belial cry,
    'Idle ye are', do ye reply,
    'We have no time to see a race,
    To spend in cards, or spend in dice.

10. 'No leisure for a fair or wake,
    No wrestlings see, no dancings make;
    No football kick, no skittles use,
    Nor tipple at a public house.

11. 'The follies vain which others seek,
    We give them up for Jesus' sake;
    And find a welcome hour to spare,
    For hearing, reading, singing, prayer.

12. 'We labour much at God's command,
    With faithful and a willing hand,
    We labour too our souls to save,
    For we must live beyond the grave.

13. 'What if e'erwhile an hour we steal
    To save our precious souls from hell?
    An even pace with you we keep;
    'Tis stolen from pastime or from sleep.'[24]

The poem, besides giving an interesting glimpse of leisure pursuits in the eighteenth century, catches something of the seriousness and earnestness associated with these eighteenth-century Christians.

Late in July 1758, Berridge was to be encouraged by a visit to Everton of George Whitefield, perhaps the greatest evangelist of modern times: Two years older than Berridge, Whitefield had been for twenty years on the road that Berridge had just begun to tread. Whitefield writes from Newcastle on his way to Scotland on 31 July 1758: 'All the last week was taken up in preaching at Everton, Saint Neots, Keysoe, Bedford, Oulney, Weston Underwood, Ravenstone and Northampton . . . Mr Berridge who was lately awakened at Everton promises to be a burning and shining light.'[25] This was the first of several visits that Whitefield made to Everton and Berridge was to preach for Whitefield in London in 1761 when Whitefield was incapacitated through illness and exhaustion. Whitefield seems always to have had a favourite meal at Everton. Writing in later years in typical fashion to a friend who was hoping to visit Everton, Berridge says, 'I will give you the same treat I always gave Mr Whitefield, an eighteen-penny barndoor fowl; this will neither burst you, nor ruin me; half you shall have at noon with a pudding, and the rest at night.'[26]

The next famous visitor to help by preaching was the indefatigable John Wesley. When he arrived at Everton on Thursday, 9 November 1758, Berridge himself was just setting out for Wrestlingworth, about four miles away. So as they rode together through Potton and up the long hill towards Wrestlingworth they had opportunity to get acquainted. In the evening Wesley preached at Wrestlingworth and he noted the church building 'well filled with serious hearers'.[27] The two men stayed overnight with Hicks and Wesley preached again early the next morning, at five o'clock. It is from Wesley that we first learn of the physical manifestations which were to develop, particularly in the following year. In the middle of the morning sermon a woman dropped down as dead. The same thing had happened with one person during the previous evening sermon. Wesley regarded these physical symptoms as signs that God was confirming his Word. 'God confirmed his own words exactly as he did at Bristol, in the beginning, by working repentance and faith in the hearers, and with the same violent outward symptoms.'[28] During Friday Berridge and Wesley returned to Everton where Wesley preached at six in the evening and at five on Saturday morning. Several were affected physically through the preaching. In December Wesley was back at Everton for his second visit, travelling down to preach on Monday, 18 December. 'The church was well filled soon after six in the evening. God gave me great liberty of speech, and applied his Word to the hearts of the hearers, many of whom were not able to contain themselves, but cried aloud for mercy.'[29]

Thus the first year of Berridge's new ministry was drawing to a close. In the previous December he had been in the throes of conversion. A year later he was in the midst of a growing revival. Whittingham tells us that during this first year he was visited by a thousand persons under 'serious impressions'.[30]

# 6.
# An important interview

Before we proceed to the second year of Berridge's evangelical ministry we shall pause to consider an important
interview that Berridge had with his bishop. We have this
account[1] through a friend of John Sutcliff, the Baptist leader
at Olney. This friend, towards the end of Berridge's life
(1792), rode over from Olney to Everton to meet Berridge.
The 'venerable old man'[2] made a deep impression on
Sutcliff's friend and he particularly remembered the prayer-
time they shared at the end of their discussions. During the
conversation Berridge related that soon after he had begun
to preach the gospel at Everton he had been called to see his
bishop.

In the eighteenth century bishops would not interfere
with the local clergy unless powerful local interests demanded some attention. N. Sykes says that one can deduce
the small degree of oversight exercised by an eighteenth-
century bishop through the few references to the bishop in
Parson Woodforde's diary. However, a bishop was powerful.
He was a temporal lord as well as spiritual, owning large
estates and possessing a major political, cultural and social
role in the life of the country. Although extenuating
circumstances have been pleaded for them, the bishops
were at the heart of the patronage system.

The case of the bishop with whom Berridge was going to
have the interview illustrates how the system worked. John
Thomas was the English chaplain at Hamburg and his
knowledge of German brought him to the attention of
George II. Through the king's interest he was appointed to
the rectory of St Vedast, Foster Lane, in the City of London,
and then was made a royal chaplain and accompanied the

king in 1740 on a trip to Hanover. He obtained from His
Majesty that summer the deanery of Peterborough, much to
the annoyance of the Duke of Newcastle, who had promised
it to someone else. The duke offered something better when
it came along, if Thomas would waive his claim, but he
refused. Three years later Thomas was rewarded for
services rendered by nomination to the see of St Asaph. He
delayed taking up the appointment and in January 1744 the
Bishop of Lincoln died. Thomas took his opportunity and
managed to obtain the king's recommendation for this
English diocese. On 20 January he was nominated to
Lincoln, where he was to remain until 1761 when he moved
to Salisbury.

When Berridge was called before John Thomas, the local
squire must have thought that he stood a good chance of
getting rid of his vicar. Berridge tells us: 'Soon after I began
to preach the gospel of Christ at Everton, the church was
filled from the villages round us, and the neighbouring
clergy felt themselves hurt at their churches being deserted.
The squire of my own parish, too, was much offended. He
did not like to see so many strangers, and be so
incommoded. Between them both it was resolved, if possible, to turn me out of my living. For this purpose, they
complained of me to the bishop of the diocese, that I had
preached out of my own parish. I was soon after sent for by
the bishop; I did not much like my errand, but I went.'[3]

This situation seems to fit exactly into the summer of
1758. We have already recorded the crowds and the beginning of the itinerant ministry and noted that Berridge had
spoken of the squire's opposition in a letter to Mr Daw in
April. Berridge also noted in his Bible: 'June 22nd, 1758
when I began to itinerate, and when my squire and Potton
vicar complained of me to the bishop.'[4] Also we saw that
Berridge spoke of 'my bishop incensed' when he began to
itinerate. The scene is still local but by the summer of 1759
Berridge's net was much wider and if the interview had been
in late 1759 this would have been reflected in the charges.
Thus I think we can assume that not long after the
complaint was made, and certainly before the bishop would
have made his way back to London for Parliament in
October, Berridge was summoned to account for his actions.

Berridge would probably have known John Thomas over many years for it is natural to assume that an urbane senior fellow of Clare College would have met his bishop at social functions and on academic occasions. In fact, Berridge may well have been one of the first to be ordained by the new Bishop of Lincoln for he was ordained deacon on 10 March 1744, the same year that Thomas was appointed bishop.

Berridge was surprised at the abruptness of the bishop's opening remark. He was clearly annoyed: '"Well Berridge, they tell me you go about preaching out of your own parish. Did I institute you to the livings of Abbotsley, or Eaton, or Potton?" "No, my Lord", said I, "neither do I claim any of their livings; the clergymen enjoy them undisturbed by me." "Well, but you go and preach there, which you have no right to do?" "It is true, my Lord, I was one day at Eaton, and there were a few poor people assembled together, and I admonished them to repent of their sins, and to believe in the Lord Jesus Christ for the salvation of their souls; and I remember seeing five or six clergymen that day, my Lord, all out of their own parishes upon Eaton bowling green." "Poh!" said his lordship, "I tell you, you have no right to preach out of your own parish; and if you do not desist from it, you will very likely be sent to Huntingdon gaol." "As to that, my lord," said I, "I have no greater liking to Huntingdon gaol than other people; but I had rather go thither with a good conscience, than live at my liberty without one." Here his lordship looked very hard at me, and very gravely assured me that I was beside myself, and that in a few months time I should either be better or worse! "Then", said I, "my lord, you may make yourself quite happy in this business; for if I should be better, you suppose I shall desist from this practice of my own accord; and, if worse, you need not send me to Huntingdon gaol, as I shall be provided with an accommodation in Bedlam."'[5]

Although, as Berridge recounts the story thirty years later, we can sense that he is enjoying himself and answering in a manner reminiscent of his debating days at Cambridge, this challenge of prison or madhouse made a deep impression on him. Later he was to mention to a young friend enquiring about preaching the difficulties which faced him at this time: 'Then I saw, if I meant to itinerate I

must not confer with flesh and blood, but cast myself wholly
on the Lord. By his help, I did so and made a surrender of
myself to Jesus, expecting to be deprived, not only of my
fellowship and vicarage, but also my liberty. At various
times, complaints or presentments were carried to my
college, to successive archdeacons and bishops; and my
diocesan frankly told me I should either be in Bedlam or
Huntingdon gaol by and by.'[6]

Probably because of their previous contacts over many
years and possibly because of Berridge's position in the
university, the bishop now changed his approach. Instead of
threatening him, he began to entreat him as a friend:
'"Berridge," he said, "you know I have been your friend,
and I wish to be so still. I am continually teased with the
complaints of the clergymen around you. Only assure me
that you will keep to your own parish; you may do as you
please there. I have but little time to live; do not bring down
my grey hairs with sorrow to the grave."'[7]

At this point the interview was interrupted by the
announcement of two visitors who wished to see the bishop.
The bishop requested that Berridge go back to his own inn
and return to dine with him at an appointed time. It was
true that the bishop was an old man, sixty-seven years of
age, with few years to live, and Berridge found this change
of approach more difficult to counter. He says he could 'bear
threatening, but knew not how to withstand entreaty;
especially the entreaty of a respectable old man'.[8] When he
arrived at his inn he immediately put the matter into the
hands of God and when the appointed time arrived he
returned to dine with the bishop. 'At dinner, I was treated
with great respect. The two gentlemen also dined with us. I
found they had been informed who I was, as they sometimes
cast their eyes towards me in some such manner as one
would glance at a monster. After dinner, his lordship took
me into the garden. "Well, Berridge," said he, "have you
considered of my request?" "I have, my lord," said I, "and
have been on my knees concerning it." "Well, and will you
promise me that you will preach no more out of your
parish?" "It would afford me great pleasure," said I, "to
comply with your lordship's request, if I could do it with a
good conscience. I am satisfied the Lord has blessed my

labours of this kind, and I dare not desist." "A good conscience!" said his lordship, "Do you not know it is contrary to the canons of the church?" "There is one canon, my lord," I replied, "which saith, "Go preach the gospel to *every creature!*" "But why should you interfere with the charge of other men? One man cannot preach the gospel to all men." "If they would preach the gospel themselves," said I, "there would be no need of my preaching it to their people; but as they do not, I cannot desist." His lordship then parted from me in some displeasure. I went home, not knowing what would befall me, but thankful to God that I had preserved a conscience void of offence.'[9] As Berridge rode home verses from a hymn which he was later to write would have suited his need:

Lord, make me dead to all below,
Content to have the world my foe,
Content to hear them blast my name,
Nor turn my head aside from shame.

Keep worldly prudence from mine eyes,
And let me only Jesus prize.
Tread in the track by Jesus given,
Pursued by scorn quite up to heaven.[10]

As the report of the interview reveals, Berridge, in his memory and interpretation of those events some thirty years later, saw the issue in terms of following men and the traditions of men or treading 'in the track by Jesus given'. There is something of the apostle Paul's passion of 'Woe is me if I preach not the gospel' in Berridge's discovery of the true meaning of the gospel and the necessity of its proclamation. He 'dare not desist', as he told the bishop.

Berridge looked upon what followed as divine providence, for he says that he took no measures for his own preservation. One of his friends at Clare College, who had put difficulties in Berridge's way when he began to preach the gospel and had caused some ecclesiastical privileges which he had enjoyed to be withdrawn, had a change of heart when he thought that Berridge might lose his vicarage. He therefore wrote to Thomas Pitt, nephew to William Pitt the

outstanding British politician who was at that time
Secretary of State: 'Our old friend Berridge has a living in
Bedfordshire, and, I am informed, he has a squire in his
parish, that gives him a deal of trouble, has accused him to
the bishop of the diocese, and it is said, will turn him out of
his living. I wish you could contrive to put a stop to these
proceedings.'[11]

Thomas Pitt, who had recently finished at Clare, spoke to
the nobleman to whom the bishop owed his promotion.
When the bishop was in London this nobleman made it his
business to see him. '"My lord," said he, "I am informed
you have a very honest fellow, one Berridge, in your diocese,
and that he has been ill-treated by a litigious squire who
lives in his parish. He has accused him, I am told, to your
lordship, and wishes to turn him out of his living." The
bishop was astonished, and could not imagine in what
manner things could have thus got round; it would not do,
however, to object; he was obliged to bow compliance, and
so I continued after, uninterrupted in my sphere of
action.'[12]

C. Smyth's conclusion that the story is not wholly
edifying seems justifiable. A system which depended on
patronage was open to abuse from all sides. It is as if the
truth of God depends not on his Word but on the manipul-
ations of politicians in London. The story, however, reveals
something of Berridge's attitude to the established church,
and this will be examined in more detail later. He was
thankful for the opportunity to preach, he felt the call to
preach, but church dignitaries must not tell him where,
when and how he should preach.

# 7.
# Sensational reports

The second year of Berridge's evangelical ministry deserves detailed treatment. It is surprising that after the passing of over two hundred years so many details of this particular year remain. It was significant for Berridge as he started preaching in the open air and expanded his sphere of service. The renewed religious interest continued to draw people from the surrounding countryside. The physical symptoms associated with some of the hearers, which had begun on a small scale in the previous year, were to rise to a peak in the summer of 1759. Opposition continued, but the work in this second year drew widespread attention. Evangelical leaders came from London to investigate its authenticity and Berridge himself received an invitation to preach before the University of Cambridge towards the end of the year.

On Thursday 1 March 1759, John Wesley again called at Everton. He arrived at Everton at about four in the afternoon and as Berridge did not expect him until the next day he decided it would be wise if he preached in Berridge's house. One can imagine how the news would quickly spread round the village and people would come in the evening to hear Wesley preach. Wesley writes that 'The next evening the church was well filled, and my mouth was filled with arguments, which I trust God applied for the conviction of some and the consolation of others.'[1] This seems to have been an ordinary meeting, with no mention of any of the swooning, trances or crying which were to be so much in evidence during the following two months. Wesley writes to Lady Huntingdon on 10 March saying that he had 'found great satisfaction in conversing with those instruments

49

whom God has lately raised up'.[2] Presumably her ladyship had asked about Berridge because Wesley gives a brief report. He had visited Everton three times and one would think that this is not a hurried evaluation: 'Mr Berridge appears to be one of the most simple as well as most sensible men of all whom it pleased God to employ in reviving primitive Christianity. I designed to have spent but one night with him; but Mr Gilbert's mistake (who sent him word I would be at Everton on Friday) obliged me to stay there another day, or multitudes of people would have been disappointed. They come now twelve or fourteen miles to hear him; and very few come in vain. His word is with power; he speaks as plain and home as John Nelson, but with all the propriety of Romaine and the tenderness of Mr Hervey.'[3] Thus Wesley confirms Berridge's communicative gifts and gives independent evidence of the crowds of people going to Everton.

It was not long before Berridge took the important step of preaching in the open air. Whittingham says that it was on 14 May 1759 that Berridge first preached in the open air. Hicks and Berridge were on their way to Meldreth, a small village a few miles south of Cambridge, when they broke their journey at a farmhouse. Berridge reports to Wesley: 'After dinner I went into his yard, and, seeing near a hundred and fifty people, I called for a table, and preached, for the first time, in the open air. Two persons were seized with strong convictions, fell down, and cried out most bitterly. We then went to Meldreth, where I preached in a field to about four thousand people. In the morning, at five, Mr Hicks preached in the same field to about a thousand. And now the presence of the Lord was wonderfully among us. There was abundance of weeping and strong crying, and, I trust, besides many that were slightly wounded, near thirty received true heart-felt conviction.'[4] Berridge's phraseology shows that he looked for no superficial, emotional reaction, but for a work of conviction of sin.

On their return journey Hicks and Berridge called again at the farmhouse where Berridge preached in the yard. Berridge says, 'Seeing about a dozen people in the brewhouse, I spoke a few words. Immediately the farmer's daughter dropped down in strong convictions. Another also was miserably torn by Satan, but set at liberty before I had done prayer.'[5] From Berridge's account we judge that these particular physical symptoms were not the product of a long psychological process or the result of mass hysteria, there being very few persons present in the brewhouse. However, they may have been copied from the previous day when two had fallen down and 'cried out most bitterly'. Whatever the psychological explanation, Berridge felt at this stage of his ministry that these physical symptoms were evidence of the unseen world and were due to conviction of sin. Hicks and Berridge did not stay long at the farm because he records that he preached at his own house at four in the afternoon where 'God gave the Spirit of adoption to another mourner'.[6] Until now physical accompaniments to the preaching had been random, spasmodic and individual. It seems that from now on and throughout the summer these physical occurrences were to increase greatly. According to C. Smyth it is this period, as recorded in Wesley's *Journal*, that formed the basis of the negative evaluations of Berridge by the historians Southey and Lecky.

Wesley wrote in his journal towards the end of May that 'About this time the work of God exceedingly increased under the Rev. Mr Berridge, near Everton.'[7] He then includes an eyewitness account, probably contributed by a Mrs Blackwell of Lewisham, of the events at Everton in the last third of the month, and a letter from Berridge describing events from 13 to 21 May. Mrs Blackwell's report is mainly taken up with describing the events of Sunday, 20 May. Berridge was ill during this weekend. Mrs Blackwell describes him as 'feeble and sickly'[8] and he retired to bed after giving a word of exhortation in the vicarage after the afternoon meeting, leaving his many visitors. 'We continued praising God with all our might, and his work went on as when Mr Berridge was exhorting.'[9] After hearing Hicks and Berridge preach several times at this period Mrs Blackwell says that 'Neither of these gentlemen have much eloquence, but seem rather weak in speech,'[10] which would suggest that Berridge was well below par. In fact on Monday, 21 May he felt so ill that he had to dismount and walk when on his way to preach at Shelford.

On this Sunday Mrs Blackwell was very tired and did not
attend the first service, which was presumably at seven in
the morning. Her husband did attend and 'observed several
fainting and crying out while Mr Berridge was preaching'.[11]
In the later packed morning service Mrs Blackwell 'heard
many cry out, especially children, whose agonies were
amazing. One of the eldest, a girl ten or twelve years old,
was full in my view, in violent contortions of body, and
weeping aloud, I think incessantly during the whole service.
And several much younger children were in Mr Blackwell's
view, agonizing as this did.'[12] She describes the afternoon
meeting as equally crowded. The building was packed to the
extent that people were crowded around Berridge in the
pulpit and the windows 'were filled within and without'.

She reports that although Berridge was unwell his voice
was for the most part distinguishable in the midst of all the
outcries. She notes that there were three times more men
than women and that many of the hearers had come from
other towns and villages in the area. Thirty had come from
thirteen miles away, having set off at two in the morning.

Berridge's text for the occasion was 2 Timothy 3:5:
'Having a form of godliness, but denying the power thereof.'
Mrs Blackwell writes, 'The presence of God really filled the
place. And while poor sinners felt the sentence of death in
their souls, what sounds of distress did I hear! The greatest
number of them who cried or fell were men; but some
women, and several children, felt the power of the same
almighty Spirit, and seemed just sinking into hell. This
occasioned a mixture of various sounds, some shrieking,
some roaring aloud. The most general was a loud breathing,
like that of people half strangled and gasping for life. And
indeed almost all the cries were like those of human
creatures dying in bitter anguish. Great numbers wept
without any noise; others fell down as dead; some sinking in
silence, some with extreme noise and violent agitation. I
stood on the pew-seat, as did a young man in the opposite
pew, an able-bodied, fresh, healthy countryman. But in a
moment, while he seemed to think of nothing less, down he
dropped, with a violence inconceivable. The adjoining pews
seemed shook with his fall. I heard afterwards the stamping
of his feet, ready to break the boards, as he lay in strong

convulsions at the bottom of the pew. Among several that were struck down in the next pew was a girl who was as violently seized as him. When he fell, Blackwell and I felt our souls thrilled with a momentary dread; as when one man is killed by a cannon-ball, another often feels the wind of it. Among the children who felt the arrows of the Almighty I saw a sturdy boy, about eight years old, who roared above his fellows, and seemed, in his agony, to struggle with the strength of a grown man. His face was red as scarlet; and almost all on whom God laid his hand turned either very red or almost black.'[13] Although Mrs Blackwell thought that it was probable that there was more than one conversion in this meeting, only one who professed conversion came to speak of it at the house afterwards. When she returned to the vicarage after a walk she found it full of people. She speaks about a word of exhortation by Berridge and similar reactions by people to those in the church service. One girl whom she had seen unconscious in the service now recovered and rejoiced in God. Her friend also was soon singing praises. Mrs Blackwell and her husband were themselves caught up in laughter of extreme joy with other Christians and with 'some of those who were waiting for salvation; till the cries of them who were struck with the arrows of conviction were almost lost in the sounds of joy'.[14] Some well-dressed young women who had shown no interest up till then began to cry aloud. The house was visited by the local squire and probably the Duke of Manchester. 'They seemed inclined to make a disturbance, but were restrained, and in a short time quietly retired.'[15] Mrs Blackwell mentions another young woman filled with 'unspeakable joy' and 'John Keeling, of Potton, who fell into an agony; but he grew calm in about a quarter of an hour, though without a clear sense of pardon'.[16] A stranger who had come forty miles 'fell backward to the wall, then forward on his knees, wringing his hands and roaring like a bull. His face at first turned quite red, then almost black. He rose and ran against the wall, Mr Keeling and another held him.'[17] He too soon had peace. A 'gipsy-looking girl' of eleven or twelve was deeply affected and later rejoiced. Mrs Blackwell comments on the joyful faces and how those who were newly converted embraced one another, weeping for joy. She concludes the account of this Sunday by saying that although she may have omitted some, one man, two women and three children were converted in the house.

This part of the report to Wesley includes a visit to Wrestlingworth on Thursday 24 May to hear Mr Hicks: 'While he was preaching, fifteen or sixteen persons felt the arrows of the Lord, and dropped down. . . A few of these cried out with the utmost violence, and little intermission, for some hours; while the rest made no great noise, but continued struggling as in the pangs of death. I observed, besides these, one little girl, deeply convinced, and a boy, nine or ten years old. Both these, and several others, when carried into the parsonage-house, either lay as dead, or struggled with all their might. But in a short time their cries increased beyond measure, so that the loudest singing could scarce be heard. Some at last called on me to pray, which I did; and for a time all were calm. But the storm soon began again. Mr Hicks then prayed, and afterwards Mr Berridge. But still, though some received consolation, others remained in deep sorrow of heart.'[18] This sensational section of the report concludes by speaking of the opposition of the rich, the death of three farmers who had opposed the work, of pews and benches being broken because of the violent struggling and the fact that some people were unaffected in the gatherings but became unconscious on the way home or in Berridge's garden.

On Monday, 21 May Berridge and Hicks journeyed to Shelford, a village four miles north of Cambridge. Berridge was still very unwell. He was greatly surprised when he arrived, as a table had been set on the common and a huge crowd (Berridge thought 10,000), with many students from Cambridge, had gathered. Hoarse with a cold, Berridge experienced extreme nervousness as he stepped up on the table. When he was settled he relaxed and gave out his text from Galatians which summarized his new theological position: 'For as many as are of the works of the law are under the curse: for it is written, "Cursed is every one that continueth not in all things which are written in the book of the law to do them." But that no man is justified by the law in the sight of God, it is evident: for the just shall live by faith' (Gal.3:10-11). He paused to think of an arresting start and his mind went blank. He writes, 'The Lord so confounded me (as indeed it was meet, for I was seeking not his glory, but my own) that I was in a perfect labyrinth.'[19] As soon as he was able to get one word out his thoughts returned and he was able to speak for nearly an hour 'without any kind of perplexity; and so loud that everyone might hear'.[20] He felt refreshed and the audience had given him a good hearing with no disturbances. He went into a house and spoke to about two hundred people who had shown interest in the message. The next morning, probably at the normal time of five o'clock, Berridge preached to about a thousand and it was announced that Hicks would preach at Orwell Field in the evening and that Berridge would preach at Grantchester, one mile from Cambridge, on the following Monday.

Berridge wrote to Wesley on 16 July 1759. He reported that he had taken to 'preaching in the fields' and that 'the power of the Lord is wonderfully present with the word'.[21] Nearly twenty towns had received the gospel and fresh invitations were coming in at frequent intervals. Success was mainly in the eastern part of his neighbourhood and accordingly he was concentrating on this area. 'The word is everywhere like a hammer, breaking the rock in pieces. People fall down, cry out most bitterly, and struggle so vehemently, that five or six men can scarcely hold them down. It is wonderful to see how the fear of the Lord falls upon unawakened sinners. When we enter a new village, the people stare, and laugh, and rail abundantly; but when we have preached night and morning, and they have heard the outcries of wounded sinners, they seem as much alarmed and terrified as if the French were at their doors.'[22] As soon as a few received convictions, Berridge describes how they would meet together two or three nights a week. At first they would only sing, whereas later they would read and pray together. Singing was obviously an important activity in the revival and Berridge was at this time working on a hymn-book for congregational use. Singing also aided the preaching, for he recounts that both at Orwell and Grantchester people gained strong convictions of sin simply through hearing the small societies singing hymns. These societies, although numerically small and weak, were experiencing

conversions in their midst. Berridge finishes his letter by
describing 'a wonderful out-pouring of the spirit of love
amongst believers',[23] which affected them so much physically that they became unconscious and were not able to
work hard for a few days. He also asks Wesley not to
publish the account of Ann Thorn which John Walsh had
sent him as it would 'only prejudice people against the
Lord's work in this place, and I find our friends in town
begin to be in great pass about the work. They are very slow
of heart to believe what they do not see with their own eyes.
Indeed these things seem only designed for the spot on
which they are wrought. What men see or hear they will be
brought to credit. Men's attention is raised, and the prejudices against what is called a new doctrine removed by
them. And thus the design of God is answered. But where
people lie out of the reach of the doctrine, you will find them
lie out of reach of conviction. These signs are not for them,
and so are disregarded by them.'[24] This passage clearly
shows Berridge's attitudes towards the 'signs' at this early
stage, but it also reveals the problems that the reports were
causing for other Christians.

The reports of strange occurrences caused Lady Huntingdon in London to send two of her chaplains, Martin
Madan and William Romaine, to gain a first-hand impression. John Walsh from Bedford accompanied them and
his enthusiastic report was included by Wesley in his
*Journal*. It is clear that Walsh did not share the reservations
and natural caution of the visitors from London.

At Potton the visitors met John Keeling and others who
related their experiences. Both Keeling and his wife were
deeply affected on 'that memorable Sabbath' (25 May),
although they had no assurance until ten days later. Ann
Thorn, another native of Potton, spoke of depression after
her visions, but stated that she was still visited 'with such
overpowering love and joy, especially at the Lord's Supper,
that she often lay in a trance for many hours'.[25] As they were
speaking they were called into the garden where another
young woman, Patty Jenkins, had entered a trance. She
appeared asleep with her eyes open uttering praise in a low
voice and when words failed, 'she frequently laughed while
she saw his glory'.[26] Mr Madan did not know whether it was

of God or the devil. Walsh sat down beside her, whereupon he himself entered into an ecstatic state. When it was time to depart to hear Mr Hicks preach at Cockayne Hatley, a village a short distance away, Patty Jenkins regained her strength and they all walked together, sixteen in number, 'singing to the Lord as we went along'.[27] Walsh thought that Hicks' sermon on the strait gate was excellent and there is no report of any unusual occurrences. Walsh with Madan and Romaine probably stayed overnight at Wrestlingworth at the home of Hicks because on the next morning Walsh copied a page from Hicks' journal. It was the page for 6 June, reporting in detail two people suffering contortions and finally being released through visions.

The next day, Friday, 13 July, both Madan and Romaine were still in doubt as to whether the strange occurrences were of God. Walsh says that they were convinced by the testimony of Alice Miller (aged fifteen) and Molly Raymond (aged eleven) who had been converted on 20 May. Although perhaps they were impressed with these testimonies it is difficult to believe the words of Walsh that they were 'fully convinced' by them. Their evaluation was based on wider evidence. A. Seymour says that 'At first they were astonished, and for a time doubted whether the work was genuine; but after they had conversed with several of those who had fallen in violent convulsive fits, and had accompanied Mr Berridge and Mr Hicks in some of their itinerant excursions, and witnessed the effects of their preaching, they were filled with a solemn awe, and felt fully convinced the work was of God, though occasionally mingled with the wild-fire of enthusiasm.'[28]

On Saturday, 14 July, Berridge was ill and he asked Walsh to exhort a few people who had come to the house. On Sunday at seven in the morning Berridge's servant Caleb Price spoke to about two hundred people. Walsh reports, 'The Lord was wonderfully present, more than twenty persons feeling the arrows of conviction. Several fell to the ground, some of whom seemed dead, others in the agonies of death, the violence of their bodily convulsions exceeding all description. There was also great crying and agonizing in prayer, mixed with deep and deadly groans on every side.'[29]

In the later morning gathering Berridge preached and
Walsh with many others stood in the churchyard to make
room in the building for those who had come from a
distance. He therefore saw little but heard the 'agonizing of
many'.[30]

Because of the crowds Berridge preached in the afternoon
in his own 'close', and again Walsh tells us nothing of the
content of the sermon or the manner in which it was
delivered, but dwells on those who were physically affected:
'Some of those who were here pricked to the heart were
affected in an astonishing manner. The first man I saw
wounded would have dropped, but others, catching him in
their arms, did, indeed, prop him up, but were so far from
keeping him still that he caused all of them to totter and
tremble. His own shaking exceeded that of a cloth in the
wind. It seemed as if the Lord came upon him like a giant,
taking him by the neck and shaking all his bones in pieces.
One woman tore up the ground with her hands, filling them
with dust and with the hard-trodden grass, on which I saw
her lie, with her hands clinched, as one dead, when the
multitude dispersed. Another roared and screamed in a
more dreadful agony than ever I heard before. I omitted the
rejoicing of believers, because of their number, and the
frequency thereof, though the manner was strange; some of
them being quite overpowered with divine love, and only
showing enough of natural life to let us know they were
overwhelmed with joy and life eternal. Some continued long
as if they were dead, but with a calm sweetness in their
looks. I saw one who lay two or three hours in the open air,
and being then carried into the house, continued insensible
another hour, as if actually dead. The first sign of life she
showed was a rapture of praise intermixed with a small,
joyous laughter.'[31]

On Tuesday, 17 July Walsh and others walked to Harston, a village a few miles from Cambridge, which was in the
heart of the area being affected by gospel preaching. They
were overtaken by Berridge, who was exhausted and
depressed, so much so that he felt he must leave off field
preaching. Walsh records about three thousand hearers and
that strength returned to Berridge in the preaching. 'Incess-
ant were the cries, groans, wringing of hands, and prayers of

sinners, now first convinced of their deplorable state.'[32] Walsh notes that vicars in this area had preached against Berridge, who would probably not have gone to the area except for the sermons preached against him.

One of these places was Stapleford, about five miles from Cambridge, where Berridge had been curate before moving to Everton. An astonishing scene occurred there the next day, Wednesday, 18 July. Walsh reports that in the evening 'About one thousand five hundred persons met in a close to hear him, great part of whom were laughers and mockers. The work of God, however, quickly began among them that were serious, while not a few endeavoured to make sport by mimicking the gestures of them that were wounded. Both these and those who rejoiced in God gave great offence to some stern-looking men, who vehemently demanded to have those wretches horse-whipped out of the close . . . However, in a while, many of the scoffers were weary, and went away; the rest continued as insensible as before.'[33]

Walsh was walking around the crowd praying when he 'heard a dreadful noise on the farther side of the congregation, and turning thither, saw one Thomas Skinner coming forward, the most horrible human figure I ever saw. His large wig and hair were coal black; his face distorted beyond all description. He roared incessantly, throwing and clapping his hands together with his whole force. Several were terrified, and hasted out of his way. I was glad to hear him, after a while, pray aloud. Not a few of the triflers grew serious, while his kindred and acquaintance were very unwilling to believe even their own eyes and ears. They would fain have got him away, but he fell to the earth, crying, "My burden! My burden! I cannot bear it!" Some of his brother scoffers were calling for horse-whips, till they saw him extended on his back at full length . . . When Mr Berridge had refreshed himself a little he returned to the close and bid the multitude take warning by Skinner, who still lay roaring and tormented on the ground. All the people were now deeply serious, and several hundreds, instead of going when Mr Berridge dismissed them, stayed in Mr Jennings' yard. Many of these, especially men, were truly broken in heart.'[34]

Berridge talked with as many as could make their way into the house, but so many continued outside that he sent Walsh to pray with them. After this Walsh was called to a John Dennis, who suffered from fits and lay stiff on a table praying. He seemed to pray with deep understanding although since he had begun to do this three weeks previously, he remained ignorant of the prayers when he recovered. Walsh returned to his lodgings and witnessed a young man crying aloud as one of the women read a hymn.

On the next day Walsh reports on a meeting with Mr Jennings who had just returned from hearing Berridge at Grantchester: 'I never saw a man sweat in such a manner – the large drops seeming fixed all over his face, just like beads of glass. The congregation at Grantchester this morning consisted of about one thousand persons, among whom the Lord was wonderfully present, convincing a far greater number now than even last night. Mr Jennings was a mild, good-natured Pharisee, who never had been awakened; but he was now thoroughly convinced of his lost estate, and stood for a time in utter despair,with his mouth wide open, his eyes staring, and full of huge dismay. When he found power to speak he cried out, "I thought I had led a good life; I thought I was not so bad as others, but I am the vilest creature upon earth; I am dropping into hell! Now, now; this very moment!" He then saw hell open to receive him, and Satan ready to cast him in; but it was not long before he saw the Lord Jesus, and knew he had accepted him. He then cried aloud in an unspeakable rapture, "I have got Christ! I have got Christ!" For two hours he was in the visions of God; then the joy, though not the peace abated.

'I had left Mr Jennings but a little while when I heard John Dennis loudly praising God. I no sooner kneeled by him than the consolations of God came upon me, so that I trembled and wept much. Nor was the Spirit poured out upon us alone; all in the house were partakers of it. John Dennis was kneeling when his fit came. We laid him on the ground, where he soon became still as last night, and prayed in like manner. Afterwards his body grew flexible by degrees, but was convulsed from head to foot. When he was quite recovered he said he was quite resigned to the will of God, who gave him such strength in the inner man that he did not find any of these things grievous, neither could ask to be delivered from them.'[35]

Later on this same day Walsh walked with twenty others from Stapleford to Triplow, a village about five miles away from the present-day Duxford airfield, to hear Berridge. He 'saw many other companies, some before, some behind, some on either hand, going the same way ... Fifteen hundred or two thousand were assembled in the close at Triplow. The only unpolished part of the audience were a few gentlemen on horseback. They were much offended at the cries of those in conviction, but much more at the rejoicing of others, even to laughter; but they were not able to look them in the face for half a minute together. I looked after service at every ring which the people made about those that fell under the Word. Here and there was a place with only one, but there were generally two or three together, and on one spot no less than seven who lay on the ground as if slain in battle.'[36]

Berridge went into a house which was full of serious people, many also filling the adjoining orchard. He spoke with them until he was exhausted and called on Walsh to pray. Walsh says that 'An hour after, most of them were still in the house or orchard – sighs and groans, prayers, tears, and joyful praise being intermixed on every side.'[37]

The next morning, Friday, 20 July, Walsh overslept and missed the early morning meeting. Berridge had so many enquirers that he sent for Walsh at seven. Walsh reports: 'Three times more persons were struck with convictions this morning than had been last night,'[38] and he describes in detail the physical contortions of the local prostitute and a young beggar girl, seven or eight years old. Later in the day Walsh returned to Everton (eighteen miles) very tired and depressed. As he came into Everton Berridge was preaching and Walsh was refreshed. 'I shook from head to foot, while tears of joy ran down my face, and my distress was at an end.'[39]

At the Sunday meetings Walsh rejoiced to see many from Cambridgeshire. In the morning, 'The church was quite filled, and hundreds were without. And now the arrows of God flew abroad. The inexpressible groans, the lamenting, praying, roaring, were so loud, almost without intermission, that we who stood without could scarce help thinking all in the church were cut to the heart. But, upon enquiry, we

found about two hundred persons, chiefly men, cried aloud
for mercy: but many more were affected, perhaps as deeply,
though in a calmer way ... Mr Berridge preached in his
close this afternoon, though in great bodily weakness; but
when he is weakest God so strengthens him that it is
surprising to what a distance his voice reaches.'[40]

Within two weeks of Walsh's report the situation was
becoming quieter. On Sunday, 5 August Wesley arrived
between eight and nine in the morning. He records that
'During the prayers, as also during the sermon and the
administration of the sacrament, a few persons cried aloud;
but it was not from sorrow or fear, but love and joy. The
same I observed in several parts of the afternoon service. In
the evening I preached in Mr Hicks' church. Two or three
persons fell to the ground, and were extremely convulsed;
but none cried out. One or two were filled with strong
consolation.'[41]

The next day Wesley talked with Ann Thorn and two
others about their trances. In the late afternoon Alice Miller
fell into a trance and Wesley records, 'I made a motion as if
going to strike, but they [her eyes] continued immovable.
Her face showed an unspeakable mixture of reverence and
love, while silent tears stole down her cheeks. Her lips were
a little open, and sometimes moved, but not enough to
cause any sound. I do not know whether I ever saw a human
face look so beautiful.'[42]

Sometimes she was filled with joy, at other times she was
in distress as she thought of the sad state of unbelievers.
When she returned to her senses she said she had been with
her Saviour in glory. Wesley's notes are full and he even
took her pulse at one stage. In the evening at eight Wesley
preached the text: '"The wicked shall be turned into hell,
and all the people that forget God." The whole congregation
was earnestly attentive; but not above one or two cried out,
and I did not observe any that fainted away, either then or in
the morning.'[43] The service was later than usual because of
the harvest, and the next morning's, at which Wesley
preached, was an hour earlier for the same reason (four
o'clock).

Wesley again visited Everton on Tuesday 28 August,
coming from the society at Bedford. When he preached in

the evening he was 'unusually heavy, and hardly expecting to do any good there. I preached on those words in the Second Lesson, "We know that we are of God." One sunk down, and another, and another. Some cried aloud in prayer. I would willingly have spent some time in prayer with them; but my voice failed, so that I was obliged to conclude the service, leaving many in the church crying and praying, but unable either to walk or stand. One young man and one young woman were brought with difficulty to Mr Berridge's house, and continued there in violent agonies, both of body and soul. When I came into the room the woman lay quiet, wrestling with God in silent prayer. But even the bodily convulsions of the young man were amazing; the heavings of his breast were beyond description – I suppose equal to the throes of a woman in travail. We called upon God to relieve his soul and body, and both were perfectly healed. He rejoiced in God with joy unspeakable, and felt no pain, or weakness, or weariness. Presently after, the woman also was delivered, and rose rejoicing in God her Saviour.'[44] Thus it seems that convulsions were still occurring, but not to the same degree.

# 8.
# Hysteria or conviction of sin?

Berridge's and Hicks' strenuous gospel preaching and the often sensational physical accompaniments to that preaching attracted considerable attention. Evangelical leaders such as Lady Huntingdon had sent aides in order to investigate the phenomenon. Wesley had been in touch personally and also through the reports of Mrs Blackwell and Mr Walsh. Besides local squires and clergymen, Berridge's university wanted some account of these strange teachings and happenings.

The Master of Corpus Christi College and Dean of Lincoln was giving time and attention to writing a critique of Berridge's confession of faith *Justification by Faith Alone*, an account of his conversion which was freely circulating in the area. John Green writes, 'I am disposed to think well of your good meaning, yet there are many appearances in your conduct, if credit may be given to some of your hearers, which look a little untoward, and are difficult to be accounted for; you are attended it seems in those frequent harangues, with a constant number of groaners, fighters, tumblers and convulsionists. These occasionally break out into such a dreadful concert of screams, howlings and lamentations, as surprises and shocks the sober part of your audience, who are in doubt whether to ascribe those sudden explosions to the catching nature of enthusiasm, or the unusual power of methodistical oratory. You are reported to use on these occasions some strange expressions which, accompanied with a loud tone of voice, vehement gesture, wild looks, and that terrible relievo which is sometimes given to the cheeks and eyes of a field-preacher, must strongly operate on weak minds, and strike terror into an ignorant and unexperienced multitude.'[1]

Berridge's regular preaching at Grantchester took place only one mile from the university and academics such as Green would have received reports of their once-respected colleague turned Methodist and field preacher, and of the accompanying interest amongst ordinary people. In consequence Berridge was invited to preach before the university in Great St Mary's. The normal arrangement at that time was not for the preaching of one sermon only, but for a sermon on four consecutive Sundays. These sermons, which Green thought Berridge intended to publish, the university allowed 'to pass without any reprehension',[2] even though some of the remarks were construed as offensive to the university. Berridge reports on one of these Sundays that 'Several dropped down, but made no noise, and the whole congregation, young and old, behaved with seriousness.'[3]

On Saturday, 24 November Wesley arrived at Everton, Berridge having already gone to Cambridge to preach. Wesley notes, 'Many people come to his house in the evening, and it was a season of great refreshment.'[4] Wesley wondered on the Sunday whether he would have enough strength to administer the Lord's Supper to such a large number of communicants, but all went well, with Hicks starting his own service early and coming over to help him. Wesley gives evidence of the decrease in physical symptoms: 'In the afternoon God was eminently present with us, though rather to comfort than convince. But I observed a remarkable difference since I was here before as to the manner of the work. None now were in trances, none cried out, none fell down or were convulsed; only some trembled exceedingly, a low murmur was heard, and many were refreshed with the multitude of peace.'[5]

On the following Monday evening Wesley preached at Wrestlingworth and at ten the next morning with the same feeling that a change had occurred: 'The people were deeply attentive but none were so affected as when I was here last.'[6]

Wesley would have expected these changes: 'I have generally observed more or less of these outward symptoms to attend the beginning of a general work of God ... but after a time they gradually decrease, and the work goes on more quietly and silently.'[7] Wesley wanted a middle line:

'The danger *was* to regard extraordinary circumstances too much, such as outcries, convulsions, visions, trances; as if these were essential to the inward work, so that it could not go on without them. Perhaps the danger *is* to regard them too little, to condemn them altogether; to imagine they had nothing of God in them, and were a hindrance to his work.'[8] Although these may be pretence, 'even this should not make us either deny or undervalue the real work of the Spirit. The shadow is no disparagement of the substance, nor the counterfeit of the real diamond.'[9]

The atmosphere at Everton, however, was definitely moving away from the approval of such physical occurrences. When Wesley visited Everton a little over a year later, in February 1761, he says that 'Few of them are now affected as at first, the greater part having found peace with God. But there is a gradual increasing of the work in the souls of many believers.'[10] At Wrestlingworth there was a 'large and serious congregation'.[11] Wesley expressed his worry the next year when he spent two Sundays at Everton, Berridge being in London preaching for Whitefield. On Sunday, 3 January 1762 he wrote, 'I read prayers and preached, morning and evening, to a numerous and lively congregation. I found the people in general were more settled than when I was here before, but they were in danger of running from east to west. Instead of thinking, as many then did, that none can possibly have true faith but those that have trances or visions, they were now ready to think that whoever had anything of this kind had no faith.'[12] Thus Wesley presents evidence for both the dying away of the physical occurrences and the changed attitude at Everton towards them.

Berridge in these early days had a positive attitude towards these physical paroxysms. He suggests that these signs were part of God's design to remove prejudices against what seemed like a new doctrine. The only claim that Berridge actively encouraged the physical manifestations comes from John Green, a hostile witness, who claims that one of Berridge's hearers reported Berridge as saying, 'Fall! Won't you fall! Why don't you fall? Better fall here, than fall into hell.'[13] Of course, we cannot put much store by hearsay evidence quoted in a hostile pamphlet, particularly in the light of eyewitness reports which mention no encouragement from Berridge and, perhaps more important, the fact that these signs came upon people while others besides Berridge were preaching and also happened independently of religious meetings. They occurred inconsistently with Berridge, Hicks, Wesley, Caleb Price, in church buildings and in the open air, in private houses and gardens, in religious meetings and when people were alone. Berridge obviously welcomed a good hearing by a serious congregation indoors or out of doors, but if physical paroxysms occurred he took these to be the work of God in bringing conviction.

As we have seen, Wesley was a frequent visitor at Everton and it would have been normal for Berridge to lean somewhat on Wesley's view and explanation on account of his own inexperience and immaturity as an evangelist, as compared with Wesley. Wesley's advice to preachers in Berridge's situation, with outward symptoms occurring, runs: 'Those whom it pleases God to employ in his work ought to be quite passive in this respect; they should choose nothing, but leave entirely to him all the circumstances of his own work.'[14] Why then did Berridge change his mind about these phenomena and thus cause Wesley to be troubled by Everton's opposition to outward signs early in 1762, as already mentioned? Was it that by the end of 1759 they were dying out, which in itself caused a revaluation by Berridge? Did his conversations with Madan and Romaine make him more cautious? Were the divisions over the matter in the congregation at Everton more pronounced than are hinted at in Wesley's *Journal*? Our guesses must remain unanswered, as Berridge in later years did not write about his understanding of that early period. However, one key comment made in a letter to Lady Huntingdon ten years afterwards would suggest that he felt that the physical experiences of 1759 nearly ruined the work at Everton by introducing pride and self-confidence rather than humility and dependence on God: 'I cannot wish for transports, such as we once had, and which almost turned our heads; I do long to see a spirit poured forth of triumphant faith, heavenly love, and steadfast cleaving to the Lord.'[15] There were perhaps several factors in this recognition. He had time to evaluate the long-term effects; he was to develop theologically, particularly in his understanding of sanctification, and move away from Wesleyan theology generally; and perhaps Green's criticism made at the beginning of 1760, with his charges of subjectivism and emotionalism, helped Berridge to place more emphasis on the objective work of Christ. The people converted needed to be fed and taught and the teacher had to develop different emphases if he wished to succeed.

J.C. Ryle says that the utmost that may be said against Berridge on the subject is that he 'at first attached more value to them than they deserved', and he goes on to say that because 'The whole subject, like demonical possession, is a very deep and mysterious one'[16] we ought to be content to leave it. A. Skevington Wood accepts the strange phenomena as 'signs following' to demonstrate the work of the Holy Spirit.[17] Both S. Carpenter and Marcus Loane can see no reason for their occurrence.[18] A. Dallimore, speaking as a Christian historian of similar experiences, meets the issue head on: 'Experiences of this kind raised important questions. It was evident that a mighty work of the Spirit of God was being done in sinners' hearts, but it was equally evident that much of the extreme emotion was humanly engendered. Where was the line to be drawn and how was one to know what was of God and what was not?'[19] No doubt Berridge sought to warn against mere emotionalism and imitation of spirituality, as many writers had done following the earlier outbreaks in America, but only an examination of the long-term results in the lives of those affected would demonstrate the true nature of the work.

Berridge must have been continually facing this problem during the year 1759. Although many hundreds professed conversion during this year and in the next decade, and many congregations were started or revived through his itinerant preaching, Everton's vicar was a man looking for real and lasting results. He wrote in 1770 to a friend in London, 'You have lived to see, I make no doubt, many hopeful plants wither, many souring professors dwindle away, and many Christian mariners wrecked. What a mercy it is we are yet in the ship, and bound for Canaan! Well, hitherto the Lord hath helped us, glory be to his grace; not unto us, not unto us, but unto him be all the praise. How charmingly the blossoms look, and how pleasantly they smell in a gospel spring; but how little fruit is found at the vintage! Some are running back to Egypt for its onions and garlic; others are living upon doctrines, sucking the shell and never cracking the nut; and a few, oh, very few, are feeding on Christ. Some are wholly withered, some are mighty confident, and a few are watchful and prayerful, walking and looking like men that are waiting for the Lord. Indeed, where the gospel comes, it makes or mars men effectually, proves a savour of life or of death; either makes men the salt of the earth or the refuse of all things. Come, my friend, let us trudge on with circumspection. There are many pillars of salt on our right hand and left which bid us be cautious, and a good Christ is before us, who bids us be bold. Let us lean on his arm, and tread in his steps, taking his word for our rule, and his Spirit for our guide.'[20]

However we view the physical occurrences of 1759, there is little doubt that many Christians were professing their new-found faith and making progress. Not only did Wesley find the congregation at Everton in early 1762 numerous, responsive and more settled, but he noted a change in the area. Speaking of nearby Potton he says, 'What has God wrought here since I saw this town twenty years ago! I could not then find a living Christian therein, but wild beasts in abundance. Now here are many who know in whom they have believed, and no one gives us an uncivil word! I preached at six to a very numerous and serious congregation.'[21] Whatever the place of the physical paroxysms, a powerful religious revival movement had been established, centring on this obscure village of Everton, but spreading out into a wider neighbourhood. The work would grow and change, and Berridge himself was to undergo many changes while preaching the same Christ whom he had discovered in late 1757.

**Note on report in Wesley's journal**
It is difficult to evaluate the report in Wesley's *Journal* concerning this early period at Everton. Wesley presumably made up this composite report because its lack of criticism and its often ecstatic tone reflected his own viewpoint. By

concentrating on the sensational these reports have opened the floodgates for unbalanced interpretation. For example, C.E. Vulliamy speaks of a stranger going to Everton and thinking that 'every other man was a lunatic or a drunkard'.[22] C. Abbey and J. Overton,[23] as well as G.M. Trevelyan,[24] give the impression that paroxysms were a constant feature of Berridge's preaching rather than confined to the initial period. E. Walker's reconstruction of Berridge's preaching[25] owes more to literary imagination than historical research. William Sargant thought that Berridge had inadvertently laid bare the 'basic mechanics of the sudden conversion process'.[26]

It is important to emphasize the unbalanced nature of the reporting which makes evaluation difficult. We read about the noise, crying and groaning, but nothing about the content of the sermons. People fall to the ground and turn black or red, but we do not read whether such people gained a clearer appreciation of Christ and his merits. We learn nothing about how the teaching was delivered or how people were counselled. There are no interviews with the less dramatic converts or with those who felt unhappy about the idea that the physical occurrences were works of God. Such people are dismissed as troublers in Israel. We learn nothing of how societies were established and maintained. Both Mrs Blackwell and John Walsh, who probably contributed most to the report that appeared in the *Journal*, were deeply and emotionally involved in the events and this obviously resulted in a lack of detachment. Also Walsh's account is characterized by egoism and lack of fundamental Christian understanding. However, the reports were by eyewitnesses and, whatever the difficulties of interpretation, they show clearly the great religious interest that was occurring at Everton and the surrounding area.

# 9.
# Academic criticism

Soon after his conversion Berridge wrote a long letter to a fellow clergyman in Nottinghamshire. This letter, which was later published by Berridge under the title *Justification by Faith Alone being the substance of a letter to a clergyman in Nottinghamshire; giving an account of a great work wrought in the author's own heart*, was dated 3 July 1758 and spoke of Berridge's conversion and his discovery of being right with God through faith in Christ alone. The letter seems to have been sent unsealed and many copies were made on its journey into Nottinghamshire. So much so, that when a person from Grantham decided to publish it against the wishes of Berridge, he could say, 'Numberless copies . . . are handed about in this neighbourhood.'[1]

The Rev. John Green, D.D., Master of Corpus Christi, Dean of Lincoln and earlier Regius Professor of Divinity at Cambridge, was given a copy by a friend and produced as a result *The principles and practices of the Methodists, considered in some Letters to the Leaders of that Sect. The first addressed to the Reverend Mr Berridge wherein are some remarks in his Two letters to a Clergyman in Nottinghamshire, lately published.* Thus two years after his conversion and after opposition from local clergy and squires, Berridge was to receive a carefully argued and sustained criticism of his account of his conversion and his understanding of the meaning of justification, made by one of his own academic contemporaries, who was shortly to be his bishop.

The opportunity for Green to make a public reply to Berridge came as a result of an unofficial publication of the letter. Green says in a note that 'This epistle, which I had preserved as an invaluable treasure in manuscript and had

71

made a few remarks upon at the request of some country friends, where it was much handed about, is lately published; and on that account I write to you in this public manner.'[2] The 'epistle' to which Green refers was published without Berridge's permission and entitled *A Fragment of the True Religion, being the Substance of two letters from a Methodist Preacher in Cambridgeshire to a Clergyman in Nottinghamshire.* The editor of this work assured the reader: 'That these excellent letters are the genuine productions of the author, to whom they are ascribed. But though copies of them are now in a thousand hands, and the more hands they are in, of the more extensive use they will be; yet the writer refused to consent to the publication of them, which one of my female acquaintance here much wished for, and offered to undertake. This refusal indeed one may attribute to his great reserve and known modesty; qualities which though very commendable in themselves, yet ought not to be too much consulted in matters of public concern and utility. He, who in spite of all discouragements, is indefatigable in spreading those important and interesting truths, which I and everybody ought to know, cannot really be offended with me for carrying out the same useful design.'[3]

Berridge's reasons for opposition to the publication may have been twofold. Firstly, the publisher seems to have no understanding of the gospel that Berridge was preaching. He was probably an Antinomian, as suggested by certain passages in his preface and by his signature, 'Faith Workless'. The editor of Berridge's own version of the letters certainly thought that 'Faith Workless' had no real sympathy with Berridge and had endeavoured 'as much as possible, to degrade and lessen the character of that sincere, honest and worthy minister of Jesus Christ, the Rev. Mr Berridge'.[4] Perhaps this is an over-reaction, for 'Faith Workless' does not openly attack Berridge although his comments are capable of innuendo. He speaks of his difficulties of getting the letter copied, particularly as the copier was hoping to enter the established church and was angered at Berridge's derogatory comments on the universities. He gives an account of the large crowds that Berridge attracted and Berridge's untidy appearance: 'I have heard him preach many an excellent discourse, when, poor man! he was sadly out at the elbows, and his shirts, I declare, were almost as black as the chimney.'[5] He also includes the explosive reactions to Berridge's teaching of the local parson, who turned red and was in a great rage after he read the letter, promising to answer it from his pulpit and endeavouring 'to preserve his flock from so dangerous an infection'.[6]

A second objection to publication may have been the secret copying of the letter. Berridge's first letter to the Nottinghamshire clergyman had not received a favourable response partly because of the publicity attached to it and partly because of its doctrine. Berridge apologized for the copying but not for the doctrine and hoped in the following summer to convince his friends that he was neither Moravian nor mad, (he had been charged with both 'faults'). Berridge writes, 'The letter was designed for your perusal; copies were taken of it, without my leave, or even my knowledge; and I was as much displeased as yourself could be, when first I heard it had been copied.'[7] Thus the privacy of a personal letter is sufficient reason for Berridge not wishing for its publication. However, once publication had occurred and the document was circulating with an erroneous preface, Berridge felt obliged to publish his own edition within a year. This quickly ran through three editions. It contained a preface written by a friend of Berridge restating the doctrine of justification by faith alone in the light of the original unofficial publication.

Berridge's letter enables us to understand the changes in his religious views. It covers his pre-conversion religious life and his attempts at Cambridge to seek to establish his own righteousness. It deals with his misgivings and doubts about his doctrine and his prayer for light, also with his conversion through taking Christ as his sole Saviour. The reaction to his new message is portrayed, together with his views on the state of the national church of which he was a member. There are also some personal challenges to his correspondent, in the light of his own experience of being zealous but in error for many years, to seek God about these matters. In view of the fact that the letter was written so soon after his change of attitude, it certainly stands the test of time. It throbs with life and the passion of a man who sees things in

a new light. Once Berridge had started the letter he
confesses he got carried away: 'When I sat down to write, I
did not intend to have filled more than half a sheet, but
when I took my pen in hand, I knew not how to lay it aside. I
have written my sentiments with great freedom, and, I hope,
without offence. May God give a blessing to what I have
written; may he enlighten your eyes, as he hath done mine,
adored be his mercy; may he lead you by his Spirit to the
knowledge of the truth as it is in Jesus, and make you
instrumental in bringing souls from darkness into light, and
translating them out of the kingdom of Satan into the
glorious kingdom of his dear Son. Amen. Amen.'[8]

Green presents three areas of criticism in his seventy-
eight-page pamphlet replying to this letter. He criticizes
Berridge's method in arriving at his new views, evaluates
what he considers to be the real reasons for Berridge's
success and presents substantial criticisms of Berridge's
main doctrinal thrust of justification by faith alone. In all
these areas he is a model of moderate and reasonable
argumentation.

After summarizing the contents of Berridge's letter,
Green focuses attention on what he considers the subjective
and existential basis of his argument. He feels that some of
Berridge's arguments are not clear or conclusive 'because
the force of them chiefly depends on your own feelings, and
is not founded on any methods of human reasoning, which
are in use among us'.[9] He cannot really enter into debate
with him because the claims that Berridge is making are, he
feels, beyond the test of reason, and although God can send
a revelation in a special way, such impressions must match
other parts of God's administration. He reminds Berridge
that all the leaders of the new sects among the Roman
Catholics had extraordinary illuminations, calls, visions
and voices. Many of Berridge's brethren in Methodism,
Green argues, live on the supernatural and the abundance
of such pretensions has brought ridicule from sensible
people.

Green counsels caution in the light of mature thought:
'You, Sir, are also a man; a great one indeed, but fallible;
subject to like passions and liable to the same infirmities
with others. You presume, on your having been so highly

favoured as to have had a mistake, you had long been under, rectified by an extraordinary revelation "by a voice or what seemed like a voice from heaven": a great distinction, but not experienced by common Christians, nor promised under the gospel covenant; a means of conviction, not suitable to the ordinary course of God's dispensations, and therefore not to be believed by yourself without the fullest assurance, nor to be credited by others without the clearest evidence.'[10] Thus Green employs a kind of psychological explanation by suggesting that Berridge makes too much of his personal experience of illumination which, Green believes, is not backed up by the tests of reason, prudence or church authorities. However, Green fails to take into account the wider background of Berridge's conversion by focusing attention purely on Berridge's description of his illumination rather than on his intellectual struggles over a period of years and his new understanding of the Scriptures. Green ignores Berridge's dissatisfaction with his doctrine before conversion and his prayer for God to show him the right way. Berridge tells us how he was sitting in his own house meditating on the Scriptures when 'The following words were darted into my mind with wonderful power, and seemed indeed like a voice from heaven: "Cease from thy own works!"'[11] This passage could have given rise to Green's interpretation that Berridge's view was based on extraordinary revelation, although the rest of Berridge's letter completely negates such an idea. Although there was a point of climax for Berridge with this illumination that he must cease from relying on his own righteousness, he does not argue for the truthfulness of the illumination, however dramatically presented, but because he came to see that this is what the Scriptures taught. This conviction, Berridge believed, was a real work of God. It led to brokenness of heart for sin and an understanding of the hopelessness of his natural condition by the Spirit of God and, by God's grace, faith in Christ alone as the only answer. Berridge spends pages presenting the scriptural evidence, as he saw it, for such a view in contrast with a mere couple of sentences describing the point of tension or climax which Green seized upon.

Berridge did indeed have a new view of the place of reason in man's approach to God. A new view of oneself would lead to a new approach; the point of reference was no longer man but God: 'Now I saw that nothing had kept me so much from the truth, as a desire of human wisdom. Now I perceived that it was difficult for a wise or learned man to be saved, as it was for a rich man or a nobleman (1 Cor. 1:26). Now I saw that God chose the foolish things of this world to confound the wise, and the weak things to confound the mighty, for two plain reasons: first that no flesh should glory in his presence (1 Cor. 1:29); and secondly, to show that faith did not stand or was produced, by the wisdom of man, but by the power of God (1 Cor. 2:5). Now I discerned that no one could understand the Word of God, but by the Spirit of God (1 Cor. 2:12). Now I saw that every believer was anointed by the Holy Spirit, and thereby led to the knowledge of all needful truths (1 John 2:20).'[12] It is a pity that Green did not deal with the wider context of Berridge's conversion rather than purely focusing attention on Berridge's description of his realization of his fundamental problems.

Another criticism by Green is that Berridge takes the success of his new preaching to be an indication of the blessing of God when in fact there were possibly other reasons for what was happening. He suggests that the novelty of open-air preaching attracted crowds and particularly encouraged Antinomians. Attacks on the self-interest and corruption of modern preachers he thought would also be popular: 'No diversion tickles the fancy of the mob so much (a circumstance which you doubtless have found out) as when one of their betters is brought in to be baited.'[13] He feels that the doctrines of free grace, election and reprobation would be particularly popular with the poor, although he is grieved to think that to give 'the vulgar too high notions of their favour and interest in heaven'[14] may lead to revolution here on earth. Berridge's gospel was an easier gospel and therefore more popular: 'It is much easier to take hold of eternal life by a confident persuasion that they are the elect and the accepted and to be warmed into holy raptures by the contemplation of this glorious prospect, than to seek it in the beaten track of gospel obedience, by treading the dead fiat of duty, and dragging on in the insipid sameness of a sober and religious life.'[15]

The physical occurrences amongst Berridge's audiences, which Green had heard about but not witnessed, did not impress him and he asks Berridge whether he really knows the source of such occurrences: 'We know not enough perhaps of our own frame, or the secret operations of nature, to judge with certainty about some unusual appearances, or to pronounce whether they are the effects of enthusiasm and a disordered constitution, or the artifices of imposture, or the workings of some invisible power.'[16]

Green reserves his strongest language – he speaks of being 'chilled with horror'[17] – for Berridge's claim for his message that there is only one way to God and that a doctrine based on trusting Christ and works means that a person is not in the way of salvation. To Green this is preposterous and is similar to papistical claims 'in excluding from salvation all those who happen to differ from you in opinion'.[18] Green feels that Berridge does not exhibit 'that humility of mind, that candour of judgement, that goodwill towards your brethren',[19] which are the characteristics of those who are truly regenerated. It is understandable that Green, moderate and reasonable as he was, failed to grasp the fundamental shift in Berridge's life and thought.

In his substantive theological criticism directed at Berridge's understanding of justification by faith alone Green wished to make his appeal to the Scriptures. Green was convinced that the texts from the apostle Paul so often quoted in support of Berridge's arguments needed to be qualified by reference to the conditional aspects of much of the rest of the Scriptures and by the acknowledgement that the apostle Paul was writing to correct particular and special abuses (the relationship of the Mosaic covenant to the Christian community) which no longer exist. God's compassion 'is never exercised in a capricious manner, without any regard to the moral qualifications of the object, or some wise ends to which it may be subservient'.[20] Green had a weaker view of justification than Berridge. He saw it in terms of deliverance and speaks of two sorts of justification: 'Several passages, applicable only to the admission of converts to the privileges of the gospel, by which they were freely justified, that is, acquitted from the guilt, and released from the punishment of their former sins, you and your brethren are wont to apply to that justification of Christians, by which they are to obtain happiness in a future state of being. To the want of this proper distinction indeed is to be ascribed a good deal of that perplexity in which this question has been lately involved. Many were received into this state of salvation by faith and without any previous qualification of a holy life; but without improving under these means of grace, without making some proper attainments in holiness "no man shall see God": or be finally approved and accepted by him.'[21]

Berridge's pamphlet shows that justification, as the word is used in Scripture, is a far more positive concept than Green allows, involving as it does a new relationship with God, God's eternal acceptance through the work of Christ, peace with God, the gift of faith, the Spirit of God bearing witness with the believer's spirit, a changed life – and much more.

In his conversion the truths of the New Testament had come alive for Berridge, whereas for Green these were to a degree inapplicable: 'If justification in this lower sense were promised to such, who in after ages should be converted from heathenism to Christianity, yet it could hardly have place in a country where we are educated and trained up in the principles of Christianity. But many expressions, used by you and your soul-brethren, would almost make one think that you were dispensing your instructions to a nation of pagans.'[22]

Of course, to Berridge there were no half-Christians. It was the lack of assurance that was inherently involved in Green's view of God's work that had led Berridge to years of uncertainty and caused him to seek to justify himself before God by his own works. Green continually stresses the commands that are set forth, but Berridge, as later in the seventies in debate with Arminian brethren, would argue strongly for the necessity of good works, not as a *condition* of salvation but as a *fruit* of the salvation in Christ. Green was in the same state as Berridge had been while a curate at Stapleford. Speaking of eternal life Green says that it 'is said to be the gift of God, and to have been obtained for us through the merits and intercession of his Son; this is granted to us freely, but yet conditionally; it is on many accounts ascribed to the grace and mercy of God, but requires some qualifications on our part to fit and prepare us for the reception of that mercy. For Christ is expressly declared the Author of salvation to them only who obey him (Heb. 5:9).'[23] But Berridge's conversion had taught him that grace was unconditional and it was his ceasing to rely on his own efforts and placing his trust in Christ alone that led not only to theological release but to a new message and joy and peace in his own heart.

There is little doubt that Green's pamphlet was intended to show that the new enthusiasm of 'Methodism', as revealed in the message and the keen evangelical effort of Berridge, was misguided and theologically heretical. Berridge himself made no reply, but pressed on with his immediate concern to reach people with his message. Little did he know that through illness and enforced inactivity he would himself return to these same issues within a few years.

# 10.
# The riding pedlar and his 'shops'

By the beginning of the 1760s Berridge had made his important decisions on itineracy and open-air preaching. During 1759 he had concentrated on the villages east of Everton towards and around Cambridge, but although his main influence was always to be in rural Cambridgeshire, his circuit was to extend in future years into the neighbouring counties of Hertfordshire, Essex, Huntingdonshire and Bedfordshire, with evidence of forays yet further afield. In 1773 he writes, 'The work of God has extended itself by means of field-preaching, into four counties, viz. Bedfordshire, Hertfordshire, Essex and Cambridgeshire. Near forty towns have been evangelized, many of which lay at a great distance from each other, and two lay preachers ride from town to town, preaching morning and evening every day.'[1]

Berridge used the commercial image to describe his own activities. 'He called himself a "Riding Pedlar" because his Master, as he used to express himself, employed him to serve near forty shops in the country, besides his own parish.'[2] The work lacked the sensational interest of the mid-1750s but it was steady and many churches stemmed from it. Towards the end of the decade Berridge was incapacitated through serious illness, but because of his attitude to true ordination and calling, the work, far from collapsing, progressed through his workers, supported through his own money and friends in London.

Berridge writes to Lady Huntingdon in 1767 indicating the kind of work in which any substitute whom she might provide would be involved: 'I do not want a helper merely to stand up in my pulpit, but to ride round my district; but I fear my weekly circuits would not suit a London or a Bath divine, nor any tender evangelist that is environed with prunello. Long rides and many roads in sharp weather! Cold houses to sit in, with very moderate fuel, and three or four children roaring or rocking about you! Coarse food and meagre liquor; lumpy beds to lie on, and too short for the feet; stiff blankets, like boards, for a covering; and live cattle in plenty to feed upon you! Rise at five in the morning to preach; at seven, breakfast on tea that smells very sickly; at eight mount a horse with boots never cleaned; and then ride home, praising God for all mercies. Sure I must stay till your academy is completed, before I can have an assistant.'[3]

While at Everton and during days of health Berridge's pattern was to go out on Monday and return home on Saturday, usually preaching in the evening and early morning at his stopping places. Whittingham states that he used to preach on average from ten to twelve sermons a week on his circuit and that he frequently travelled one hundred miles in so doing. These travels continued for many years, except when he was ill, until extreme age limited him in the late 1780s. The extent of the work can be seen when Berridge was confined to Everton through illness and had appealed to Lady Huntingdon for help. He writes that Mr Glascott 'is going about Everton this week. Afterwards he goes out on Mondays and returns on Saturdays. In six weeks' time he will be able to visit not all, but most of my churches. I hope you can spare him so long at least.'[4]

Berridge certainly lived a busy life and perhaps he physically and emotionally overstretched himself. The normal pleasantries of life, like reading and writing letters, took second place. Little wonder that Berridge compares the preacher to a pen that sometimes runs out of ink: 'Sometimes you perceive the pen is exhausted and almost dry . . . lift up your hearts in prayer for the poor pen and say, "Lord, give him a little more ink." '[5] Berridge believed in no half measures. Just as he had studied assiduously at Cambridge, he would now give himself fully to reaching people with the message.

Although Berridge during these years visited towns further afield, his main work was visiting his 'shops', as he called his congregations. One of these must have been at

Waterbeach, a few miles from Cambridge, first visited by
Berridge in 1759. We have a brief record of his first visit in
September 1759, when he preached on the green close to
where the old cage and stocks used to be: 'The service
commenced with a hymn and a prayer. The men and women
left the beerhouses and the fighting rings, and gathered
round in blank astonishment. My great-grandmother,
finding the sale of her damson plums over, resolved to go
and hear the preacher for herself and while listening to his
message she was pricked in her heart and went home to
pray.'[6] The work there grew steadily in the 1760s. Cole, a
high churchman, came from Bletchley in 1767 to take up the
living and he was depressed with what he found: 'The town
is above half full of Methodists, made so by Mr Berridge of
Clare Hall. If I had known as much at first I believe I should
not have thought of it.'[7] In December of that year, having
moved in, he married two disciples: 'Married William
Baxter to Mary Howell, two Methodists, with whom this
parish swarms.'[8] Cole felt deeply about Berridge's influence: 'The grief is that the parish swarms with Methodists –
look which way I will the same heresy stares me in the face.
Yet such is my wretched situation that I am obliged to be
more than ordinary civil to these enemies of the church and
clergy.'[9] Such converts not only closely associated themselves with Berridge and his fellow workers but imitated his
attitude to evangelism. A contemporary speaks of a 'numerous seminary of the disciples of Mr Berridge of Clare Hall,
called from him "Berridges" and who to this day send out
preachers, gardeners, collar-makers, shop-keepers, etc., into
many of the adjacent villages.'[10]

Berridge's 'rambles' included Steeple Morden over the
border in Hertfordshire. A report in the *Congregational Magazine* informs us that the gospel was reintroduced in this town
about 1765 by Berridge, who opened a place in Flax Lane
which was built by a Mr W. Chesham. Berridge regularly
preached there for thirty years until towards the end of his
life a Mr Sharp succeeded him.[11] A barn was fitted out at
Bassingbourn and this gathering was to develop into a
Congregational church with a building capable of seating
several hundred. Berridge himself helped by recommendation to raise the money for the building.[12] Rooms were

licensed at Ely which were later to develop into a chapel in
connection with the Countess of Huntingdon.[13] At Harston,
three miles from Cambridge, there was another example of
an 'independent church, which owes its existence to the
painful and zealous exertions of John Berridge of Everton.
Here, as usual, he fitted up a barn, in which he preached for
the last time in 1781, from the text Luke 5:15.'[14] This
meeting constituted itself into a Baptist church in 1785. A
shepherd at Duxford, who had started preaching in a barn
and was experiencing difficulties, was encouraged by
Berridge, who preached there regularly himself and encouraged one of his assistants to visit once a fortnight. A
meeting-house was erected just after Berridge's death and
Mr Pyne, its first minister, called Berridge 'the apostle of
Cambridge'.[15] At Bottisham, about twenty-four miles from
Everton and four miles outside Cambridge, he took possession of a deserted barn which had formerly been occupied by
the Presbyterians and later took another at his own cost.
'Here he and his colleague Mr Hicks, with some others,
preached occasionally for some years. They stationed there
Mr Price.'[16] This presumably was Berridge's manservant
who had stood in for Berridge when Berridge was ill, as
recorded in Wesley's *Journal*. One of Berridge's lay preachers visited Streatham. For a time the work there was
accommodated in a barn, but soon afterwards moved into
an old meeting-house and later in 1772 with the help of
Berridge a new meeting-house was erected.[17] These details,
with their emphasis on congregations founded, come from
reports sent in 1818-20 to the *Congregational Magazine*, which
was compiling a statistical review of dissenters. In the light
of the material C. Smyth comments that 'In the county of
Cambridgeshire alone dissenting congregations at Bassingbourn, Bottisham, Lode, Croydon, Duxford, Ely,
Grantchester, Hadenham, Harston, Steeple Morden, Great
Shelford, Stretham, Swavesey and Waterbeach were either
planted or revived by Berridge.'[18] These presumably were
some of his forty 'shops'.

Soon after conversion Berridge had modified his views on
who could preach. He had gone to university and had
applied himself to study, believing 'human learning to be a
necessary qualification for a divine, and that no one ought

to preach unless he had taken a degree in the university'.[19] After conversion he recognized that no one could understand the Word of God but by the Spirit of God and 'That every believer was anointed by the Holy Spirit, and thereby led to the knowledge of all needful truths and, of course, that every true believer was qualified to preach the gospel, provided he had the gift of utterance'.[20] Berridge was a great encourager, both through word and action, of those who had his ability of communication and in many ways he encouraged what would be called 'team ministry' today.

It was not only Berridge's changed views about true ordination that came into play, but also the practical necessity of fulfilling the demands of the call. 'Doors are open, and ears are open everywhere, but messengers are wanting. There are several serious students at both universities, but I fear they are very prudent and very doctrinal, and such would not suit me.'[21] If one wanted to be ordained one must not break the rules, and itinerate or associate with men like Berridge. Rowland Hill associated with Berridge and adopted the same philosophy about field-preaching and it cost him dear both in terms of a career in the Church of England and of the affection of his family. With few exceptions Berridge did not get any help from men trained at college.

Right from the beginning, Berridge turned to workers from the same background as his hearers. In 1760 when Howell Harris was passing through Potton he noted, 'The Lord has begun a gracious work by a clergyman, one Mr Berridge, who joins none and sends three laymen out.'[22] No training could produce a preacher without diving commissioning. These helpers in the work were often very poor but Berridge believed they were called. For Berridge the use of poor labouring men to preach the gospel vindicated the ways of God who uses the weak and foolish to carry out his purposes.

> Ways seeming base and weak
> A God of might will try,
> Such ways his presence speak,
> And tell his arm is nigh;

His finger in the work is shown.
And glory springs to God alone.

But witlings of a span
Will think the Lord a fool;
They judge of God from man,
And measure by that rule;
The likely means a man will use,
And such they think a God will choose.

Where sundry servants wait
In some capacious hall,
On various matters meet,
The master useth all;
Sometimes the chaplain will employ,
But oftener calls the stable-boy.

Why may not Jesus too
Send servants at his will?
And servants high or low,
His pleasure best fulfil;
An angel's wing or ass's tongue
Alarm the giddy flirting throng.[23]

Berridge gives an account to John Thornton of his lay workers. Two full-time men were allowed £25 each a year by Berridge to provide themselves with horses and clothes and to pay the turnpike expenses. There were also at this time six Sunday preachers who received support from Berridge. 'By this means the gospel is preached without charge to the hearers. No collections are made, which mightily stoppeth the world's clamour.'[24]

Johnny Stittle, one of these helpers, was born at Madingley in 1727. He was a hedger and thatcher by occupation, uneducated but naturally gifted. He was converted under the preaching of Berridge and later learnt to read although he was never able to write. Because of his natural gift of preaching Berridge engaged him as one of his preachers.

Berridge was joined in society with converts, but not in societies with strict rules and regulations such as were favoured by John Wesley and others. When Howell Harris spoke with Berridge about rules Berridge said that it was 'taking the work out of the Saviour's hands'.[25] Congregations which had been formed and converts who attended other churches were in a loose association which allowed different groups to develop as they wished. During the sixties two lay preachers joined dissenting congregations and this annoyed Berridge. However, after calm thought he confessed that he 'did humbly conceive the Lord Jesus might be wiser than the old vicar'.[26] The common bond amongst the 'shops' was that many owed their conversion to Berridge or his fellow labourers. Berridge was always delighted that people gathered to hear the gospel: 'It would delight you to see how crowded my cathedrals are, and what abundance of hearers they contain, when the grain is threshed out. I believe more children have been born of God in any one of these despised barns than in St Paul's Church or Westminster Abbey.'[27]

Much of this local evangelism lies hidden for ever, only to surface in the histories of nonconformist chapels. Perhaps it is for this reason that Berridge's 'importance in the history of village nonconformity has not been sufficiently recognized'.[28]

# 11.
# Wider service

In the 1760s Berridge was not only to pursue an active preaching and teaching ministry throughout his own area; he was also to get to know more evangelical leaders of his day and start his regular habit of preaching in London during the winter months. Both Berridge and his theology were to undergo changes; in particular his friendship with John Wesley would experience strain. This period starts with a lengthy criticism by John Green and finishes with a severe illness which stopped his activity and caused a complete re-evaluation of his life and theology.

The first new contact was with John Fletcher (1729–1785), a native of Switzerland who had come to England as a tutor and had obtained ordination in the Church of England. He was on intimate terms with both the Wesleys and had no doubt heard of the work of God at Everton from them. Fletcher was later to become famous for his work at Madeley and for the support he gave Wesley in disputation. Fletcher writes to Charles Wesley from Dunstable on 1 March 1760 that 'The fine weather invites me to execute a design, I had half formed, of making a forced march to spend next Sunday at Everton, Mr Berridge's parish ... Don't forget to present my respects to the Countess. If I continue any time at Everton I shall take the liberty of giving her some account of the work of God in these parts; if not I will give it her in person.'[1]

When he arrived and was introduced Berridge recognized who he was from his accent and quickly arranged for him to preach the next day. Fletcher must have communicated with Lady Huntingdon because three days of special services were arranged, with the countess, Martin Madan and Henry Venn arriving to join Fletcher at Everton. A. Seymour reports that 'The arrival of Lady Huntingdon at Everton, and the preaching of the ministers who accompanied her, was quickly reported for many miles around, and awakened considerable attention, insomuch that on the following day it was judged ten thousand at least assembled to hear.'[2] Lady Huntingdon persuaded Berridge to accompany her back to London with the aim of introducing him 'to the religious circles of the metropolis, with a view to his spiritual improvement'.[3] Madan consented to remain at Everton until Romaine would come and relieve him. During this absence from home Seymour reports that Berridge preached two or three times in city churches and every morning and evening at Lady Huntingdon's home, besides one or two other houses.

Berridge was in London again, preaching for George Whitefield, in early 1761. Whitefield, exhausted from his years of preaching and on the verge of a physical breakdown, was happy with Berridge's help. He writes on 23 February 1761 that 'A new instrument is raised up out of Cambridge University. He has been here preaching like an angel of the churches indeed,'[4] and on 14 March Whitefield adds a postscript to a letter: 'One Mr Berridge lately Moderator of Cambridge hath been preaching here with great flame.'[5] This shows the progress that Berridge had made in a comparatively short time. He could not only communicate with country people; he could preach with power to the more sophisticated town congregations and also gain the praise of perhaps the most gifted English preacher of all time.

The next year Berridge was back in London. Whitefield was still finding preaching difficult and to add to his problems he had fallen from his horse. Whitefield writes on 8 January that 'Mr Berridge is here and preaches with power. Blessed be God that some can speak though I am laid aside.'[6] Berridge had helped John Wesley on Friday 1 January at the society at Spitalfields and Wesley supplied for Berridge at Everton for the next two Sundays.[7] Berridge probably welcomed this opportunity of preaching in London as it would have been very difficult for him to itinerate at home during the winter. Whittingham says that he 'continued to renew it every year to the close of his valuable life'.[8] Thus Berridge preached in the capital for over a period of thirty years, mainly at Whitefield's Tabernacle and Tottenham Court Road Chapel. This aspect of Berridge has been largely ignored, but it surely shows his homiletical skills and his flexibility in sustaining an interest over such a long period. In his last sermon at the Tabernacle preached on 1 April 1792 he looks back over the many years at the Tabernacle and entrusts the church to God: 'And now, Lord, I must take leave of this chapel which I have long visited. Oh, keep them continually in thy fear; and bless them abundantly with all spiritual blessings! May they evermore delight in the Lord, and the Lord delight in them to heal them.'[9]

Lady Huntingdon had obviously enjoyed a visit that Berridge had made to Brighton, for she requests him to come again. In November 1762 Berridge writes a frank letter saying that he has no guidance to come a second time:

My Lady,

I cannot see my call to Brighthelmstone; and I ought to see it for myself, not another for me. Was any good done when I was there? It was God's doing, all the glory be to him. This shows I did not then go without my Master, but it is no proof of a second call: many single calls have I had to villages when some good was done, but no further call. I am not well able to ride so long a journey; and my heart is utterly set against wheel-carriages on these roads. Indeed I see not my call; I cannot think of the journey; and therefore pray your ladyship to think no more of it. I write plainly, not out of forwardness, I trust, but to save your ladyship the trouble of sending a second request, and myself the pain of returning a second denial. You threaten me madam, like a pope, not like a mother in Israel, when you declare roundly, that God will scourge me if I do not come; but I know your ladyship's good meaning, and this menace was not despised; it made me also attend to the state of my mind during its deliberation, which was as follows. Whilst I was looking towards the sea, partly drawn thither with the hope of doing good, and partly driven by your Vatican bull, I found nothing but thorns in my way; but as soon as I turned

my eyes from it I found peace; and now whilst I am sending
a peremptory denial, I feel no check or reproof within, which
I generally do, when I am not willing to go about my
Master's business,

J.B.[10]

Yet the next summer Berridge went to Sussex again after
the death of Lady Huntingdon's youngest daughter. This
loss occasioned four letters from Berridge in the space of
half a month. The first two are worth quoting in full as they
show his epistolary style and the quality of relationship he
had with Lady Huntingdon.

*Everton June 23rd, 1763*

My Lady,

I received your letter from Brighthelmstone, and hope
you will soon learn to bless your Redeemer for snatching
away your daughter so speedily. Methinks I see great mercy
in the suddenness of her removal; and when your bowels
have done yearning for her, you will see it too. Oh, what is
she snatched from? Why, truly from the plague of an evil
heart, a wicked world, and a crafty devil, snatched from all
such bitter grief as now overwhelms you, snatched from
everything that might wound her ear, afflict her eye, or pain
her heart. And what is she snatched to? To a land of
everlasting peace, where the voice of the turtle is ever heard,
where every inhabitant can say, 'I am no more sick.' No
more whim in the head, no more plague in the heart; but all
full of love and full of praise, ever seeing with enraptured
eyes, ever blessing with adoring hearts, that dear Lamb who
has washed them in his blood, and has now made them
kings and priests unto God for ever and ever. Amen. Oh,
madam! What would you have? Is it not better to sing in
heaven, 'Worthy is the Lamb that was slain' etc., than
crying at Oathall, 'O wretched woman that I am!' Is it not
better for her to go before, than to stay after you; and then to
be lamenting, 'Ah, my mother!' as you now lament 'Ah,
my daughter!' It is not better to have your Selina taken to
heaven, than to have your heart divided between Christ and
Selina? If she was a silver idol before, might she not have
proved a golden one afterwards? She is gone to pay a most

blessed visit, and will see you again by and by, never to part more. Had she crossed the sea and gone to Ireland, you could have borne it; but now she is gone to heaven, 'tis almost intolerable. Wonderful strange love this! Such behaviour in others would not surprise me; but I could almost beat you for it, and I am sure Selina would beat you too, if she was called back but one moment from heaven to gratify your fond desires. I cannot soothe you, and I must not flatter you. I am glad the dear creature is gone to heaven before you; lament, if you please, but glory, glory, glory, be to God, says,

J.B.[11]

*June 27th, 1763*

My Lady,

My poor clay ever wants to teach God how to be a good potter; and may not your Dresden have something in it which resembles my delf? You would not, like Uzziah, lay your hand on the ark of God; but may you not be too solicitous about a driver of the cart, and a blinder hobgoblin than myself you need not desire. Indeed I am so dissatisfied with my own carting, that, if I durst, I should throw the whip out of my hands. Every hour I lose my way; every day forget what I learnt the day before; neither instruction nor corruption mends me. Yea, verily, though I know myself to be a most stupid ass, yet at times I am a most conceited one. Though not fit to drive a dung-cart, yet at some certain seasons I can fancy myself qualified to be the king's coachman. And nothing so much discovers to me the sovereign hypocrisy of my heart, as when anyone is so cruelly kind as to tell me that all the mean things I say of myself are very true. Nay, if your ladyship should send me word that you really think me that hobgoblin which I seem to think myself to be, it might put me so much out of conceit with you, as to fancy that your Dresden was now no better than delf. Oh! I am sick, sick, mighty sick of this self. How can you but rejoice for that happy creature who was delivered from this self, almost as soon as she felt the curse of it!

J.B.[12]

A. Seymour tells us that William Romaine came to relieve Berridge at Everton on 1 August when Berridge immediately

set out for Lady Huntingdon's new home at Oathall. After a
short stay he proceeded to London to preach at the Tottenham Street Chapel. He had to rush back home to Everton
at the end of August because of the sudden death of Hicks'
wife. Presumably after comforting his brother he returned to
London because he writes to a Mr Reynolds[13] at Everton on
23 September from Tottenham Chapel asking him that if
through a mistake or mishap there should be no preacher on
Sunday would he please preach in Berridge's orchard both
morning and afternoon?

After Berridge's return to Everton another evangelical
leader paid him a visit. Howell Harris had been a prominent
leader with Whitefield and since experiencing a breakdown
had been quietly living in Trevecka in Wales where a
Christian community had been established. Harris had
already heard of the work at Everton because he passed
through Potton in August 1760. While at Bath on 1 November 1762 he wrote in his diary of 'a great work done by Mr
Berridge near Cambridge'.[14] Harris arrived at Everton on
Saturday, 29 October 1763 to find Berridge 'prejudiced
against me about the work at Trevecka'[15] – Harris disagreed
with Berridge for not being in union with Whitefield. At the
Saturday night meeting held in Berridge's house Harris was
asked to speak in spite of his critical comment that in the
discussions that afternoon he felt that Berridge 'did not
receive one word I said'.[16] They had disagreements about
the value of ministers' meetings and rules for societies, both
being opposed by Berridge. Berridge was also against
Moravian teaching and Wesley's perfectionism. On Sunday
the morning meeting started at nine. Harris notes in his
diary: 'Mr Berridge preached most excellently on Psalm
66:1,2. I dined with him. To Evening Prayers, and he
preached a most excellent sermon. Saw the uncommon
glory and power on him and the people; some crying out
and he affected all the while.'[17] In the evening Harris
discussed with Berridge what had caused his demise from
the prominent position he had once held and how he
blamed both Whitefield and Wesley for exposing the
Moravians to the world. Although Berridge laughed at
Harris' title 'Captain and Esquire' and disagreed with his
having a chaise, Harris writes, 'Vast love to Venn and him

here – Berridge – for they are the first among the clergy in their spirit, sight and usefulness.'[18]

Berridge's fellowship at Clare College, Cambridge was vacated on 1 June 1764[19] and it was towards the end of this year that he was to establish contact with a student at the university who was to become a future evangelical leader and to have a particularly warm relationship with Berridge. Rowland Hill (1745–1835) was the sixth son of Sir Rowland Hill of Hawkstone in Shropshire. He had been converted while at Eton through the influence of his elder brother. At Cambridge he found his position as an evangelical lonely and difficult. However, news of his witness must have reached Berridge because while preaching at Grantchester on 18 December 1764, one mile from the university, Berridge sent a note to Hill:

> Grandchester, Tuesday Morning,
> December 18th, 1764.
>
> Sir,
> Mr Thomas Palmer was at my house last week and desired me to call upon you when I went to Cambridge. I am now at Grandchester, a mile from you, where I preached last night and this morning, and where I shall abide till three in the afternoon – will you take a walk over? The weather is frosty, which makes it pleasant under foot. The bearer of this is Mr Matthews, who lives at Grandchester mill, at whose house I am. If you love Jesus Christ, you will not be surprised at this freedom taken with you by a stranger, who seeks your acquaintance only out of his love to Christ and his people. I am, for his sake, your affectionate servant,
> John Berridge.[20]

Hill, who had only been at Cambridge a term, accepted this frank invitation and as a result spent Christmas at Everton. His family, although they rejoiced in his meeting with fellow Christians, were worried about his new association. His sister writes that 'My brother Hill and myself both think it proper to give you a caution how you go too frequently to Mr Berridge, for should that be discovered, I need not tell you the storm it would raise.'[21] However, such prudent advice in terms of getting ordained did not deter

Rowland Hill 'from cultivating the friendship of the despised apostle of the eastern counties'.[22] Hill spent practically every Sunday at Everton, riding over early in the morning and making sure that he returned in time for college chapel in the evening. They became lifelong friends. Hill wrote later, 'Many a mile have I ridden and many a storm have I faced to hear good old Mr Berridge, for I felt his ministry when in my troubles a blessing to my soul . . . affectionate old man; I love him to my heart.'[23] Although committed to the Church of England, Hill never obtained a living and later established Surrey Chapel.

It is interesting to note that while a strong evangelical work was being developed in the villages around Cambridge, the university itself was not only unaffected, but was positively hostile to those who were tinted with Methodism. Hill helped to organize a small club that met together to read the Greek New Testament and religious books. He wrote later that 'The university was almost then in total darkness. No wonder, therefore, if for such exercises and for some other strong symptoms of a 'Methodistical bias' we were speedily marked and had the honour of being pointed at as the curiosities of the day.'[24] By 'other symptoms' was probably meant preaching in barns and houses in the surrounding villages – an activity which resulted for Hill in a threat from the master of his college of refusal of testimonials needed in order that he could be ordained. The friendship of Berridge and the sympathy of Whitefield only confirmed the authorities' worse fears. Hill's friendship with Berridge was to blossom while Hill remained at Cambridge and Hill himself was to catch Berridge's love of itinerating and preaching the gospel on every possible occasion.

Another visitor to Everton was a cousin of Lady Huntingdon, Walter Shirley (1725–1786). Shirley, who was to take a prominent part in the Calvinism controversy of the 1770s, came to Everton during January and February of 1765 presumably while Berridge was in London preaching. As Berridge probably left Everton before Shirley arrived he left some written directions to help him orientate himself to the country situation. They reveal Berridge's mixture of humour and earnest seriousness:

## Family

Prayers at nine in the morning, and nine in the evening; first reading a chapter, and singing a hymn, the hymns always sung standing. On Saturday evenings the serious people of the parish come to my house about seven. I first sing a hymn, then expound a chapter, then sing another hymn, then pray, and conclude with singing on my knees, 'Praise God from whom, etc.'

## Diet

You must eat what is set before you, and be thankful. I get hot victuals but once a week for myself, viz. on Saturday; but because you are an honourable man I have ordered two hot joints to be got each week for you, with a pudding each day at noon, some pies and a cold ham, so you will fare bravely; much better than your Master with barley bread and dry fish. There is also ale, port, mountain, and a little Madeira to drink; the liquor suits a coronet. Use what I have just as your own. I make no feasts, but save all I can to give all I can. I have never yet been worth a groat at the year's end, nor desire it. I hope you will like your expedition; the people are simple-hearted. They want bread and not venison; and can eat their meat without sauce or a French cook. The weekday preachings are in the evening at half-an-hour past six. If you can preach in a house the method with us is, first to sing a hymn, then pray, then preach, then sing another hymn, then pray again, then conclude with 'Praise God from whom etc.'

The Lord bless you, and make your journey prosperous!
Your affectionate servant

J.B.[25]

In the autumn of 1765 Berridge preached at Brighton and he refused two requests by Lady Huntingdon to attend the opening of a new chapel at Bath. By 1767 Berridge was having doubts about his wider ministry, believing that he should concentrate more on his own area. After having been out preaching all week he sat down on Saturday, 26 Decem-

ber, to reply to Lady Huntingdon who had written asking
him to preach at Bath: 'Verily you are a good piper; but I
know not how to dance. I love your scorpion letters dearly,
though they rake the flesh off my bones; and I believe your
eyes are better than my own, but I cannot yet read with your
glasses. I do know that I want quickening every day, but I do
not see that I want a journey to Bath. I have been whipped
pretty severely for fighting out of my proper regiment, and
for rambling out of the bounds of my rambles; and whilst
the smart of the rod remains on my back, it will weigh more
with me than a thousand arguments. All marching officers
are not general officers; and everyone should search out the
extent of his commission. A gospel minister who has a
church will have a diocese; and let him, like (*episcopos*) an
overseer or bishop of that diocese, and like faithful
Grimshaw, look well to it. An evangelist who has no church
is a metropolitan or cosmopolitan, and may ramble all the
kingdom, or all the world over; and these are more highly
honoured than the other, though they are not always duly
sensible of the honour. They are nearest to the apostolical
character of any.'[26]

Berridge thought highly of the travelling evangelist but
the main thrust of his own work was to be confined to his
own area, where evangelism was to be thoroughly linked
with pastoral care and with church reviving and planting.

# 12.
# Relationship with Wesley and changing theology

Wesley, who at first described Berridge to Lady Huntingdon as 'one of the most simple as well as most sensible men of all whom it has pleased God to employ in reviving primitive Christianity',[1] was later to change his evaluation of Berridge and of the revival at Everton. Berridge's gradual move towards a more explicit Calvinistic theology during the late sixties reinforced divisions that had occurred. Berridge's independence of character and his opposition to Wesley's doctrine of Christian perfection were the more immediate causes of a wedge between them. This estrangement meant that although Wesley would visit places around Everton we have no record of his ever coming to Everton after early 1762.

The background to the lack of development of their relationship was the radical change in self-image that Berridge was undergoing during the 1760s and particularly during his severe illness at the end of that decade. He confesses to John Newton in 1771: 'My heart, I knew, was bad enough, but I scarcely thought there was half the baseness in it which I find, and yet I know not half its plague. How sweet is the mercy of God, and how rich is the grace of Jesus, when we have had an awful peep into our hearts! This makes us prize the gospel, embrace the Saviour, and fly to his cross. At times I am so overwhelmed with the filth and mire of my nature, that I can scarcely look through it unto Jesus. And when he has put on a little of his eye-salve, and scoured off my films, I stand amazed to think he can touch such a leper. And yet when the sun shines clear for a season, and my dunghill is covered with snow, I forget my leprosy, or become a leper only in speculation. I think it perhaps, but do not feel it, nor am humbled by it. What a heap of absurd contradiction is man, and most of all the perfect man cast in the foundry! Well might the Redeemer say, I am God and not man; and therefore ye children of Jacob are not consumed.'[2]

Berridge sees himself as full of contradiction and Wesley at his meeting centre in London was equally a contradiction, in spite of his teaching on perfection. Whittingham includes a report of a visit of a Mr Hobbs to Everton in June 1791, near the end of Berridge's life, which shows how the then very old man viewed these problems: 'I took the opportunity of informing him of the death of the Countess of Huntingdon, which had occurred a few days before. "Ah," said the good man "is she dead? Then another pillar is gone to glory. Mr Whitefield is gone, Mr Wesley and his brother are gone, and I shall go soon." I replied, "Yes Sir, it is not probable you will long survive them: and although some little differences in opinion existed between you here, I have no doubt you will unite in perfect harmony in heaven." He then, with a placid smile answered, "Aye, Aye, that we shall; for the Lord washed our hearts here, and he will wash our brains there."[3]

Eighteen months after his first visit to Everton and before their more serious difficulty, Wesley wrote a fairly blunt letter to Berridge from Ireland on 18 April 1760. Wesley interpreted Berridge's choice of remaining unconnected with others as tacit condemnation of others, whereas Berridge may simply not have wished to come under the umbrella of Wesley or anyone else. Berridge's view that converts should only read the Scriptures, (which was to be modified later) upset Wesley, as all his preachers were encouraged to sell the literature of the movement wherever they preached. Wesley was also disturbed to find Berridge rewriting parts of his brother's hymns. Although a classicist, Berridge had strong views about the Latin language, which he considered to be a weed choking simple English. Understandability and the practical need for each line to have a completed sense, as the hymns were sung line by line due to illiteracy and the lack of hymn-books, seem to have been Berridge's motives in such revision. He says in his first hymn-book, 'In making this collection care has been taken to avoid enthusiastic rant, to throw out hard words, and to make the sense end or nearly end at the proper pauses. All the hymns have been revised, and many of them almost new made.'[4]

What does show Wesley in a very bad light is the publication twenty years later of this letter in the new magazine he had founded without Berridge's reply and with his own criticisms emphasized in italics. The only motive that Wesley could have had in publishing this twenty-year-old letter without the reply at a time when Berridge was a well-known and respected preacher every winter in London was to bias people against Berridge. At the same time as Wesley published this letter he wrote to a Mr B. Collins, who was assisting Berridge at Everton, showing his doubts about the work there: 'A few years ago the people at and around Everton were deeply alive to God and as simple as little children. It is well if you find them so now.'[5] Whatever the evaluation of Wesley's substantial criticisms in the 1760 letter, his eventual publication of this letter must be seen in the light of his prejudiced view of Everton, and by impli-cation of Berridge, which had developed in the years that followed.

Dublin,
April 18th, 1760

Dear Sir,

Disce, docendus adhuc quae censet amiculus; and take it in good part, my mentioning some particulars which have long been on my mind: and yet, I knew not how to speak them. I was afraid it might look like taking too much upon me, or assuming some superiority over you. But love casts out, or, at least, overrules that fear. So I will speak simply, and leave you to judge.

It seems to me that, of all persons I ever knew (save one) you are the *hardest to be convinced*. I have occasionally spoken to you on many heads; some of a speculative, others of a practical nature; but I do not know that you were ever convinced of one, whether of great importance or small. I believe you retained your own opinion in every one and did not vary a hair's breadth. I have likewise doubted whether you were not full as *hard to be persuaded*, as to be convinced:

whether your will do not adhere to its first basis, right or
wrong, as strongly as your understanding. I mean with
regard to any impression, which another may make upon
them. For perhaps you readily, too readily, change of your
own mere motion; (as I have frequently observed great
fickleness and great stubbornness meet in the same mind) so
that it is not easy to please you long, but exceeding easy to
offend you.

Does not this imply the *thinking* very *highly* of *yourself*?
Particularly of your own understanding. Does it not imply
(what is always connected therein) something of *self-
sufficiency*? 'You can stand alone; you care for no man. You
need no help from man.' It was not so with my brother and
me, when we were first employed in this great work. We were
deeply conscious of our own insufficiency; and though, in
one sense, we trusted in God alone, yet we sought help from
all his children, and were glad to be taught by any man. And
this, although we were really alone in the work; for there
were none that had gone before us therein. There were none
then in England, who had trod that path, wherein God was
leading us. Whereas *you* have the advantage which we had
not; you tread in a beaten path. Others have gone before
you, and are going now in the same way, to the same point.
Yet it seems you *choose* to stand alone; what was necessity
with *us*, is choice with *you*. You like to be unconnected with
any, thereby tacitly condemning all. But possibly you go
farther yet. Do not you explicitly condemn all your fellow
labourers, blaming one in one instance, one in another, so as
to be thoroughly pleased with the conduct of none? Does not
this argue proneness to condemn? A very high degree of
censoriousness? Do you not censure even *peritos in sua arte*?
Permit me to relate a little circumstance to illustrate this.
After we had been once singing a hymn at Everton, I was just
going to say, 'I wish Mr Whitefield would not try to *mend* my
brother's hymns. He cannot do it. How vilely he has mur-
dered that hymn, *weakening* the sense, as well as marring the
poetry!' But how was I afterwards surprised to hear it was
not Mr Whitefield but Mr B. In very deed, it is not easy to
mend his hymns any more than to imitate them.

Has not this aptness to find fault frequently shown itself
in abundance of other instances? Sometimes with regard to

Mr Parker, or Mr Hicks; sometimes with regard to me. And this may be one reason why you take one step which was scarce ever before taken in Christendom: I mean the discouraging of the new converts from reading, at least, from reading anything but the Bible. Nay, but get off the consequence who can: if they ought to *read* nothing but the Bible, they ought to *hear* nothing but the Bible, so away with sermons, whether spoken or written! I can hardly imagine that you discourage reading even our little tracts out of jealousy, lest we should undermine you, or steal away the affections of the people. I think you cannot easily suspect this. I myself did not desire to come among them; but you desired me to come. I should not have obtruded myself either upon them or you; for I have really work enough; full as much as either my body or mind is able to go through; and I have (blessed be God!) friends enough, I mean as many as I have time to converse with; nevertheless, I never repented of that I spent at Everton: I trust it was not spent in vain.

I have not time to throw these thoughts into a smoother form: so I give them just as they occur. May the God, whom you serve, give you to form a right judgement concerning them, and give a blessing to the rough sincerity of, dear sir, your affectionate servant,

John Wesley[6]

Berridge was not offended by such a letter from his relatively new friend, although there is a hint that he bit his lip before replying. His reply was warm and loving, facing up to the problems of disagreement. The letter was not published until after both men were dead.

Everton,
November 22nd, 1760

Dear Sir,

I received your letter from Ireland, and purposely delayed my answer till your return to England, that I might not write in a spirit unbecoming the gospel. I wish all that love the Lord Jesus Christ were perfectly agreed in their religious sentiments; but this, I find, is a matter rather to be wished than expected. And perhaps a little disagreement, in nonessentials, may be designed as one part of our trial, for the exercise of our candour and patience. I discourage the reading of any books, except the Bible and the Homilies, not because of the jealousy mentioned by you, but because I find they who read many books usually neglect the Bible, and soon become eager disputants, and in the end turn out Predestinarians. At least, this has so happened with me. If my sentiments do not yet altogether harmonize with yours, they differ the least from yours of any others. And as there is nothing catching or cankering in those sentiments of yours which are contrary to mine, I am not only willing but desirous you should preach at Everton, as often as you can favour us with your company. Last week, I was at Bedford, and preached to your society; from whom I heard you were returned from the west, and purposed to come amongst us soon. Will you call at Everton, as you go to, or return from Bedford? You will be welcome. My invitation is sincere and friendly; accept of it.

I send my love to your brother, and to all that labour among you. May grace, mercy, and peace be multiplied on you, and your affectionate servant,

John Berridge[7]

Wesley took up the invitation and was at Everton early the next year (4 February 1761), making his last visit in the following year, taking two Sundays for Berridge who was deputizing for Whitefield in London. As Berridge states in his letter, there was much agreement between the two men at this stage of their relationship. Berridge, like Wesley, clearly opposed the doctrine of election. His early contacts with those of the Calvinist school in his own area left him perplexed and annoyed. He wrote in his 1760 hymn-book warning Christians about these matters: 'Are your ministers alarmed and disquieted? Perhaps you have given them some reason, by going often to hear strange doctrines, from all which we beg you turn away; because we would not have you be tossed about, like a wave of the sea, with every wind of doctrine; among which, that of unconditional election is remarkably strange to us, with whom you are now joined in society, or at least assemble yourselves to hear the gospel. I believe the Lord has some disciples who hold predestination; yet it is a perpetual bar against our following on with them, or they with us; but whilst we all follow the crucified Redeemer, it can be no bar against our loving each other as he hath loved us. And this we shall find easier to do, by considering the shortness of time; for yet a little while, and our difference of opinion will subsist no more. No device of Satan can divide us in Paradise; but here on earth we had better never meet, than waste our precious time in disputing. When the Lord first opened my eyes, I was much visited by predestinarians from far and near. I then took notice, that instead of desiring to join in prayer, discoursing of the love of God, or exhorting me to press forward and strive to enter in at the strait gate, they made an endless clutter about election and reprobation, speaking the same things a hundred times over; so that after a conference held with one, I knew what every other person had to say. Can this be called lifting up the hands which hang down? Was it not more like the coming of foxes, to spoil the tender grapes? For my part I seek no strange Lord, not predestination, but Jesus be my God! Thus, being weary of disputers, I refused to converse any longer with them. So do ye my brethren, or no rest will you find to your souls. It is no wonder Satan bestirs himself about election; for nothing serves his purpose better. Christ says, "Strive to enter in at the strait gate" (Luke 13:24). But Satan, perceiving his opportunity, says to the weary predestinarian, "Strive not at all; for if thou art ordained to salvation, saved thou must be, whether thou strivest or not. Then, soul, take thine ease; it is good for thee to eat, drink and be merry, for thou canst cope with God, whose decrees are unalterable, and his power irresistible." I shall conclude this head, my brethren, with a few questions to each of you. Is it reasonable to think that God would send his only Son to die a cruel and accursed death, for the human race, if the lot of each individual was determined before the world was made? I take it for granted that such is the doctrine of predestination; which, if true, is not all preaching, and all hearing vain? Is not every soldier of Christ beating the air? Could you believe the far greater part of mankind to be pre-ordained for hell, and yet cry out, with Abraham of old, "Shall not the Judge of all the earth do right?" or with St

John, "God is love"?'[8] Although Berridge was to change from
this early position on election and so obviously to
consolidate the differences between Wesley and himself, in
the light of Wesley's strong feelings against Calvinism, it
was Berridge's developing views on sanctification and
Wesley's teaching on Christian perfection that were the
cause of the initial theological, as opposed to personal,
strain.

By October 1763 Howell Harris on a visit to Everton
records that Berridge was full against 'Mr John Wesley's
Perfection'.[9] In March of that year Wesley wrote to Lady
Huntingdon naming Berridge with many other notable
leaders who were opposing him. The event that caused the
opposition was the débâcle of George Bell and his followers
who, building on Wesley's teaching of 'entire sanctification', claimed to be as holy as angels and incapable of
sinning and prophesied the end of the world on 28 February
1763. Although Wesley disclaimed any responsibility, the
incident brought Methodism into disrepute. Wesley himself
said that Bell and Maxfield, two of the leaders, had by their
actions 'made the very name of Perfection stink in the
nostrils even of those who loved and honoured it before'.[10]
Charles Wesley thought that the movement was in danger
of being drowned in enthusiasm. Although Wesley
dismissed Bell and Maxfield and many left his society at the
Foundery, Wesley's teaching remained the same. Romaine
felt the point strongly when he said, 'I pity Mr John from my
heart. His societies are in great confusion; and the point
which brought them into the wilderness of rant and mad-
ness is still insisted on as much as ever.'[11] R. Knox agrees
with Romaine's evaluation that the theory of sinless perfection was responsible for this crisis and that Wesley
continued preaching the doctrine to the end of his days.[12]

This crisis, and particularly the part played by Bell, must
have been one factor in Berridge's articulated opposition to
perfectionism. Whittingham says that Bell had occasionally
visited Everton and just before the final burst of enthusiasm
in London 'he began to entertain the idea that he was a
peculiar favourite of heaven and that he should be distinguished above other Christians in his exaltation to heav-
en'.[13] He claimed that he would ascend up to heaven in a

chariot of fire. The next time Berridge was in London he
requested that Bell would call on him and after some
conversation Berridge said, "'I have heard, Mr Bell, that
you say, you shall be carried up to heaven in a chariot of
fire." "So I shall," replied Mr Bell, in a tone of uncommon
exultation. "Indeed," added Mr Berridge, "then you will be
highly honoured. May I request one favour of you? Having
always given you a cordial reception when you have visited
me at Everton, I have some small claim on your kindness."
"Most assuredly," answered Mr Bell, "shall I be ready to
grant you any favour that is in my power." "When you are
carried up to heaven in a chariot of fire," replied Mr
Berridge, "I request that you will grant me the honour of
being your postilion." This, being spoken in a sarcastical
manner, roused the spirit of the enthusiast, and he
exclaimed in a loud tone of voice that he had spoken
blasphemy. After raving for a while, in a wild strain, he
quitted the room.'[14] Whittingham says that it was soon after
this that Bell made his prophecy.

Before 1763 Berridge was certainly influenced by
Wesley's 'entire sanctification' teaching. For example, he
tells us in 1761 that he did not realize that 'Christ was to be
my whole strength, as well as righteousness; I saw his blood
could purge away the guilt of sin, but thought I had some
native might against the power of sin; accordingly I laboured to cut my own corruptions, and fray away my own
will, but laboured in the fore. At length, God has shown me
that John Berridge cannot drive the devil out of himself; but
Jesus Christ, blessed be his name, must say to the legion,
"Come out." I see that faith alone can purify the heart as
well as purify the conscience; and Christ is worthy to be my
all in wisdom, in justification, sanctification and redemp-
tion. Prayer and faith are two handmaids never to be
separated, are to carry me through the wilderness; and
whilst I am diligent in God's appointed and blessed
ordinances, I am then to sit still, and quietly wait for the
salvation of God, and see clearly that he can as fully remove
all the corruptions of my heart, as the guilt of sin; that he
can as perfectly restore me to his image, as his favour. And I
believe that Jesus Christ is called the second Adam, because
he is to restore the whole of what he died for; and I know it is

God's good will, because I have his word for it that we should be renewed in the spirit of our minds (Eph. 4:23). For this my spirit waiteth, for this my soul longeth, for this my heart and flesh cry out to the living God. Come, Lord and fill me, take me, and make me wholly thine.'[15] In seeking this Berridge was disappointed and he moved away from this simplistic and non-biblical view of sanctification as he faced up to the realities of the inner man and his own sinful nature.

In 1768, two years before Wesley put forward his propositions at the 1770 conference on the dangers of Calvinism, Berridge wrote to Wesley seeking reconciliation:

Jan. 1st, 1768

Dear Sir,

I see no reason why we should keep at a distance, whilst we continue servants of the same Master; and especially when Lot's herdsmen are so ready to lay their staves on our shoulders. Though my hand has been mute, my heart is kindly affected toward you. I trust we agree in essentials, and therefore should leave each other at rest with his circumstantials. I am weary of all disputes, and desire to know nothing but Jesus; to love him, trust in him, and serve him; to choose and find him my only portion: I would have him my meat, my drink, my clothing, my sun, my shield, my Lord, my God, my all. Amen.

When I saw you in town, I gave you an invitation to Everton; and now I repeat it, offering you very kindly the use of my house and church. The Lord accompany you in all your journeys. Kind love to your brother. Adieu

John Berridge.[16]

This warmth may appear surprising in view of Berridge's opposition to perfectionism and the shift towards what might be called more liberalized principles in theology which Wesley was undergoing from 1763 onwards. Perhaps Berridge was unaware of the trends in Wesley's thinking on assurance and justification, for 'there can be little doubt that Wesley's notion of justification altered to the place where simply to fear God and work righteousness revealed an acceptance by God and a degree of faith'.[17] These issues would be made more public in two years' time through the Calvinist controversy, by which time Wesley would write in his own copy of his published works in 1771 opposite the entry for February 1738 'not converted', 'I am not sure of this.' And against the entry on the same day, 'I am a child of wrath', he writes, 'I believe not.'[18] Holiness of life showed whether there was true justifying faith even if the theology of justification by faith alone was denied by the person. Whatever the theological differences between Berridge and Wesley, it was Wesley's perfectionist views at this time that would stop any practical reconciliation between the two men. Two months after Berridge's invitation Wesley wrote to John Fletcher: 'I seldom find it profitable to converse with any who are not athirst for full salvation; and who are not big with earnest expectation of receiving it every moment.'[19] Berridge, with his more realistic view of sin, would always be outside the circle. This view, developed after years of painful experience, can be seen in a letter to John Thornton in 1773, ten years after he had rejected perfectionist approaches:

Dear and Honoured Sir,

I owe you many thanks and many prayers, and a letter beside; but the debts I owe to God are without number, and a daily increasing sum, and exceedingly heinous. Everlasting thanks for a Surety, whose blood is of infinite value, and who can save to the uttermost. Ten years ago I hoped to be something long before this time, and seemed in a promising way; but a clearer view of the spiritual wickedness in my heart, and of the spiritual demands of God's law, has forced me daily to cry, 'O wretched man that I am! God be merciful to me a sinner.' I am now sinking from a poor something into a vile nothing; and wish to be nothing, that Christ may be all. I am creeping down the ladder from self-complacence into self-abhorrence; and the more I do abhor myself, the more I must hate sin, which is the cause of that abhorrence. A legal heart may strive against sin, through fear of hell; or strive against sin to glorify himself, as laying a foundation for merit; but a gospel-broken heart strives against sin, through a loathing of it, as the filthiness of his spirit, the image of the devil, and a contradiction to

God's holiness ... God says he will dwell with a broken
heart; but a heart cannot be broken where there is a sense of
merit, it is only broken down by a dread of sin, or by a
loathing of it. First, we are taught to loathe ourselves, on
account of our sinful nature. As the heart is more washed,
we grow more sensible of its remaining defilement: just as
we are more displeased with a single spot on a new coat,
than with a hundred stains in an old one.[20]

Thus Berridge had reached a more spiritual view of law
and a more clear view of sin in his own heart. He began his
book *The Christian World Unmasked* with an analysis of the
nature of sin and it was this that formed the basis of his
Calvinistic views and made separation from Wesley inevit-
able. Berridge believed that 'Men are strangers to the
spiritual nature of God's law, and to the woeful depravity of
the human heart and therefore entertain a meagre notion of
religion, and a lofty thought of their own ability.'[21] For
Berridge, 'Truth is called for in the inward parts.'[22] The
inner life was the true test of spirituality. Henry Venn sums
up Berridge's view by observing that 'He is often telling me
that he is sick of all he does, and loathes himself for the
inexpressible corruption he feels within: yet is his life a
pattern to us all and an incitement to love and serve the
Lord with all our strength.'[23] Obviously Everton's vicar had
emerged from his troubles a more knowledgeable man. He
would call himself the 'old ass of Everton',[24] 'daily praying
to know more of my blindness, helplessness and vileness'.[25]
There would be a constant warfare until the end of his life
and, apart from all else, this warfare convinced Berridge
that he was a child of God. Towards the end of his life he
wrote a letter published in *Cheerful Piety* which described this
spiritual battle in an open way. He was convinced that 'God
never justifies but he sanctifies, Election is God's mark to
know his own children by. Calling and sanctification are our
marks, by which we come to know that we ourselves are his
elected children. Oh, then set forth the work of the Spirit in
a rebellious will, a blind understanding, a hard heart, a
stupid conscience, and vile affections; renewing and
sanctifying all these powers, and so proving it to be truly the
work of God and not man.'[26]

That Wesley was disappointed in the broken-hearted Berridge is shown in Wesley's attitude to the value of the revival at Everton and his failure to visit Berridge even when in his neighbourhood. For example, Wesley visited St Neots, six miles from Everton, for the first time in 1775. There were a further eight visits before 1790 and yet Wesley made no contact with Berridge. In the eighties he paid visits to Hicks, Berridge's early preaching companion at Wrestlingworth, and yet there was no contact. The reason was probably Wesley's attitude to the work at Everton. We have already seen how in 1780, writing to Collins, he had suggested a lack of development in the spiritual life at Everton, but a more theological evaluation is found in Wesley's comparison of the Everton revival with that in Weardale (County Durham), where, as in the early days at Everton, there were sensational happenings. Wesley thought the Weardale revival, which occurred ten years after that at Everton, was more of a work of God. He felt that more people were converted at Weardale and that there were not the satanic counterfeits found at Everton. Wesley emphasizes the difference in the leaders of the work in both places: 'Not one of those in or near Everton had any experience in the guiding of souls. None of them were more than "babes in Christ", if any of them so much. Whereas in Weardale, not only the three preachers were, I believe, renewed in love, but most of the leaders were deeply experienced in the work of God, accustomed to train up souls in his way, and not ignorant of Satan's devices. And hence we may easily account for the grand difference between the former and the latter work; namely, that the one was so shallow, there scarce being any subjects rising above an infant state of grace; the other so deep, many, both men, women and children, being what St John terms "young men" in Christ. Yea, many children here have had far deeper experience, and more constant fellowship with God, than the oldest man or woman at Everton which I have seen or heard of.'[27]

Berridge's opposition to Wesley's second-blessing teaching after his initially being influenced by it and his developing knowledge of the reality of his own heart meant that he and the people at Everton were classed as second-class Christians who had not progressed. It is not surprising that their relationship was at an end even before Berridge's trenchant and articulated attack on Arminianism. True friendship is based on respect and integrity and while we wait for our brains to be washed it does us good to reflect on the weaknesses of the human heart even or especially amongst those who follow the Lamb.

# 13.
# Illness and learning to be a passive servant

From 1768 to 1773 recurring illnesses confined the once energetic and enthusiastic field-preacher to his own home for long periods. He usually succeeded in taking the church services on Sunday, but sometimes even that was beyond his powers. Although he fretted and suffered depression at first he came to bless God for these years of difficulty and trial. Enforced rest led to a serious evaluation of himself and of his theology. The way forward for Berridge was the path of difficulty and all his writings after this period give evidence of a more knowledgeable and spiritual man.

Berridge suffered from asthma. It probably started when he was a young man, for he writes in 1775, 'We have been house keepers every summer for forty years.'[1] It is completely wrong to suggest, as Ryle does, that Berridge 'seems to have possessed one of those iron constitutions which nothing but old age can quite break down'.[2] Berridge lived with intermittent asthma most of his life and in fact he died as a result of an attack. Sometimes it was debilitating, when he would be 'much weighed down with coughing and phlegm, sometimes almost strangled with it, which has wasted and weakened my body, and narrowed and bleached my face'.[3] He comments later that 'My disorder seems to be asthmatic, and is attended with a deep cough and much phlegm.'[4] Berridge called his illness a 'nervous fever', meaning a sinuous illness which proved obstinate and did not yield to medicine.[5]

After years of great activity he was seized with a serious attack in the early summer of 1768. For five months he was completely incapacitated. Other attacks, although often milder, were to remain with him and stop him itinerating until 1773. Attacks were much worse in the summer months. In 1771 he writes, 'In the winter I am somewhat braced; and can make a poor shift to preach on the Sabbath, but nothing more. As soon as the hot weather comes in, I am fit for nothing but to sigh and yawn.'[6] In the summer of 1770 he did not preach for four months. He wrote to Rowland Hill, 'I have had a miserable summer, Jesus flogging, and poor Jack pointing and snarling. I am now better, and can preach once a week, blessed be God; and have some hopes that the Master will send out his old ass once more to alarm the devil and the minor prophets of Cam with his bray by and by.'[7]

The following summer, 1771, Berridge managed a very curtailed programme although he was fearful of what the summer might bring. Writing to his friend John Newton at Olney, he notes that 'When the warm weather first set in, I began to sink apace, and was apprehensive I should soon be laid aside, but through mercy I am somewhat braced up again, and again enabled yet to do whole duty on the Sabbath. I can bear very little exercise in walking or riding, and a gentle hurry overturns me; but I can still bear quiet company, and am refreshed by it.'[8] In the same letter he makes the remarkable statement that 'By a token received, I expect to be kept an invalid two summers more.'[9] In another letter of the same period he says that 'The Lord gave me notice of this sickness nine months before it came, following me first with these words, "Thou shalt be dumb for a season," and then with these words, "Thou must have fellowship with Christ in his sufferings."'[10] By this time Berridge was coming to terms spiritually with his disability. He had come to acknowledge that his spiritual pride had brought him this discipline. He was thankful for the day of small things: 'Whether this strength will continue, when the hot season returns, I know not, nor is it needful to know at present; this only do I know, that all my troubles are of my own procuring; my pride sets my feet in the stocks and brings fresh rods and more furrows on my back. I know Jesus loves me, and therefore takes the trouble to scourge me soundly. I feel the furnace humble my heart, and yet I seem full of pride still.'[11]

This was not his first response. At first he was irritated and depressed. Whittingham says that 'To be laid aside in the plenitude of his success was so irritating to his nature, that like Jonah, *his heart fretted against the Lord*, and he wished he had never been employed in the work of the ministry. To such a pitch of criminal exasperation was he carried against the government of God, for checking his ministerial career, that he could not even endure the sight of his Bible, nor bear the people sing in his adjoining church.'[12]

Berridge was now to learn to be a passive servant rather than a very active one: Although Whittingham's summary may be exaggerated, something of Berridge's early reaction is seen when he describes himself as 'a scalled miserable indeed, just able at times to peep into my Bible' and undergoing 'cloudy days and moonless nights; only a little consolation fetched down now and then by a little dull prayer'.[13] Berridge declares, 'Woefully weary I am of myself, but know not how to live and feast daily upon Jesus. A treasure he is indeed, but lies hid in the field, and I know not how to dig in the dark.'[14] He confesses to Whitefield that he 'cannot kiss the rod'[15] and that he is like a poor toad spitting at everything that annoys him. He had periods when his heart was broken and he saw more of the grace of God and thought that he would grumble no more. But these periods were short and he soon slid into misery.

Berridge thought that his great success during his ten years of gospel preaching had increased his pride and independence. His response to difficulty in the form of illness showed him the true nature of his heart. In 1772 he wrote, 'My Master has been tying me to a whipping-post for four years and has chastised me smartly with rods and scorpions. Indeed, they were both sorely wanted; for I have a very saucy will, and a sad, proud heart, and was grown in my own conceit almost as good a man as my Master. He sent me out to preach; and because he was pleased to do wonders by his Word and Spirit, I stole all his laurels from him, and girt them around my own temples. But the Lord was jealous of his own honour, and has taken me to task roundly, and made me willing not only to throw the pilfered laurels at his feet, but to cast my scoundrel self there. He has lowered my top-sail, beaten down my masts, ransacked my vessel, and battered its sides so wonderfully, that I am escaped like a mere wreck into haven. I can now feel as well as call myself vile, and can submit to lay my hand upon my mouth and to thrust my mouth in the dust. Dear sir, how sweet is poverty of spirit and brokenness of heart!'[16]

This illness thus proved a watershed in Berridge's experience. His own abilities were nothing; the work was God's. Others noticed the change. Henry Venn had seen the heady days of 1760 when he had accompanied Lady Huntingdon and preached with Madan and Berridge to thousands gathered at Everton. Venn noticed a vast difference in Berridge since the early sixties when he came to live nearby: 'Summer differs not more from winter than this dear man from what he was ten years ago; he is now broken in heart, yet fervent in spirit.'[17]

There is no doubt that Berridge was depressed on various occasions during this period. The discovery of pride in his life, as seen in his fretting and questioning God, brought him soul trouble.

> Full many a year
> I seem'd to be sound,
> Was lighter than air
> And sprung on the ground:
> I trod on a mountain
> And lofty was seen,
> And wanted no fountain
> To wash my heart clean.
>
> But now I am sick,
> And full of complaint,
> Exceedingly weak,
> And ready to faint;
> My heart an old den is
> Of filth and deceit;
> And all its revenues
> Spring out of conceit.[18]

He longed for a closer relationship with God, not that which flowed from the sensational but one which was based on increased faith. In March 1770 he replies to Lady Huntingdon, thanking her for a helpful letter: 'These many months I have done little else but mourn for myself and others, to see how we lie among the tombs, contented with a decent suit of grave clothes. At times my heart has been refreshed with these words: "On the land of my people is come up briars and thorns, until the Spirit be poured out upon them from on high," but the comfort soon vanisheth, like gleams of a winter sun. I cannot wish for transports, such as we once had, and which almost turned our heads; but I do long to see a spirit poured forth of triumphant faith, heavenly love, and steadfast cleaving to the Lord.'[19]

He could be brought low in spirit because of the great need: 'I would fain prattle a little for him [Christ] in the pulpit this summer; for we have now large congregations, and it is sad, very sad, to have them broken up, and to be laid aside myself altogether, as a broken vessel.'[20] Perhaps the basis for his depression was in part physical, for it may well be that he was suffering from nervous exhaustion (as well as his asthma) as a result of his unremitting work for ten years. However, God can and often does turn our weakness into strength and Berridge was to learn the lesson of 'not resting on feelings, but leaning on grace'.[21]

In May 1773 he began to itinerate 'after a five years' discontinuance through illness, and kept on, though with much feebleness, for two months, when I was seized with a smart attack of my old complaint, I am now, as the world acounts, a scold miserable, but lying at Jesus' gate, and am reduced to a mere Sunday preacher; the Lord be praised that I am not wholly laid aside.'[22] In the summer of 1773 Berridge was not able to go outside his parish for five months. 'Since the cool weather set in I am growing better, through mercy, and hope to be on horseback shortly, and preach a little in the neighbourhood.'[23] That Berridge was not fully recovered is seen in that he only travelled 'two or three days in a week to preach'[24] in the two months before another attack. He was, however, delighted with the abundance of hearers at this time. His illness was recurring and formed a continual backdrop to all his activities to the end of his life.

After his initial rebellion at being laid aside Berridge was to develop a positive attitude towards this affliction. It was part of taking up the cross daily: 'The Lord be praised for past sickness, and returning health. Whilst we dwell in

houses of corrupt clay we shall need continual correction. . .
Expect the cross daily, and it cannot surprise you, nor much
hurt you when it comes. It will come from every quarter just
as it is wanted; and it comes with a rough and lowering
countenance, but brings a blessing secretly in its .hand for
you. We are often simple enough to think that any other
cross were better for us than the present; yet since Jesus is a
kind and wise physician, he always sends the most suitable
medicine. He lays a blister on the proper part; yea, and
takes it off too when it has done its work. Afflictions have
been to me some of my greatest mercies.'[25]

Berridge saw his illness as directly from the Lord for his
own benefit: 'I do not love this fever friend; yet he is
certainly the best earthly companion I have. No lasting gain
do I get but in a furnace. Comforts of every kind, in the
issue, make me either light or lofty, and swell me, though
unperceivably, with self-sufficiency. Indeed, so much dross,
native and acquired, is found in my heart, that I have
constant need of a furnace; and Jesus has selected a suitable
furnace for me, not a hot and hasty one, which seems likely
to harden and consume me, but one with a gentle and
lingering heat, which melts my heart gradually, and lets out
some of its dross. Though I cannot love a furnace, nor bask
in it like a salamander, yet the longer I live, the more I see of
its need and its use. A believer seldom walks steadily and
ornamentally, unless he is well furnaced. Without this his
zeal is often scalding hot; his boldness attended with
fierceness, or rather rashness; and his confidence at times
more the result of animal spirit than the fruit of the Spirit;
but a furnace consumes these excrescences, and when
sweetly blown with grace, will make a Christian humble,
watchful, and mellow; very censorious of himself, and full of
compassion for others.'[26]

During these difficult years Berridge did not vegetate. He
preached when he was able. He wrote over three hundred
hymns. He clarified his views on the sovereignty of God and
summarized his views in *The Christian World Unmasked*. He
was able to develop relationships with friends, particularly
Lady Huntingdon, Rowland Hill, John Thornton and John
Newton. He was encouraged with help received from one of
Lady Huntingdon's chaplains in the summer months. John

Thornton sent books for evangelism, medicine and gifts. Rowland Hill had caught Berridge's love of itinerating and Berridge was able to encourage him when he received opposition. John Newton was a visitor during these years and Berridge reminds him not to pass Everton 'without warming a bed and a pulpit'.[27]

This period of difficulty and trial formed a watershed in Berridge's life. He came through it with a new view of himself and, more importantly, a renewed appreciation of Christ.

# 14.
# Berridge and women

Some writers have misinterpreted Berridge's view of women and marriage. They have fallen into the trap of extending his view that evangelists should not get married to cover a condemnation of all married relationships. This is a sad misrepresentation in the light of Berridge's obvious delight in female company and his joy in the happy marriages of his friends. He was conscious, however, that as marriage required commitment from both partners the evangelist, with his prior attachment to travelling preaching, was unable to live with two dividing commitments. For young couples marrying at Everton he wrote the verse:

> In purest love their souls unite,
> And link'd in kindly care
> To render family burdens light,
> By taking mutual share.[1]

There could be no mutual share for a man with Berridge's commitment to itinerant preaching.

Berridge believed that he had divine guidance for not getting married. In the early 1760s he described himself as 'having been grievously tormented with housekeepers' and adds, 'I truly had thoughts of looking out for a Jezebel myself.'[2] He adopted a method of guidance on very special decisions by praying for direction and letting the Bible fall open. At the first attempt he met with the words: 'When my son was entered into his wedding chamber, he fell down and died' (2 Esdras 10:6). This caused him concern but he soon realized that the book was apocryphal and therefore did not have the same weight as authentic Scripture. Again he fell on his knees and asked for a sign from the canonical Scriptures. His eyes fell directly on the words found in Jeremiah: 'Thou shalt not take thee a wife, neither shalt thou have sons or daughters in this place' (Jer. 16:2). This satisfied his mind and he henceforth no longer made marriage the subject of his prayers.

Whittingham relates that soon after this, when Berridge had begun to preach in London, he was visited by a lady who had come down from London to Everton in her carriage to solicit Berridge's hand in marriage, assuring him that the Lord had revealed to her that she was to become his wife. Berridge paused for a few moments and then replied, 'Madam, if the Lord has revealed it to you that you are to be my wife, surely he would also have revealed it to me that I was designed to be your husband; but as no such revelation has been made to me, I cannot comply with your wishes.'[3] The lady returned to London disappointed.

As an itinerant preacher, Berridge held strong views about marriage. He shared his views freely with one of Lady Huntingdon's preachers who was helping him at Everton. 'Before I parted with honest Glascott, I cautioned him much against petticoat snares. He had burnt his wings already: sure he will not imitate a foolish gnat and hover again about the candle. If he should fall into a sleeping lap, he will soon need a flannel nightcap, and a rusty chain to fix him down, like a church Bible to the reading-desk. No trap so mischievous to the field preacher as wedlock and it is laid for him at every hedge corner.'[4]

According to Berridge the man who was committed to itinerant preaching would be hindered by marriage. He wrote to his young friend Rowland Hill exhorting him that 'Now is your time to work for Jesus; you have health and youth on your side, and no church or wife on your back.'[5] The itinerant preacher was despised and any wife would be linked with that dishonour. Hill was honest in the matter when approaching his future wife: 'Can you be contented to see a despised pilgrim for my once despised Master, rejected for my labours, and reproached for my God?'[6] After Hill's marriage Berridge rejoiced that he was wrong: 'I was somewhat afraid lest orders and a petticoat would cure you of rambling – but my fears were groundless, and all is well.'[7]

At the conclusion of this letter he says how much he liked
Hill's wife when they met in London and he sends his kind
love to her. However, perhaps Berridge was right over the
longer term, for Hill was destined in the future to lead a
settled work at Surrey Chapel in London.

Most of Berridge's comments on women are positive and
show his powers of love and friendship. One exception
seems to be his comments on Job's wife, where he does not
mince words. Writing to a friend, a curate at Lakenheath,
who was being worried by the prospect of his vicar removing
him, Berridge counsels patience and trust and reminds him
of Job who 'lost more than sixty pounds by his disaster, he
lost his all; nothing was left except a froward piece of
furniture in his house, without a name, but not without a
tongue, a very crooked rib, and much unlike yours'.[8] On the
other hand he rejoiced that Margate had helped the wife of
a friend and Berridge noted that 'She is a favourite of mine,
and give my love to her, but do not be jealous.'[9] He was
happy in the marriage of another friend: 'I wish you both
joy, yea much joy, but all in the Lord. Perhaps you do not
know that you have married my sister. Indeed she is as like
me as if we had been born of one mother. Well, you are
married into a good family, but I trust, adopted into a
better; and though you have given your hand to my sister
Bateman, I hope your heart, as well as hers, is given to my
Lord Jesus.'[10]

He included wives in his greetings and speaking to
Newton he asks that the Lord would 'bless the dear partner
of your bosom'.[11] He speaks with affection of the wife of
Samuel Wilks as he was her spiritual father. He was thrilled
at the spiritual experiences of a daughter of Henry Venn:
'Kitty had a wonderful breathing of the Holy Ghost upon
her three or four years ago, which continued for many
months. A spirit of prayer was given in rich abundance with
divine consolations, and her heart seemed wholly taken up
with God.'[12] He thought that another daughter, Jenny, had
wonderful abilities: 'She visits all the sick in the parish,
makes up their medicines, delights in the work, and would
make a good parson's wife.'[13]

Berridge's letters to women show that he discussed any
issue with them with no hint of patronizing. He wrote on

terms of equality. He found a letter from Lady Huntingdon a spiritual encouragement and told her so. Berridge's relationship with Lady Huntingdon seemed very open and both could speak plainly to each other. Finally, although Berridge did not marry he did not live alone, as Ryle states, for he had servants and refers to 'my family'. Like any family there were trials and in 1780 he speaks of a maid suffering insanity, who was later to recover. He writes rejoicingly to a. Miss L. on returning to Everton after London commitments that 'Through the Lord's protection I came safe to Everton on Tuesday, the 11th at half-four, and found my servants all well, and everything well about me.'[14] Thus it would appear that Berridge was at ease with women and that the spiritual dimension, and not that of gender, was the important sphere to him.

One comment by Berridge has ensured him a bad press concerning marriage. In a passage to Lady Huntingdon, speaking about the dangers of matrimony for a field preacher, Berridge comments adversely on the marriages of other evangelical leaders. He says that 'Matrimony has quite maimed poor Charles, and might have spoiled John and George, if a wise Master had not graciously sent them a brace of ferrets. Dear George has now got the liberty again and he will escape well if he is not caught by another tenterhook.'[15] It is doubtful if marriage was the only reason that discouraged Charles Wesley from itinerating although it is true that after his marriage Charles did little itinerant preaching. John Wesley often felt that he had been deserted by his younger brother. Charles Wesley's views on the importance of the national church may have caused him to reassess his role in Methodism. However, in Berridge's opinion a happy and comfortable home had blunted the edge of his evangelistic desires. 'Maimed' is too strong a word for us, but not for Berridge who saw preaching the gospel as his priority.

John Wesley held a similar view to that of Berridge on the value of celibacy for those engaged in service for God. In his tract *Thoughts on a Single Life*, he states that every man can receive this gift and that there are so many advantages for the Christian, including, 'You may give all your time to God without interruption, and need ask leave of none but yourself so to do.'[16] Wesley's main nineteenth-century biographer concluded after reading this tract that a man holding such views should not have married. Perhaps Berridge himself formed his own views from the tragedy of Wesley's unhappy marriage. Whoever was the most sinned against – the unfortunate Mrs Molly Vazeille, the well-off widow whom Wesley married, or Wesley himself – it was certainly true that a miserable domestic background formed the background to his itinerant preaching. If the man who believed no Methodist preacher should 'preach one sermon or travel one day less in the married than in the single state'[17] had realized the implications of such a position, much unhappiness would have been avoided. Berridge's image of the ferret is strong but it reflected what actually happened. Wesley himself thought that 'If Mrs Wesley had been a better wife, he might have been unfaithful in the great work to which God had called him.'[18]

Dallimore criticizes Berridge for linking Whitefield's wife with Wesley's wife. However, Whitefield held basically the same views as Wesley and Berridge and although he valued a marriage partner as a help in his ministry, he started married life with the clear intention that there should be no change in life-style for himself. Although Dallimore suggests that the marriage over the years was tolerably happy, Berridge only knew Whitefield in the last years of his married life and it is in these years that Whitefield may have been happy to itinerate. Dallimore himself speaks of the difficulty of Mrs Whitefield balancing her personal needs with her husband's ministry, entailing as it did long absences. Whether or not Berridge was right in his own evaluation of Mrs Whitefield, one must remember that the remarks were made in a private letter in the context of Berridge's view that a wife is a danger to a field preacher.

Berridge seems to have equally valued men and women. His views on the dangers of marriage for a travelling evangelist seem realistic and in this matter he was able to follow his own advice. Let us remember, however, that an evangelist is equally a danger to a God-fearing woman if he determines to live the same type of life that he lived before he was married.

# 15.
# Controversy and Calvinism

Berridge had a love for all true Christians and a correspondingly deep hatred of sectarianism and party spirit. Whittingham points out that he felt strongly that, just as Satan had divided man from God in the beginnings of sin, so he made it 'his constant aim and endeavour to divide the followers of Christ, or to prevent the continuance of brotherly love. Thus he foments animosity and ill-will, and thereby furnishes ground for the entertainment of infidel principles and irreligious conduct.'[1]

Berridge expresses his antisectarian views in a hymn:

> One cries, I am for Paul;
> And one Apollos takes:
> Each thinks his leader all in all,
> And wild dissension makes.
>
> If carnal feuds appear,
> Where gospel truth is taught,
> Sweet love is quickly banish'd there,
> And Jesus Christ forgot.
>
> The gospel suffers harm,
> And infidels blaspheme,
> When fierce disciples lift their arm,
> And raise a party flame.
>
> Yet oft, full oft we see,
> Much unbecoming strife;
> Nor sheep nor shepherds can agree
> To lead a peaceful life.

From thy disciples, Lord,
Such carnal strife remove,
Subdue them by thy gracious word,
And teach them how to love.[2]

Whittingham stresses that Berridge was not indifferent to
the essentials of salvation and would welcome fellowship
with all those who had exercised repentance, trust towards
Christ, and who inculcated holiness of life, whatever their
church affiliation. 'They had a place in his affectionate
heart, however distinguished by different modes of worshipping God.'[3]

Berridge's attitude towards the damaging effects of public
controversy was persistent and, except for his entry into the
Calvinistic controversy of the 1770s with *The Christian World
Unmasked* (1773), a consistent one. In his early hymn-book of
1760 he cautions his fellow ministers against 'disputing and
reading many books, which would make you neglect the
Bible'.[4] Berridge had seen the effects of barren argumentation, particularly in the visits of Calvinists trying to
convince him about election soon after his conversion.

Soon as the gospel sound
Was published all abroad,
The din of party echoes round,
And clogs the gospel road.[5]

He wrote to Wesley, 'I am weary of all disputes, and
desire to know nothing but Jesus.'[6] He was concerned about
his friend Newton researching into the controversies of the
first few centuries. Berridge thought these controversies
'had better lie buried'.[7] He was painfully aware of the
tendency of the human heart to trust in doctrines and
positions rather than Christ. 'Now one soars up with the
cloud of perfection, crying out, I am a queen! and becomes
the devil's goddess. Another falls asleep and snores hard in
election; God's truth, indeed, is often made the devil's
cradle.'[8] A hymn summarizes his convictions:

Some wise men of opinions boast,
And sleep on doctrines sound;

But, Lord, let not my soul be lost
On such enchanted ground.

Good doctrines can do me no good,
While floating in the brain;
Unless they yield my heart some food,
They bring no real gain.

Oh, may my single aim be now
To live on him that died,
And nought on earth desire to know
But Jesus crucified.

Disputings only gender strife,
And gall a tender mind;
But godliness in all its life
At Jesus' cross we find.[9]

Berridge was convinced that the 1770 controversy was
detrimental. 'Religious controversy has hurt the work much;
religious gossipping hurts it still more and deep-mouth
Calvinism loves sitting and hearing much better than
kneeling and praying.'[10] As Berridge grew older he recognized that 'Controversy usually goes on briskly, but gospel
work goes on heavily, at least amongst us.'[11] Three years
before his death he was looking forward to heaven: 'Blessed
be God for a prospect of peace; much wrangling here about
things civil and sacred, but no belligerents above. One
heaven holds all; and one temple serves all; and one Jesus
feeds all with his own love, joy and peace.'[12]

Even at the very time of the publication of *The Christian
World Unmasked* Berridge was doubtful of such a polemical
role for himself: 'Whatever Mr Fletcher may write against my
pamphlet, I am determined to make no reply. I dare not trust
my own wicked heart in a controversy. If my pamphlet is
faulty, let it be overthrown; if sound, it will rise up above any
learned rubbish that is cast upon it. Indeed, what signifies
my pamphlet or its author? While it was publishing I was
heartily weary of it; and have really been sick of it since.'[13]

Three years later he reinforces this doubt, writing to a
friend in London: 'I cast away all controversial writers, and

betake myself to the Word of God and prayer; this is my chief employment, and my best delight; and I would advise you to do the same; for controversy will puzzle you, and may tincture you with a controversial spirit, which is generally a bad one, even when engaged in a good cause.'[14]

It is clear that by 'controversy' Berridge meant boastful attitudes and postures rather than humble discussion. Thus he was grateful that he had 'neither the ability nor inclination for controversy which often proves a gospel bear garden, when the combatants are bruising each other, and he that deals hardest blows seems the cleverest fellow'.[15] Berridge thought that public controversy was a poor witness to the world. As the patient in *The Christian World Unmasked* says, 'It makes us titter when we hear a cry of fire, and see some engines from the Foundery playing on the tabernacle pulpit. . . Such frays make us laugh delightfully and yield a venison feast for the squire and the vicar.'[16] He expressed his fear to Thornton that Fletcher and Toplady 'were setting the Christian world on fire and the carnal world in laughter, and wished they could both desist from controversy'.[17]

Whittingham, curate at Everton for the last period of Berridge's life, says that Berridge became indifferent to the reading of controversial works. He tells a story of Berridge being visited by an eminent minister, who asked him if he had read certain works on the different points of Arminianism and Calvinism. Berridge replied, 'I have them on my shelves in my library, where they are very quiet; if I take them down, and look into them, they will begin to quarrel and disagree.'[18] Whittingham then sums up Berridge's mature thought: 'He regarded controversy, being often conducted with acrimony, with no favourable opinion, regarding it as injurious to heavenly-mindedness, as well as to a peaceful state of mind. Where controversy proceeds from a dispassionate disposition, and breathes the air of Christian charity, it may be useful in settling the minds of those who are fluctuating . . . on account of the various and contrary opinions which engage their thoughts.'[19]

Berridge well knew the truth that what we criticize in others is often present in ourselves. Mr Richard Hill, one of the leading writers in the early days of the controversy on the Calvinistic side, disapproved of his younger brother,

Rowland, engaging in travelling open-air preaching, against the canons of the Church of England as he saw it. He went to Bristol to rebuke his brother but arriving during preaching was himself prevailed upon by his younger brother to preach. On returning to London he wrote a very severe letter to his brother. Berridge comments, 'Oh, what is man! But how easily we spy the vanity and inconsistency of the creature in another, and how hardly we discern it in ourselves! The foulest stain and highest absurdity in our nature is pride. And yet this base hedgehog so rolls himself up in his bristly coat, we can seldom get a sight of his claws.'[20]

In discussing controversy concerning the deity of Christ and his own experience at Cambridge, when he had been involved in much discussion of this issue, Berridge says to Thornton, 'You judge exceedingly right, to stand still, and avoid disputings; they only gender strife, and stir up pride. A sweet behaviour, joined with secret prayer, will do more in this matter than a thousand eager disputations.'[21] This was written in 1773, the year of the publication of *The Christian World Unmasked*. A few months later he was writing to Rowland Hill, 'Avoid all controversy in preaching, talking or writing; preach nothing down but the devil and nothing up but Jesus Christ.'[22]

The evidence about Berridge's view on controversy raises two fundamental questions. Firstly, why have some historians painted Berridge as a lover of controversy; and, secondly, why did Berridge engage in the Calvinism controversy by writing *The Christian World Unmasked* when he held such definite views on the detrimental effects of controversy on fellow Christians, himself and the world?

Abbey and Overton speak of Berridge rushing 'into the very thick of the Calvinistic controversy',[23] Overton and Relton say, 'It would be unprofitable to quote the abusive language, both in prose and doggerel verse, with which he now assailed his old friend',[24] and E.J. Poole-Connor speaks of 'his scurrility to his theological opponents'.[25] Such views come not from a careful examination of the facts, but probably from the historian Southey, who linked Berridge on internal evidence with verses that were written in *The Gospel Magazine* called 'The Serpent and the Fox, or an

Interview between old Nick and old John'. Overton is very
nasty in his criticism of Berridge based on this abusive
poem, concluding that it was written by Berridge because of
the signature of 'Old Everton'.[26] But Elliot-Binns notes that
as Overton's claim that it was signed 'Old Everton' was
erroneous, his whole argument is false. C. Smyth, commenting on this says, 'The external evidence makes this
identification exceedingly improbable, for Berridge plainly
deplored the controversy, and would have been the last man
deliberately to inflame it.'[27] *The Christian World Unmasked* and
the letters of Berridge at the time were free from the
personal abuse which characterizes some of the controversy.
C. Smyth calls it a 'temperate performance'[28] and L.
Tyerman says that it was 'entirely free from the personal
scurrility so characteristic of others'.[29] Interestingly
enough, another historian makes a similar point about
Berridge's later hymn-book in that he found in it 'an entire
absence of bitterness found plentifully in almost every
hymn-book of that period'.[30] In *The Christian World Unmasked*
Berridge does not attack people, although he ruthlessly
attacks their ideas. However, Berridge had some regrets.
Whittingham informs us that Berridge 'regretted many
years before his death that he had introduced some doctrinal topics in an unpleasant manner; and that had he
himself re-published his Works, he would have made those
alterations which are now made in this edition'.[31] These
alterations were minor and the original does not embarrass
Berridge.

   In order to understand why Berridge involved himself in
the controversy we have to consider many factors, ranging
from the background of events and Berridge's personal
circumstances at the time, to Berridge's own move towards
a Calvinistic position and the critical importance which he
attached to the debate in the light of his own conversion
when he fled to Jesus alone for refuge. Berridge was ill from
1768 to 1773. Although for most of the time he was able to
take the Sunday services he was according to his own
standards comparatively unemployed through his asthma.
He may well have felt that the writing of *The Christian World
Unmasked* was a legitimate means of communicating the
gospel. The style and presentation would give weight to this

view. It was the prison house of illness and the passion of the Christian communicator that gave birth to this unusual book.

There is little doubt that the primary purpose of the book was to arouse the person who professes Christianity, but is spiritually dead. The patient professes himself well: 'I have my faults, as well as my neighbours; but my appetites are pretty well bridled. My heart is honest, quite willing to pay all men their due; my hands too are sometimes disposed to relieve a neighbour's want; and my feet go orderly to church on a Sunday, when the bells chime, except it proves a rainy day; and then I read the weekly paper, or a Bible chapter at home, just as suits my fancy. This I call a regular life, and it is the ground of my hope; not forgetting Jesus Christ, to help out some defects. For I am choleric, no doubt; but it quickly bloweth over; and a little apt to fib in a market, but who can help it? All my neighbours do the same. . .'[32] The physician pronounces him not just sick, but dead, and the rest of the book outlines the marks and blessings of a true Christian compared with outward decency and unreal profession.

Another factor was obviously Berridge's own move towards a Calvinistic understanding of the gospel. We must be careful not to set the issues out in black and white. Whittingham, who knew Berridge in the last decade of his life, has a tendency to set the issues out in this manner. He says that for the first few years Berridge was a very rigid Arminian and that he adopted the Calvinistic position as a result of his severe illness that flared up in 1768 and led to a long confinement. The work of God still went ahead independent of John Berridge. Whittingham says, 'In his furnace of affliction he became much more acquainted with the plague of his own heart, was led to see that the work of God could be carried on without his agency, and was convinced of the divine sovereignty in the dispensations of grace and appointments to the sacred office.'[33] This is a simplistic account of something far more intricate, although it is true that his illness and his experience in it formed the background for his settled mature views.

Even at the beginning of Berridge's evangelical experience it is difficult to stereotype him. In the preface to his

1760 hymn-book he speaks of the doctrine of unconditional
election being remarkably strange. The logical conclusion of
predestination he felt to be Antinomianism. Such a doctrine
meant that all preaching and hearing was in vain since the
decrees of God were irresistible. However, Berridge in the
very early letter to a friend in Nottinghamshire, just six
months after his conversion, had stressed the work of the
Spirit in conversion and God as the author of faith. The
sovereignty of God, particularly in his own conversion,
pervades his whole testimony. It is interesting to note that
John Green, who wrote a long criticism of this letter and of
Berridge's activities as a preacher, assumes that Berridge
preached the doctrines of free grace, election and reprobation. Thus Berridge was inconsistent at this early stage,
believing in the sovereignty of God in his own conversion,
but dismissing the doctrine of election as illogical and
divisive.

Berridge's growing struggle with the doctrine of election
is clearly seen when he deals with the subject in *The Christian
World Unmasked*, which reinforces Whittingham's comment
concerning his illness of 1768. The doctor in the book, after
being challenged by the patient that election 'is a frightful
notion, exceeding discouraging, and seemeth not consistent
with common equity' answers, 'Sir, I think the doctrine of
election never can agree with human merit. One will be
always barking at the other. Every man who seeks to justify
himself by works, will loathe the doctrine heartily, and load
it lustily with most reproachful names. Yet men reject the
doctrine, not for want of Scripture evidence, but for want of
humbled hearts. We are not willing to be saved by an
election of grace till we know ourselves, and find our just
desert.

'A furnace is the proper school to learn this doctrine in,
and there I learnt it. Nor men nor books could teach it me;
for I would neither hear nor read about it. A long and
rancorous war I waged with it; and when my sword was
broken, and both my arms were maimed, I yet maintained a
sturdy fight, and was determined I would never yield; but a
furnace quelled me. Large afflictions, largely wanted, gave
me such experience of my evil heart that I could peep upon
electing grace without abhorrence; and as I learnt to loathe

myself, I learnt to prize this grace. It seemed clear, if God had mercy for me, it could be for this gracious reason, because he would have mercy (Romans 9:18): for every day and every hour, my desert was death. . . I know the rancour of the human heart against this doctrine, for I have sorely felt it; and charitably thought that all its teachers were the devil's chaplains.'[34]

Thus Berridge saw his belief in election coming as a result of troubles which had exposed the real nature of his heart. Perhaps he wrote *The Christian World Unmasked* not only with evangelistic motives but also to help himself clarify the implications of accepting the doctrine of election. Besides the implications for preaching, which he dealt with thoroughly, he found that the doctrines of grace were the only teachings that could directly challenge the liberalizing and watering down of justification by faith alone which he saw occurring amongst some leaders in Methodism. Belief in electing grace was the only realistic outcome for someone who had for so long struggled with the relationship between faith and works, and who had recognized right from the beginning that faith was a gift of God. Although, as Henry Venn noticed in 1771, Berridge's Calvinism was experimental and practical rather than philosophical, a man with Berridge's mind must have pondered theological aspects of the teaching. By 1773, the year he published *The Christian World Unmasked*, he describes himself as a moderate Calvinist. This would suggest that the book summarized the emotional and spiritual changes that had been occurring for some time.

Another factor in the writing of *The Christian World Unmasked* must have been the current controversy and Berridge's awareness of it. Some date the beginnings of this furious and at times acrimonious debate from the publication of Wesley's *Conference Minutes of 1770*, in which he said that the Methodist movement had leaned too much towards Calvinism. The Minutes were an attempt to clarify Wesley's position. They were certainly problematic for the evangelical Christian, as Wesley seemingly came in them to conclusions radically different from his initial theology. However, the controversy had already opened up two years previously with the expulsion from St Edmund Hall, Oxford of six evangelical students on the charges of singing, praying and preaching in private houses and of holding the heretical doctrine of predestination. Whitefield himself had written in their defence and this expulsion had produced a spate of pamphlets for and against, debating whether the Thirty-Nine Articles taught predestination. At the 1771 Conference a carefully worded statement, stating that the 1770 Minutes had been wrongly interpreted to favour justification by works and restating that works played no part in purchasing our justification, although a real believer would do good works if he had opportunity, seemed to give the opportunity of peace. However, Wesley's publication of Fletcher's defence of the original Minutes made sure that the argument would continue and it was towards the end of the 1770s before it burnt itself out.

Although Berridge lived in a very quiet village the controversy did not fail to reach him. Rowland Hill would have kept him in touch with events in Oxford and Hill's elder brother wrote on behalf of the expelled students. The expulsion attracted considerable attention in the *Lloyd's Evening Post*. John Newton was in contact with one of the students. One of the main protagonists, Toplady, had contact with Berridge. Berridge was aware of the compromised statement at the 1771 conference, for he wrote to Rowland Hill showing his scepticism of the struggle for leadership as he saw it. 'The late contest at Bristol seems to turn upon this hinge, whether it shall be Pope John or Pope Joan. My dear friend, keep out of all controversy, and wage no war but with the devil.'[35] Rowland Hill did not take Berridge's advice and Berridge himself was soon to forsake his own counsel.

The evidence clearly shows Berridge as no lover of controversy; his spiritual life was dominated by his relationship with Christ. However, he had a concern for truth as he saw it and as a result of clarification that had occurred in his own outlook and the opportunity afforded by illness he was drawn into the controversy of the 1770s, only to be greatly disappointed at the quality of debate that followed his contribution. He probably saw the situation as an evangelical downgrade and felt the issues keenly as he had himself struggled with similar issues in the years leading up to his conversion.

# 16.
# The Christian World Unmasked (1773)

The solution to why Berridge wrote *The Christian World Unmasked*, in spite of his advice to others to keep out of the argument and his own views on the detrimental nature of uncharitable controversy, is to be found in the issues that were being raised. To say, as some historians have suggested, that no new ground was covered in this debate is to miss the vital point that many on both sides considered that the very nature of the gospel was at issue. Also it was not just a debate about the sovereignty of God and the freedom of man. In the light of the apparent theological changes in Wesley, it was a debate about what constituted the Christian message. Even without discussing such issues as election, Berridge would certainly have reacted to the new expressions about the place of works relative to faith. Berridge's expression of truth is often original, picturesque and perhaps to some ears blunt. One writer says that Berridge used a 'style and manner pre-eminently calculated to rouse the dullest attention, and break through that indifference with which familiarity encrusts the most solemn momentous subjects'.[1] He wrote for ordinary people and addressed them in their language. His concern was not abstract theology but vital truth; truth opposed to any form of auto-salvation.

Berridge's quaint title *The Christian World Unmasked – Pray Come and Peep* clearly portrays his aim. For Berridge, many in Christendom were resting on a false gospel, a gospel of faith and works: 'For a century past the noble building of God's grace has been propped up with legal buttresses. Moses is called in hastily to underprop his master Jesus.'[2] The patient whom the gospel doctor examines and pronounces mortally sick thinks that because of his respectable life he enjoys good Christian health. The task for Berridge is to show the unreality of such a profession in comparison with those who are the real subjects of Christ and who have been enabled 'not only to profess him, but to love and serve him, and fix their whole dependence upon him'.[3] In order for this to happen there must be a change in the self-image (broken-heartedness) and a new glorious view of Christ as the only Saviour. 'He wants no partner, and will admit of none; nor were he worthy of the name of Saviour, if salvation was not wholly from him.'[4] The true Christian's 'whole dependence must be on the Saviour's blood for pardon, and on the Saviour' grace for holiness'.[5]

Berridge's approach is premised on the comparison between the true and the counterfeit. Authentic humble Christians know Christ as King. 'They know the purchase price he paid, and having tasted of the blessings, they love his person, and adore his grace. Paul and they are now agreed, to know only Jesus Christ, and him crucified. He is their song and boast, their peace and hope, their all in all.'[6] The spiritually dead person has no real interest in prayer, communion with God or the appropriation of the promises of God: 'Glorious things are spoken in the Scripture but they make a mighty small impression on a Christian congregation. The heavenly tidings fall into their heavy ears like money dropped into a dead man's hand. No comfort is received from the money or the tidings, because they are dead, and have no interest in them.

'If you, sir, was an heir to a fine state, your bosom would be warmed with the joyful prospect; but your father's servant could not feel your joy. His bosom would not glow when the fields arc viewed, or when the rents are paid. And wherefore? Because he is not the heir.'[7]

The true function of the law is not to allot merit before God and make a sinner righteous. 'Through the weakness of his flesh, it has no power to justify or sanctify him. It shows the path of duty, but neither lends a crutch to lame travellers, not gives a heavenly title unto sinners.'[8] On the other hand, 'The law sends us unto Jesus, not with recommendations in our hand, but with condemnations in our bosom; and is meant to empty us of every fancied legal hope arising from our own obedience, and force the heart to seek salvation wholly by grace through faith . . . then it becomes a rule of life in the Mediator's hand.'[9] The true Christian is at first an awakened sinner: 'The curse of the law has now made known his guilt; the spirituality of the law has shown his depraved nature and his vain attempts to keep the law have disclosed his utter feebleness. Thus the law has prepared him for Christ. His heart is humbled and broken down with an awful sense of his guiltiness and filthiness and feebleness.'[10]

According to Berridge Christendom and its adherents had departed from the cardinal doctrine of the need for spiritual renovation and a real but secret work of the Holy Spirit and were preaching a gospel of moral reformation perhaps with some help from Christ. Such a gospel radically misunderstood the nature of the Fall. The patient thinks himself 'as good as Adam was before he fell. Why should his fall put my nose out of joint? Could he not stumble without throwing me down? Perhaps he did receive a bruise, and his ankle might be sprained, but I do not read that he broke his neck, or broke a leg, by the fall.'[11] In comparison, Berridge believed that man did indeed break his neck and 'All spiritual life ceased on the day he sinned, and his soul was dead to God.'[12] The reality of spiritual death is such that it 'strips away all power, as well as all perception. A dead body may as well restore itself to life as a dead soul. A fallen angel may as soon rekindle spiritual life and regain his first estate, as a fallen man. Nothing can produce the spiritual life and a spiritual mind resulting from it, but the Spirit of God.'[13] A real Christian indeed is a new creature and God's workmanship. The voice of Jesus will indeed raise the dead.

Man is reborn through the gift of divine faith, not by assent to doctrines, and this divine faith consists in trust in the Saviour's person and promises. 'It brings a precious view of Christ, and draweth precious blessings from him.'[14] The grace of Jesus brings salvation; and through faith, as an instrument put in the sinner's hand, the sinner is enabled to reach out; just as a beggar, by his empty cap stretched forth, receives alms. 'A pole held to a drowning man, and by which he is drawn to land, saveth him, just as faith saves a sinner. In a lax way of speaking, we are said to be saved by faith;

and so the drowning man might say he was saved by the pole, though in truth he was rescued by the mercy of a neighbour, who thrust a pole towards him, and thereby drew him safe on shore.'[15] Thus true faith in Christ, and Christ alone, brings a blessed peace which 'does not grow in nature's garden, nor can be digged out of mines of human merit. It was lost in Paradise, and is only found at Calvary.'[16] True faith will produce works and this will distinguish the Christians from those 'who frequently amuse themselves with fancies instead of faith, and think a mere assenting unto Scripture doctrines is believing in Christ Jesus'.[17] Genuine faith is shown through genuine works: 'It bringeth heavenly peace, purifies the heart, and overcomes the world. Faith is genuine where these fruits are found. The believer is a real branch of the true vine, and receives his fruit from it. The fruit shows the branch to be alive, but does not make it so – it beareth fruit, because it is alive.'[18]

The miracles are recorded in order to show the nature and use of faith and how the sinner must go to Jesus. Sinners come not to buy but to beg. 'They carry no money in their caps, and bring no merit in their mouths, to purchase blessings, but come as miserable creatures, and in a worshipping posture, to obtain an act of mercy.'[19] They come as helpless creatures expecting all their help from Jesus and as believers putting their faith in him alone. 'All that seek to Jesus Christ, with a due sense of their misery and helplessness and with a single trust on his power and mercy, will obtain what they seek.'[20] To whom does this gospel apply? To those aware of their sickness: 'Jesus Christ, the bread of life, is freely offered in the gospel to every hungry famished soul. Such are prepared for the bread, and the bread prepared for such. . . He turns no real beggar from his gate, though full of sores and vermin. . . It is the Saviour's office, as it is his honour, and his heart's delight, to save a sinner freely; to call and wash, and heal, and clothe, and feed a prodigal at his own expense. He asks no recommendation but our misery and helplessness, and does relieve his patients now, as he relieved them in Judea, out of mere compassion. All that seek in his appointed way will be saved graciously, and love the Saviour heartily.'[21]

This aim of a clear gospel message is also set in the context of Berridge's understanding of the moderate Calvinism which he had come to adopt. He therefore stresses the disabling effects of the Fall and the total inability of man to respond to God apart from God's grace: 'Nothing but the salt of grace can heal the swampy ground of nature as Elisha's salt, a type of grace, healed the naughty waters and the barren grounds of Jericho.'[22] For Berridge, justification by faith alone, effectual and final, 'is the capital doctrine of the gospel'[23] and he writes clearly against two justifications – faith plus works. Justification is not a matter of degree and although 'there are degrees in *affection and rewards of Christ*, there can be no degrees in his justification'.[24] 'Thus a believer's state of happiness is finally determined by his faith; he that believeth shall be saved; but the measure of his happiness in that state depends upon the fruits of faith. Faith alone saves a Christian; but his crown is brighter according as his faith works more obediently by love.'[25]

Besides his analysis of the primacy of faith, many pages of *The Christian World Unmasked* are a consideration of the place and value of works. For Berridge, once works were accepted as a condition rather than a fruit of salvation, this detracted from the grace of God and would leave room for man to boast. He analyses the parable of the sheep and the goats and notes that not a single sheep expected to be justified by works, yet the goats did expect it. Not that the goats had no works of charity, but they had no true interest in Jesus nor his little flock. However, although not resting on a 'broken bed of duties',[26] he expects the believer to evidence love for Christ and his words. Berridge is embarrassed at the thought of those who 'would purchase heavenly mansions with such scraps of alms as would not buy an earthly hogsty'.[27] He summarizes his view that the little flock may be rewarded *according to* their works, but not be rewarded *for the merit of* them with an illustration: 'A tender-hearted gentleman employs two labourers out of charity, to weed a little spot of four square yards. Both are old and much decrepit, but one is stronger than the other. The stronger weeds three yards, and receives three crowns; the weaker weedeth one, and receives one crown. Now both the labourers are rewarded for their labour, and according to their labour, but not for the merit of their labour. You cannot say their work deserves their wages. And yet their work deserves their wages better, an hundred thousand fold, than our poor works can merit an eternal weight of glory.'[28]

The book's section on election honestly confronts problems, but its emphasis is practical and spiritual rather than speculative. People reject the doctrine of election, Berridge says, 'not for want of scriptural evidence, but for want of humbled hearts'.[29] He confesses that he learnt it through affliction and not from man or books. Election cuts at any doctrine of merit. God is sovereign and just. A human king may spare a traitor and hang the rest. The act of grace may be shown to one or more, without a charge of injustice to those who are hanged. One has cause to bless his prince, while the others have no reason to complain. God may act in the same way and he will not be restricted by the 'cobweb words which human pride has weaved for him. He will have grace to give, and justice to conflict; and will be glorified in both. The provision of a Saviour gives no sinner right to claim the mercy of salvation. It only makes a way for God to exercise his mercy, consistently with justice; but he may exercise it when and where he pleaseth. The grace of God is called free; not because it is free for you or anyone to claim, but free for God to give to whom he pleaseth. His grace is free, just as my alms are free; and grace is heavenly alms. Now my alms are free, because they are bestowed freely, where I like. If any could demand them justly, they would cease to be an alms, an act of grace, and prove a debt.'[30]

The doctrine of election does not discourage sinners from seeking Christ. We cannot peep into the books of heaven and our business lies with the written Word and its promises. An awakened sinner has no cause to be alarmed at this doctrine, whereas a sinner fast asleep will commonly despise it. No one can come to Jesus except the Father draws him. 'Yet sinners do not perish, because they cannot come, but because they will not come.'[31] 'Salvation is of the Lord alone, and damnation wholly from ourselves.'[32]

Berridge outlines how true believers will persevere. What Jesus gives he will not take away. This doctrine 'yields no shelter to licentiousness or laziness. If perseverance is promised to the saints, then I must be found persevering in the path of duty and the means of grace, else the doctrine does condemn me, and destroy my evidence.'[33] We are to make our calling and election sure. There is need for exhortation. The parables of the ten virgins and of the sower are warnings. We must not look for short-lived impressions, but a growth in grace and in the knowledge of Christ Jesus. 'Sergeant If' stands as a watchman for the camp of Jesus: not the 'if' of legal condition to purchase man's salvation, 'but a modest gospel evidence to prove the truth of grace. He tells no idle tales that the sheep of Christ may perish, and a child of God mistake his way, while his guide is fast asleep and ramble down to hell: but knowing there are various works, which are but mimics of a work of grace, he kindly standeth in the King's highway of faith, producing peace and holiness; and telleth passengers, if you continue walking in this way, your perseverance proves your faith is true; for faith, which comes from God, endures and brings men safe to God.'[34]

Berridge also argues strongly for the imputed right-eousness of Christ to the believer, an issue strongly derided on the Arminian side, linked as it was to Wesley's perfectionist views. He 'marvels much that any who allow the imputation of Christ's death should yet object to the imputation of his life', and he feels that 'Till we see ourselves utter bankrupts, we shall go about to establish our own righteousness, and cannot rest upon the Surety's obedience, the God-man's righteousness as our legal title unto glory.'[35] True views of the righteousness of Christ do not lead to laxity but make us hate sin. Christian holiness 'is a true devotedness of heart to God, a seeking of his glory, walking in his fear and love, rejoicing in him as a reconciled Father, and delighted with his service, as the only freedom'.[36] However, the holiest Christian can put no trust in his holiness. 'Tekel is written on every duty,'[37] for his best services do not answer the demands of God's law. His refuge is only in Christ as his legal title to glory.

Berridge is well aware of the low opinion that men hold of the doctrine of grace and one of the reasons is because some abuse such teaching to sanctify their wickedness. However, 'The abuse of doctrines is no argument to prove the doctrines themselves are hurtful. The blessings of providence are fully as much abused as the doctrines of grace, yet none reject the providential blessings because of their abuse. If all my countrymen were drunkards and gluttons, this would be no argument for my rejecting food and liquor, but a good caution to use them temperately. And if my brethren, who profess the doctrines of grace, should all agree to wear them as a cloak for wickedness, this would be no reason for my rejecting the doctrines, but strong caution not to wear the cloak myself. The apostles did not reject the doctrines of grace, because a wicked use was made of them, no more should you or I.'[38]

Berridge detects a deeper reason for their unpopularity: 'The doctrines themselves are hateful, because they batter human pride, undermine all human merit, lay the human worm in the dust, and give the glory of salvation wholly unto God. Nature cannot bear this, she would not have salvation as a lost, but as a decent sinner; nor become an heir of glory by a mere election of God and faith in Jesus, but by some noble place of merit; nor would she walk in duty's path through the Holy Spirit's aid, but by her own gouty ankles. With some reluctance she endureth to go snacks [shares] with Jesus, but will never bear to be wholly saved by grace.'[39] For Berridge these doctrines received the world's indignation and censure because they attacked man's own righteousness. 'No one can truly bear the doctrines till he cannot bear himself.'[40]

Berridge was glad to have finished his 'pamphlet', as he calls it, although it extends to two hundred pages. There were two editions during 1773 and one in the following year with minor additions. There is nothing offensive or peculiar about it. On the contrary, Berridge shows his great powers of analysis, argumentation and illustration through his writing. It often shows touches of autobiographical matter, having been written from the heart as well as the head. Theologically it grapples with the major concerns of method and definition. In some circles Berridge's name was blackened, particularly because of the attacks of Fletcher, who spoke of him as being an Antinomian – a most unjust and unfair judgement. Berridge wrote to John Newton that his midway preaching stop at Bedford on the way to Olney seemed to be 'closed by the stench which my pamphlet has occasioned'.[41] His own people at Everton were not adversely affected for he says of them, 'My hearers are Bible readers, and prefer the Word of God to everything. In general, they are people of great simplicity and are Calvinists, but unpractised in disputes, and so happy as not to know what a Calvinist or Arminian means.'[42] The opposition that he received he resented at first, as he felt it misrepresented him, but he came to feel that this criticism was good for his pride: 'I believe it is a healthful thing for every author to have his head in the pillory, and the barnacles on his nose; it may help to chill his vanity, and make him sick of scribbling.'[43]

Although tempted to do so he determined to make no reply to his critics. He regretted his own entry into the controversy as disputes detracted from true Christianity: 'A Smithfield fire would unite the sheep, and fright the goats away, but when the world ceases to persecute the flocks, they begin to fight each other. Indeed the worst part of the sheep is his head, which is not half so good as a calf's head, and with this they are butting at each other. Until the millennium come, and perhaps until the resurrection, Judah will be vexing Ephraim, and Ephraim will be envying Judah. Teach me, Lord to become a child, and to have no part in this envy or vexation.'[44]

This entry into the controversy of that time taught Berridge to fear his heart even more and to concentrate on communing with God, a fact that all visitors and friends noticed.

# 17.
# John Fletcher's criticisms

Berridge first met John Fletcher in the very early days of the revival at Everton. Since that time Fletcher through his patron had acquired the humble parish of Madeley in Shropshire in spite of the offer of a far more lucrative one. Fletcher, a native of Nyon in Switzerland, was by his character and devotion to make Madeley a byword for evangelical outreach and holiness. This in spite of a long period of illness and much time spent in leading the attack for Wesley on Antinomianism (that is, the teaching that Christians are free to ignore God's law), as he saw it in the form of Calvinism. In his early ministry he tried to copy what he had seen at Everton and he says that before he saw the need of being broken before God he 'did not despair of being soon a little Berridge'.[1]

The two men moved apart theologically during the sixties over the issues of perfectionism and Calvinism. Fletcher, after the challenge to the 1770 Minutes, had engrossed himself in the controversy. His defence of Wesley was to last for the next six years and to run into many hundreds of pages of scholarly and restrained argument. Abbey and Overton comment on his 'excellent knowledge of Scripture and great ingenuity in explaining it on his own side'.[2] Fletcher was to devote the second half of the first part of the *Fifth Check to Antinomianism* to attacking a character in Berridge's book. Afterwards he produced *Logica Genevensis Continued*, or *The Second Part of the Fifth Check to Antinomianism*, explicitly criticizing Berridge.

Fletcher's criticisms and Berridge's initial response highlight two important facts. Firstly, Fletcher seems to have been carried away by his logic and grossly misrepresents Berridge by setting up a straw man of Anti-nomianism of his own creation which he then sets out to demolish. Berridge's initial response was annoyance at Fletcher's misrepresentation, followed by a deep humility at his own pride and a conviction not to pander to that pride by answering the criticisms. Even Tyerman, Fletcher's biographer, acknowledges 'that it may be fairly doubted whether he [Berridge] ever held the doctrines which Flet-cher, perhaps somewhat hardly, deduces from a few of his unguarded words'.[3] An examination of what Berridge had actually written shows, however, that Fletcher's deductions were not based on unguarded words, as Berridge had the ability to speak with clarity and precision on the issues as he saw them. Fletcher, however, effectively stopped Berridge from any more apologetic and doctrinal writing, and Berridge reverted to his low view of human scholarship, confirmed in his belief that it hindered spiritual communion. Perhaps Berridge was naïve as well as incon-sistent in producing *The Christian World Unmasked* and in thinking that Fletcher or someone else would not defend the ideas that he had attacked.

We first learn of Berridge's reactions to Fletcher's criticisms at the end of a long letter to John Thornton in August 1773, written after he had received a personal letter from Fletcher: 'In my pamphlet, I wrote something against what the world calls sincere obedience, and with a twofold view: first, to expose that insincere obedience is commonly cloaked under the name of sincere obedience, or doing what we can. Secondly, to show that obedience, where it is sincere, and the fruit of the Spirit, is no ground of merit, or cause of justification. And I thought no professor could misunderstand me; but in a letter just received from Mr Fletcher, he writes thus: "What you have said about sincere obedience has touched the apple of God's eye, and is the very core of Antinomianism. You have done your best to disparage sincere obedience, and in a pamphlet, ready for the press, I have freely exposed what you have written." Then he cries out in a declamatory style, "For God's sake let us only speak against insincere and Pharisaical obedience." Indeed, I thought I had been writing against insincere obedience throughout the pamphlet; and that everyone who has eyes must see it clearly; but I suppose that Mr Fletcher's spectacles invert objects, and make people walk with their heads downwards.'[4]

Before we examine Berridge's claim that he was being grossly misrepresented let us move on a few days to the end of that same month of August. Thornton had replied showing that he obviously thought Berridge's attitude to Fletcher was wrong. Although Berridge had every reason for feeling aggrieved he immediately took the criticism to heart: 'I thank you for the friendly admonition you gave me respecting Mr Fletcher. It made me look into my heart, and I found some resentment there. What a lurking devil this pride is! How soon he takes fire, and yet hides his head so demurely in the embers that we do not easily discover him! I think it is advisable to write to Mr Fletcher, though despairing of success. His pamphlet will certainly be published now it is wrote. Indeed I have wrote to him aforetime more than once, and besought him to drop all controversy, but he seems to regard such entreaties as flowing rather from a fear of his pen than a desire of peace. His heart is somewhat exalted by his writings, and no wonder. He is also endowed with great acuteness, which, though much admired by the world, is a great obstacle to a quiet childlike spirit. And he is at present eagerly seeking after legal perfection which naturally produceth controversial heat. As gospel and peace, so law and controversy go hand in hand together. How can lawyers live without strife? In such a situation, I know from my own former sad experience, he will take the Scotch thistle for his motto, *noli me tangere*. But his heart seemeth very upright, and his labours are abundant; and I trust the Master will serve him, by and by, as he has served me, put him into a pickling-tub, and drench him there soundly, and when he comes out dripping all over, he will be glad to cry "Grace, grace," and a little child may lead him. We learn nothing truly of ourselves, or of grace, but in a furnace. Whatever Mr Fletcher may write against my pamphlet, I am determined to make no reply. I dare not trust my own wicked heart in a controversy.'[5]

Another letter to Thornton a few weeks later reveals that Berridge did indeed write to Fletcher. Berridge told Fletcher he thought his intentions were clear from 'the whole drift of the pamphlet'[6] and that he was an enemy to controversy and would not 'raise up to fight with him, but will be a dead man before he kills me'.[7] Berridge was not hopeful of success, however, as one of the evangelical students expelled from Oxford in 1768 had called on him, after being shown by Fletcher what he had written against Berridge and was planning to publish soon.

To understand Fletcher's reaction to *The Christian World Unmasked* is to understand something of the whole Calvinism-Arminianism controversy in miniature. Antinomianism was a great enemy for Wesley, as for any other evangelical Christian. However, 'It was the absolute identification of Calvinism and Antinomianism which the Wesleyans made in the seventies – although there were evidences of this earlier – that underlay Wesleyan ferocity'[8] against Calvinism. Fletcher's charge against Berridge was that, as a Calvinist, he taught, though unintentionally, that it did not matter how a Christian lived. Fletcher's logic was simple: if one was saved in the way that Calvinists understood the keeping power of God, no sin could stop that salvation and therefore it did not matter how one lived. Fletcher therefore drew the false conclusion that Berridge attacked obedience to the law of God. Although Fletcher's logic in arriving at these deductions is understandable it is hard to see how he could charge Berridge with Antinomian tendencies when both his life (as Fletcher readily acknowledged) and his writings gave the lie to any such claim.

Fletcher seems to have introduced Berridge into his discussion of the issues so that he could produce an example from the writings of an eminent Calvinist divine which would confirm the reality of the charges he was bringing against Calvinism.[9] He cited Mr Fulsome, a character in Berridge's book, who has all the right words, but whose life belies those words. Berridge had clearly created this character as an illustration that real spiritual life will show itself in the person's behaviour. Our works do not save us, but without good works our faith is unreal. The gospel guards against licentiousness because it provides numerous ways of checking whether faith is genuine. *The Christian World Unmasked* is very clear on this, whole sections being devoted to an examination of these evidences. Mr Fulsome led a

scandalous life in spite of his profession of faith and
Berridge had clearly shown that all who lived as he did
'plainly show themselves destitute of that faith which
purifies the heart'.[10] There were indeed no grounds, except
in Fletcher's own mind, for producing Mr Fulsome as a
witness that Calvinism logically and necessarily leads to
Antinomianism. It is not only unfair but dishonest to draw,
as Fletcher did, the following conclusions from Berridge's
treatment of Mr Fulsome: 'Upon the principles of Calvinism
no logician in the world can I think find a flaw in the
following arguments of Mr Fulsome: "If I am unconditionally elected, irresistible grace will certainly save at last:
nay, my salvation is already finished; and for this tankard
and twenty more, I shall only 'sing louder' in heaven the
praises of free, distinguishing restoring grace. . ."'[11] It is
little wonder that such criticism annoyed Berridge; the
greater wonder is that Berridge was prepared to bite his lip
and not reply to such gross misrepresentation.

In the *Second Part of the Fifth Check to Antinomianism* Fletcher
again acknowledged that Berridge's life was exemplary and
admitted that he did not think Berridge intended to teach
Antinomianism: 'Mr Berridge is a good and excellent man,
therefore the Antinomian errors, which go abroad into the
world with his letters of recommendation. . .cannot be too
soon pointed out, and too carefully guarded against.'[12]
Fletcher's purpose in writing was to stop people carrying
Berridge's speculative Antinomianism, as he saw it, into
practical disregard for the laws of God. Because Berridge
believed in justification by faith alone, Fletcher charges him
with the 'heresy of Solifidianism', that is, of holding that a
man is saved by faith alone. He expresses his hope that
Berridge would reply and that he would 'no longer oppose the
dictates of reason, merely to pour contempt upon our Lord's
doctrine of a believer's justification by the words of faith'.[13]
To Berridge this must have seemed like the old mixed covenant of his pre-conversion days. Fletcher stressed the need for
his publication because Berridge's arguments against sincere
obedience as a condition of salvation were so plausible 'that
the simple can hardly avoid being deceived by them; nay, and
some of the judicious too'.[14] However, Berridge understood
the concept of 'sincere obedience' as being the doctrine of

justification by works. He added a note to the 1774 edition of *The Christian World Unmasked*, following Fletcher's claim that he had spoken against the obedience of Christians to Christ. He says, 'The judicious reader will perceive that I have not wrote against sincere obedience, as it is the genuine fruit and a necessary evidence of faith, but only decry it as a condition of salvation.'[15]

Not only was sincere obedience no condition of salvation, but Berridge had challenged those who claimed that it was to define it, maintaining that they could not do so: 'If God had made sincere obedience the condition of salvation, he would certainly have drawn the line, and marked out the boundary precisely, because our life depended on it.'[16] Fletcher argued that God had clearly defined sincere obedience in the Scriptures, drawing the boundaries as true repentance and faith unfeigned.

Berridge had concluded that the emphasis on sincere obedience necessarily leads to perfectionism, which Scripture and experience show to be false. Fletcher challenged this conclusion on the grounds that the Scriptures do indeed teach us to go on to perfection – not 'absolute perfection', but a relative dispensational perfection. Fletcher gives as an example of such perfect obedience a man who fully and sincerely uses his talents.

There is much that is complicated in Fletcher's attack but the basic problem is one of approach. He argued from reason as well as from Scripture. In short, in his view Calvinism was illogical.

To summarize this debate, it seems clear that Fletcher interpreted Berridge as teaching the unimportance of works and therefore of obedience to Christ, whereas Berridge was convinced that Fletcher and his fellow Arminians were teaching a second justification by works, which in his view attacked the heart of the gospel. In *The Christian World Unmasked* there is no evidence that Berridge was discouraging Christians from showing the fruit of faith in Christ by changed lives. Fletcher, however, took Berridge's attack on the doctrine of sincere obedience as a condition of salvation not as an attack on the insufficiency and inadequacy of such works in terms of earning salvation, but as an attack on sincere obedience to God in itself. It is difficult to evaluate the exact place Fletcher apportioned to works, but it does seem that he taught some form of second justification.

Tyerman regards Fletcher's criticisms of Berridge as 'irrefutable'[17] and says that 'Berridge is routed.'[18] Smyth gives the same judgement, saying that Berridge was outmatched by his opponent. This is not so. The tortuous arguments of Fletcher do not answer in any way the simple direct thrust of Berridge's writing. These writers seem to have forgotten that Fletcher's whole case rests on a gross distortion of Berridge's views. Tyerman does acknowledge that Berridge did not teach the doctrines that Fletcher attacks, but suggests that Berridge's 'similes, allegories, figures, and loose language might be construed by Antinomian readers in such a sense.'[19] The evidence in no way supports such a claim. The controversy of the 1770s needs to be studied afresh.[20]

Fletcher, in his concluding comments, pays his respects to Berridge. He professes his 'brotherly love and sincere respect for the ingenious and pious author ... His indefatigable labours in the Word and doctrine entitle him to a double share of honour; and I invite all my readers with me to esteem him in love for his Master and his work's sake; entreating them not to undervalue his vital piety, on account of his Antinomian opinion; and beseeching them to consider that his errors are so much the more excusable as they do not influence his moral conduct, and he refutes them himself, far more than his favourite scheme of doctrine allows him to do.'[21] Fletcher invites Berridge to preach in his pulpit, knowing that he would 'be edified, and overjoyed, to hear him enforce there the guarded substance of his book, which notwithstanding the vein of solifidianism I have taken the liberty to open, contains many great and glorious truths'.[22]

History often presents seemingly contradictory pieces of a puzzle and the future relationship between Berridge and Fletcher must be seen in that light. Whittingham includes in the *Works* a letter written by the Rev. G. Gorham of St Neots, detailing a warm, affectionate meeting between the two at Everton in December 1776. 'They embraced each other with tears of affection, at first meeting, and saluted by the endearing name of brother; surely never did two more kindred spirits meet.'[23] After leaving them alone for two hours the young Gorham and his two other friends returned to find the two former antagonists deeply engaged in conversation. The visit was finished with joint prayer, with Berridge's servants being called in. Gorham concludes that the behaviour of the two men was 'truly ornamental to their holy profession'[24] and the atmosphere of the day was firmly fixed in his mind. According to Gorham, a few months later Berridge, who was then in London, visited Fletcher at Stoke Newington, where he had gone to a friend's house because he was suffering from consumption. Gorham records of that visit that 'They met and parted, as they did at Everton, in the true spirit of Christian love.'[25]

Although there are some minor historical problems with Gorham's account, such first-hand information must speak. How then do we explain a comment by Berridge in a letter in September 1776, a few months earlier, that he had 'read very little of Mr Fletcher's works, but enough to see that he is yet a stranger to the gospel'?[26] This comment is perfectly consistent with Berridge's claim that the Wesleyan understanding of works and merit was another gospel. It was to him the gospel with plusses – plusses that to him detracted from the exalted position of Christ and justification by faith alone. How can we explain the warm meeting of December? Either Gorham is looking back with rose-coloured spectacles, for he is writing seventeen years after the event, when evangelicals were embarrassed with the conflicts of the Arminianism-Calvinism debate, or Berridge does not mean what he seems to say. Of course, there is another speculative alternative. Tyerman suggests that Fletcher had undertaken the journey to the area in order to see Berridge as well as Venn at Yelling. He was very ill, a point that Gorham records. The secret to unravelling the puzzle may lie in what the two men said to each other in the letters that prepared the visit. Fletcher had been unjust in labelling Berridge as an Antinomian and Berridge had no doubt pondered over some of Fletcher's learned and philosophical rebuttals of Calvinism and had drawn conclusions that were perhaps unwarranted. Such a meeting as Gorham describes suggests some form of reconciliation. Of course, the visit itself may well have clarified their differences and put them in some perspective.

# 18.
# The fool's cap – Berridge's humour

Two incidents recorded during these years following his illness (1774–80) draw our attention to Berridge's humour. The first occurred when he returned to Everton to find his congregation in what he called a state of 'spiritual lunacy' produced by a light-hearted preacher with style but little content. The second was occasioned by John Thornton's frank criticism of Berridge's use of humour. Constitutionally Berridge could not help putting things in an unexpected and humorous manner. The evaluation of this trait has ranged from buffoonery to a natural gift which occasionally ran away with him – both of which are unhelpful.

There is no doubt that this side of Berridge's character caused problems in his own day and particularly to his nineteenth-century biographers. J.C. Ryle spends three pages pleading for understanding in terms of the kind of rustic and ignorant audience to which Berridge preached. Far from his losing control over his humour, Ryle suggests that it was a gift he used to communicate when more sober and formal approaches would have failed: 'His grand aim was to make his hearers understand, and to attain that aim he sacrificed everything. If he made them smile, he also made them weep. If he excited them, he did not let them go to sleep. If he broke the rules of taste, and made men laugh, he also succeeded in breaking hard hearts, and making them repent.'[1] There is, I think, some truth in this evaluation, as Berridge was above all a man who knew his audience and so prepared a little seasoning that the food might be more palatable. In *The Christian World Unmasked* he acknowledges that the style may enable people to get to grips with the content. 'If my expressions ever wear an air of pleasantry, it is because I would tempt you by a smile to hear me out. My subject is weighty, but may seem too grave, as the modern taste goes, without a little seasoning.'[2] Although Thornton was opposed to Berridge's humour in the pulpit he acknowledges the argument: 'I know the apology frequently made for such language is that the common people require it, it fixes their attention, and affords matter for conversation afterwards; for a sentence out of the common road is more remembered than all the rest.'[3] This would suggest that there was a rationale.

Others have felt that Berridge lacked control of his humour. Elliot-Binns suggests that he could not help putting things in a ludicrous way.[4] D. Martyn Lloyd-Jones, speaking of those who, like Berridge, employed humour in the pulpit, said these kind of men troubled him because they allowed their humour to run away with them. Although there is little direct evidence from his sermon outlines for such views, Berridge himself acknowledges the spontaneity of his humour. He says, 'Odd things break from me as abruptly as croaking from a raven,'[5] and 'Hear, sir, how my Master deals with me; when I am running wild and saying many things somewhat rash, or very quaint, he gives me an immediate blow on my breast which stuns me.'[6]

Thornton wrote his letter of concern over Berridge's humour on 17 October 1775. After thanking Berridge for a gift he comes straight to the point:

In some discussions we have had relative to the *Christian World Unmasked*, I could not help laughing with you, though at the same time I felt a check within; your reasons silenced but did not satisfy me. Your vein of humour and mine seem much alike; if there is any difference between us it lies here: I would strive against mine, because I find the ludicrous spirit is just as dangerous as the sullen one; and it is much the same to our great adversary whether he falls in with a capricious or facetious turn of mind.

I could not forbear smiling at your humorous allegory about the tooth, and was pleased at the good sense displayed in it; yet something came across my mind – Is this method agreeable to the idea we ought to entertain of a father in Israel? It would sound mighty well in a newspaper, or in anything calculated for public entertainment, but it certainly wanted that solidity or seriousness that a Christian minister should write with. What the apostle said in another sense will apply here: 'When I was a child I spake as a child,' etc. An expression of yours in your prayer before sermon when at Tottenham Court struck me: 'that God would give us new bread not stale, but what was baked in the oven on the day'. Whether it is that I am too little, or you too much, used to such expressions, I won't pretend to determine; but I could not help thinking it savoured of attention to men more than to God. I know the apology frequently made for such language is that the common people require it, it fixes their attention, and affords matter for conversation afterwards; for a sentence out of the common road is more remembered than all the rest. This may be true, but the effect it has is only a loud laugh amongst their acquaintance; not one person is edified, and many offended by such-like expressions. Some ministers I have known run into the other extreme, and think something grand must be uttered to strike the audience; but this seems to me as unnecessary as the other, and both have a twang of self-conceit, and seem like leaning to carnal wisdom. Truth, simple truth, requires no embellishments, nor would it be degraded; we are not to add to, or take from it, but to remember the power is wholly of God. My reverend friend, as an old man, might be indulged in his favourite peculiarities, if they would stop with him, but others catch the infection: and we find young ministers and common people indulging themselves in the same way: they think they are authorized so to do by such an example. Wit in any person is dangerous, and often mischievous, when used improperly, and especially on religious subjects; for as the professing part of an audience will much longer retain a witty or a low expression than one more serious, so will the wicked part of it too, and turn it to the disadvantage of religion. I recollect but one humorous passage in all the Bible, which is that of Elijah with the Baalites; and when the time, place, and circumstances are properly considered, nothing could be more seasonable, nothing so effectually expose the impotence of their false god, the absurdity of their vain worship. The prophets often speak ironically, sometimes satirically, but I do not remember of their ever speaking ludicrously. Our Lord and his apostles never had recourse to any such methods; the short abstracts we have of their sermons and conversations are all in the serious strain, and ministers cannot copy after better examples. I dare not say, that giving liberty to a man's natural turn, or an endeavour to put and keep the people in good humour is sinful; but this I may assert, such a method is universally followed on the stage, and in all places of public entertainment; and therefore it seems to me to savour much more of the old man than of the new.

I remember you once jocularly informed me you were born with a fool's cap on: pray, my dear sir, is it not high time it was pulled off? Such an accoutrement may suit a natural birth, and be of service, but surely it has nothing to do with a spiritual one; nor ever can be made ornamental to a serious man, much less to a Christian minister. I waive mentioning Scripture injunctions, such as 'Let your speech be with grace', etc. As you know these better than I do, you will think it necessary to be more guarded; but should you think me mistaken, I trust it will make no interruption in our friendship that I am thus free with you, as it proceeds from a sincere love and regard.

The Tabernacle people are, in general, wild and enthusiastic, and delight in anything out of the common way; which is a temper of mind though in some respects necessary, yet should never be encouraged. If you, and some others, who have the greatest influence over them, would use the curb instead of the spur, I am persuaded the effect would be very blessed. Wildfire is better than no fire; but there is a divine warmth between these two extremes, which the real Christian catches; and which, when obtained, is evidenced by a cool head and a warm heart, and makes him a glorious and shining example to all around him. I desire to be earnest in prayer, that we may be more and more partakers of this heavenly wisdom, and ascribe all might, majesty and dominion to the Lord alone. I am, dear sir, yours affectionately,

John Thornton[7]

Five days later Berridge had penned the reply. The letter shows that Berridge recognized something of the validity of Thornton's criticism.

Everton, Oct. 22nd, 1775

Dear and honoured Sir,

Your favour of the 17th requires an answer, attended with a challenge. And I do hereby challenge you, and defy all your acquaintance to prove that I have a single correspondent half so honest as yourself. Epistolary intercourses are become a polite traffic; and he that can say pretty things, and wink at bad things, is an admired correspondent. Indeed, for want of due authority and meekness on one side, and patience and humility on the other, to give or to take reproof, a fear of raising indignation instead of conviction, often puts a bar on the door of my lips; for I find where reproof does not humble it hardens; and the seasonable time for striking, if we can catch it, is when the iron is hot; when the heart is melted down in a furnace, then it submits to the stroke, and takes and retains the impression.

I wish you would exercise the trade of a gospel limner, and draw the features of all my brethren in black, and send them their portraits. I believe you would do them justice every way, by giving every cheek its proper blush without hiding a pimple upon it. Yet I fear if your subsistence depended on this business you would often want a morsel of bread, unless I sent you a quartern loaf from Everton. As to myself, you know the man, odd things break from me as abruptly as croaking from a raven. I was born with a fool's cap. True, you say; but why is it not put off? It suits the first Adam but not the second A very proper question; and my answer is this: a fool's cap is not put off so readily as a nightcap. One cleaves to the head, and one to the heart. Not many prayers only, but many furnaces are needful for this purpose; and after all the same thing happens to tainted heart as to a tainted cask, which may be sweetened by many washings and firings, yet a scent remains still. Late furnaces have singed the bonnet of my cap, but the crown still abides on my head. And I must confess that the crown so abides in whole or in part for want of a closer walk with God, and nearer communion with him. When I creep near the throne this humour disappears, or is tempered so well as not to be distasteful. Hear, sir, how my Master deals with me: when I am running wild and saying many things somewhat rash, or very quaint, he gives me an immediate blow on my breast which stuns me. Such a check I received whilst I was uttering that expression in prayer you complained of, but the bolt was too far shot to be recovered. Thus I had intelligence from above before I received it from your hand. However, I am bound to thank you, and do hereby acknowledge myself reimbursed for returning your account of myself and acknowledged the obligation I owe you, I would return you the obligation in the best manner I am able.[8]

From Berridge's reply it is obvious that he was not going to change fundamentally. Humour had always been a part of his character. Whittingham notes that 'While he was at college, if it was known that he would be present at any public dinner, the table was crowded with company, who were highly delighted with the singularity of his conversation and witty sayings.'[9] However, in the pulpit his natural humour must be put in context. Smyth reminds us that his preaching style was plain, 'sometimes jocular, but never trifling'.[10] The humour influenced the way the subject matter was communicated, but the subject matter itself was serious. Balleine comments on the fact that his sermon notes have nothing remarkable about them and they are a trifle dull if one is looking for the unusual. He suggests that it was on the spur of the moment that Berridge 'interpolated so many quaint asides, homely illustrations, racy anecdotes, personal applications, and so many of those pithy proverbial sayings that the rustic loves, that he became a veritable Mrs Poyser in the pulpit'.[11] Ryle develops the same point saying that the sermon notes are scriptural, spiritual and evangelical and certainly show that Berridge was no 'mere pulpit jester'.[12] Ryle agrees that the odd things must have been the illustrations. Seymour speaks of these illustrations saying that 'His figures were new'[13] and another notes that "His addresses were remarkable, original, his style clear and expressive, his figures often quaint but forcible.'[14] As we saw, one of Thornton's doubts arose over an illustration.

The writer commemorating Berridge's death in the *Gospel Magazine* stresses that this ability to express things in a humorous way never affected his own seriousness: 'A vein of innocent humour ran through all his public and private discourses. This softened what some might call the austerity of religion, and rendered his company pleasant to people of a less serious habit; but what is very singular, it never overcame his gravity. He would often, by an unexpected sally of humour, throw a whole assembly into a sudden burst of laughter, but would himself continue solemn as death.'[15] The illustration might be humorous but the point to which the illustration was directed was serious. Berridge's humour in the pulpit and in his letters must be seen in the context of his desire to preach Christ and him crucified.

Berridge viewed public gatherings as serious occasions. They were times of humility and abasement, not entertainment.

> Thy gracious coming here we wait
> And long to view thee, as thou art;
> We bow as sinners at thy feet,
> And bid thee welcome to our heart.
>
> Our broken walls and gates repair,
> And water well thy Sion's hill;
> The feeble hearts with kind words cheer,
> And famish'd souls with good things fill.[16]

The meetings at Everton reflected this concern. Thomas Robinson of Leicester 'declared them to have been a model and a proof of what the Church of England is capable of exhibiting and effecting in a community of lively worshippers'.[17]

When Berridge returned from his winter London visit in 1775 he found his 'congregation cast into a spiritual lunacy, easily mistaken for spiritual liveliness, and such gospel junketing introduced as made Methodism exceedingly palatable to carnal taste'.[18] By 'junketing' Berridge meant entertainment and he says it was introduced by a Mr Coughlan, 'a Newfoundland divine. Such a light-spirited, vain-glorious, and Canterbury Tales' man, never crept into my pulpit before.'[19] The comments which followed show that Berridge is concerned about the dangers of mistaking light emotions for spirituality: 'How insensibly our hearts are drawn away from the right object; and when once seduced, how easily we can mistake frothy mirth for gospel joy; and yet how wide the difference! Joy in the Lord, as it is the most delightful, so it is the most serious thing in the world, filling the soul with holy shame and blushing, and drawing tears of sweetest love. Merriment and laughter compose the syllabub of human joy; and where no better can be had, this may be thought excellent: but an angel's mouth is out of taste for such syllabub; and so is a saint's mouth, when his harp is well in tune. Laughter is not found in heaven; all are too happy there to laugh; it is a disease of fallen nature, and as such infested me sorely when sunk into the lowest stage of a nervous complaint. It forced itself on me without provocation, and continued with such violence, as quite to overwhelm me; and nothing could check it, but choking it, viz. filling my mouth with a handkerchief.

'I dare say, Adam never laughed before he fell; and am sure he had no cause to laugh after; nor do we read that the second Adam ever laughed. Laughter sprung with sin; and as it makes the life of Esau's joy, it often proves the death of Jacob's comfort. More prayer would cure us of this itching disease; and make us exchange our treacle for honey, that honey which flows from the rock. The lightness and barrenness, that is found in ourselves, is owing to the want of more prayer. No divine communion can be had without it; and when the heart is destitute of that communion, it snaps at any worldly comfort.'[20] There is thus for Berridge a vast difference between frothy mirth of the world which can easily creep into the church and true gospel joy.

> But, oh, thou man of God
> This empty mirth beware;
> March off and quit the giggling road;
> No food for pilgrims there.
>
> It checks the Spirit's aid,
> And leaves the heart forlorn,

And makes thee look as Samson did,
When all his locks were shorn.

May Jesus be my peace,
And make up all my joy;
His love can yield me serious bliss,
And bliss that will not cloy.[21]

Was Berridge contradictory or inconsistent in holding
such views, or did he look back to his pre-conversion days
with warning and know the need for 'serious bliss'? He knew
that there were dangers in his humour. He also knew the
true ends of Christian preaching and his humour must be
sublimated to those ends. Berridge here, as in other things,
needed the grace of God and, as Ryle remarks, 'Never,
probably, did the grace of God dwell in a vessel of such
singularly tempered clay.'[22] Whatever the case, we only
possess touches of his humour, mainly in his letters. Only
one sermon was recorded and that is a remarkable example
of sober, serious, experimental, expositional preaching.
Perhaps this side has been exaggerated.

Berridge displayed humorous wisdom in practical matters. He advised a country clergyman to keep a barrel of ale
in the house so that when a man called on business or with a
message 'his ears may be more open to your religious
instructions'.[23]

Whittingham, as a young man when he first met Berridge,
was struck with his humorous but instructive and encouraging conversation. When he was leaving Berridge noticed
his light-coloured waistcoat and stockings and said, 'If you
come to be my curate, you must draw that waistcoat and
those stockings up the chimney.'[24] Berridge's advice to
Whittingham as a young curate was 'Lift up your voice, and
frighten the jackdaws out of the steeple; for if you do not cry
aloud while you are young, you will not do it when you are
old.'[25]

In his study Berridge had engravings of some of the
Reformers hung on his walls and a framed looking-glass of
the same size over the fireplace. 'A clergyman on his first
visit, looked at first one, and then another. "That", said Mr
Berridge, "is Calvin: and that is Luther; and that", pointing

to the one over the fireplace "is the devil." The clergyman stepped hastily to look at it and saw his own face. "Is it not", exclaimed Mr Berridge, "a striking likeness of his satanic majesty?"'[26]

Often his images are slightly shocking to our ears in their directness. Speaking of the faithfulness of Christ he says,

> Full breasts of milk, that cannot cloy
> He, like a nurse, will bring;
> And when he draws the promise nigh
> Oh, how we suck and sing![27]

Traps are laid at every hedgerow in order to catch the unwary single evangelists into wedlock. Lady Huntingdon is Dresden in the hands of the potter.

Like all humorists Berridge enjoyed punning. He thinks that Newton will want the help of a noted independent minister, Bull from Newport Pagnell, in his plans for an academy: 'Your eye is fixed, I perceive, upon a fine bull, but how will you pair him except with wild bullocks?'[28] People with no spiritual interest love a scanty sermon, 'the fagg-end of a subject'.[29]

Humorous images convey spiritual truths: 'If Jesus Christ is not Jehovah, to couple him with the Father in the same baptismal dedication is a thousand times more unseemly than to harness a snail and an elephant together.'[30] Once Berridge used Christ 'as a healthy man will use a walking staff, lean an ounce upon it, or vapour with it in the air. But now he is my whole crutch, no foot can stir a step without him.'[31]

Although Berridge sometimes made questionable comments in his letters and could at times go too far in his asides during preaching, his humour did serve rather than injure his Master. Whittingham notes that he did not enjoy trifling conversation – the things of God filled his heart and his concern. How he enthused his love was related to his own constitution. He used his wit because he had 'the desire of catching the attention'[32] of his hearers and readers and in this he was eminently successful.

# 19.
# The old gospel pedlar

The years after Berridge's incapacitating illness were
devoted to persistent preaching although his health was still
to remain a problem and would often confine him to
Everton. Berridge was now in his early seventies and
suffered the normal problems associated with old age.
However, these years were full of service to God, and
Berridge knew the truth that there is no retirement for the
Christian. He says, 'Happy are they that grow hoary in his
service, and find it more and more delightful.'[1] The few
jigsaw pieces that remain allow us to form some idea of how
he sought to exercise his gifts during these years.

After his recovery from illness Berridge immediately
resumed his annual winter preaching visits to London,
lasting from early January until the end of March. Often
these visits exhausted him and he had to rest completely
between sermons. He mentions the strain of one of these
winter visits to Rowland Hill, saying that his London trip
'almost overset the old gospel pedlar, and my Everton
friends tell me, I must go no more to the Tabernacle, unless
I mean to lay my bones there'.[2] However, although he often
found it physically difficult, God blessed his preaching.
Henry Venn writes in 1776 how that Berridge 'laboured for
three months above his strength: he had the largest congregations that were ever known, for a constancy; and
greatly was his word owned of the Lord'.[3] Any difficulties
because of health while in London Berridge saw as coming
from his God. In 1780 he was lame and so preached sitting
on a stool. He writes on returning to Everton, 'I was made to
see a need of it soon after it came, and now find a blessing
from it. The Lord be praised for past sickness, and returning

health.'[4] Berridge obviously enjoyed these visits and considered them important because of the efforts he made. However, he judged success by a real spirit of devotion, not by crowded and attentive congregations.

When Berridge resumed his local itinerating in 1774 he found a warmer reception than before his illness. He reports in a letter to John Thornton that in most places there were large crowds who were attentive and silent in comparison with the common mockings and outrages that had once occurred. He 'says that 'The living and lifeless professors receive me with more favour since my Master has cropped my ears, and turned his old ass out of doors again.'[5] Some summers proved too difficult and his health collapsed. In 1776 he was able to make a start but had to return home. He writes to Hill saying that the third week 'laid me up without preaching, and sent me home in a carriage; since then I only preach on the Lord's day, but keep eating every day of the week – so I have fourteen meals for one sermon. A poor business truly for a Methodist parson . . .'[6] In June 1778 his spring fever kept him at home and he found even writing a letter an exhausting task. The summers of 1782 and 1783 were a struggle for Berridge and he just managed to preach once each Sunday at Everton. In the summer of 1786 he was only able to walk the two hundred yards from the vicarage to the church building. He was unable to journey outside the parish.

However, there were periods of intense activity during periods of remission from his asthma. On these occasions he worked hard. As late as 1788 he gives us a hint of his activities and his spirit when he was asked by Thornton to read and edit a new edition of Bogatsky's *Treasury*: 'After my return from London my leisure hours shall be employed on your *Treasury*, but itinerant preaching affords me only one spare day in the week: and sometimes I am so jaded with riding and preaching, that I seem fit for nothing on that spare day but to catch wasps, kill gnats, and count my teeth. However, I will do my best, and hope for your favourable acceptance of it. Oh, dear sir, every year makes me more ashamed of my worthless self! Eternity is just at hand, yet how lazy and lifeless I seem!'[7] Berridge, now in his seventies, never lost his vision for evangelism.

Such open-air preaching was used to communicate the gospel. Grantchester was always a favourite spot for Berridge and in July 1785 he reports preaching there 'to a very numerous audience, among whom were several gracious young students, and three Masters of Arts. One of the Masters, who had been a zealous Socinian, came to see me after preaching, and embracing me with tears, thanked me for the sermons I had preached last summer at Wistow and Harston, in Cambridgeshire, and for the private discourse before and after sermon. From what I saw and heard of him, I hope he is coming home to Jesus.'[8] What an encouragement for Berridge, who himself had been through the Socinian scheme!

In terms of the Christian work at Everton and in the area, Berridge had encouragements and disappointments during these years. Friends in London continued to support him financially and he was able to help the poor and the preachers associated with him who toured the circuit. He writes to Benjamin Mills, who helped support these workers financially, thanking him and those in society with him for their yearly gift. He says, 'I know not what my poor lay-evangelists would do without some assistance received from yourself and your society. They are labouring men whose paws maintain their jaws, and two of them have seven children, and their wives are kindling every year. They seem the only free grace preachers in the land; for they do preach free grace freely, without money, and without price, having nothing for their preaching but a plain dinner, and sometimes not even that.'[9] These men encouraged Berridge and he thought that God used them to quicken dead souls more than all the boasted wisdom of Cambridge preached in the university church.

Berridge was asked to preach at Ickleford near Hitchin by a newly converted rector whose preaching had driven the squire from the church. Berridge thought that any reputation that the rector might have amongst neighbouring clergy would not survive his own visit. He also rejoiced at a more sympathetic attitude amongst students at the university. In 1782 he met Charles Simeon, who was destined to lead the evangelical cause at Cambridge and further afield.

The Venn family at Yelling caused Berridge to rejoice. He was delighted with their devotional times and the whole behaviour of the family. At the beginning of this period, soon after Henry Venn had arrived at Yelling, Berridge had persuaded Venn to join him in itinerant preaching, even though Venn was concerned about the charge of irregularity by preaching in a parish other than his own. Such help encouraged Berridge. However, later he was to mourn Venn's acting in a hypocritical manner, when he influenced Charles Simeon, whom Berridge had encouraged to preach at Bluntisham without permission of the local vicar, to desist from such irregular preaching.

There were, of course, other disappointments during this period. At the start of the eighties there are several references to a lowering of spiritual life at Everton. In December 1780 Berridge was in prayer for latter rain: 'Our skins are growing dry; the spiritual pulse beats very low; and grey hairs are sprinkled upon us.'[10] Two years later he says that 'Church work goes on heavily here: many of the old sheep are called home and few lambs drop into the fold.'[11] In another letter a week later Berridge puts some of the blame on those who had been helping him: 'My church at present is in a decline, and seems consumptive. Mr Hicks supplied my church from September last till the following Easter; and fairly drove away half my congregation. My present curate is a stop-gap, but no assistant. He cannot preach without notes, nor read handsomely with notes; so my hearers are dwindling away, and transporting from Everton Church to Gamlingay Meeting.'[12]

With the improvement in Berridge's health by the middle of the 1780s he was able to report a full congregation: 'My church is usually very full in afternoons, and the people are awake and attentive, but the congregation is almost a new one. Many old sheep are housed in the upper fold; and many, who live at a distance, are dropped into neighbouring meetings, and only pay occasional visits to Everton.'[13]

Perhaps the improvement was also due to Richard Whittingham, who seems to have joined him in October 1782 as his curate, for nearly all the banns and marriages are penned with Whittingham's signature until 1790, when they are shared with a John Elard until Berridge's death. Until

1782 Berridge had found it difficult to get a suitable curate. He wrote to John Newton in December 1780 asking his opinion on a certain recommendation that he had had: 'Is he moral; is he also evangelical? Can he preach without notes; and will he condescend to visit some neighbouring country town once a week, and give a sermon or an exhortation in a barn or a house?'[14] The same problem seemed to arise in 1788 when in a letter to Thornton we learn that Whittingham had obtained a living of his own: 'My curate cannot help being glad at having a living of his own, but he is himself in no haste to be gone, and our sorrow will be mutual at parting, whenever it be.'[15] It seems that Whittingham did stay until 1789 and then returned to help when needed in Berridge's declining years. Berridge had a high opinion of Whittingham and he found him to be a worker and a communicator.

Besides his asthma, Berridge makes reference in his letters to the ageing process. In 1780, when sixty-four years old, he writes, 'Old age, with its winter aspect, creeps on me apace.'[16] In the summer of 1786 he lost his hearing for three months so that he could not converse and his eyesight was deteriorating: 'At first I prayed daily to the Lord for my hearing, but with submission to his will, and on Sunday fortnight he gave me a better pair of ears, thanks be to his grace, not perfectly restored; yet so as to make me able to converse with comfort; and they seem still to be mending. This has encouraged me to ask for a better pair of eyes. And why should I not? Jesus has eyes to give as well as ears, and he can bear dunning, nay, is never better pleased than with a thousand duns at his door. Well, my eyes are somewhat better, thanks again to my healer, and I keep praying on.'[17]

Age affected Berridge's gift of projecting his voice, a necessary ability when speaking to large congregations. Venn records a visit Berridge paid to Yelling in December 1782 and noted that his voice was weaker. Six years later Venn wrote to his son, telling him that he had gone to Everton on Sunday and shared the preaching with Berridge, Venn taking the afternoon service and Berridge the morning: 'We both perceived how our voices were weakened; but had a sweet interview, while we talked together of the pity and tender love of our adorable Master towards all his aged ministers, when they are almost past the service of office. He told me he could pray little out of his own mind; but the method he used was, to read his Bible, and as he read, to turn the word into prayer for himself.'[18]

The loss of an upper tooth caused Berridge trouble, for he found that he could not speak without hissing. He wrote to Thornton asking for the large sum required in London for a new tooth and acknowledged the struggle he had had with his pride both in putting his case before Thornton and also in feeling ashamed in appearing ridiculous when speaking. He tried to solve matters himself by filling up the cavity on the Sunday with white wax, 'which served indifferently well in the morning, but my pellet dropped out in the afternoon service during sermon and made me conclude abruptly'.[19]

Berridge's attitude to his infirmities was completely different from his initial reaction to his illness back in 1768. In 1786, before the improvement in his hearing and sight, he wrote to John Thornton who had just returned from a visit to the seaside: 'Infirmities, I find, are growing upon me: but they come at the Lord's bidding, to make them room in the heart; and come with his blessing, to make them welcome. My ears are now so dull, they are not fit for converse; and my eyes are so weak, I can read but little, and write less. Old Adam, who is the devil's darling, sometimes whispers in my eyes (and he can make me hear with a whisper), "What will you do, if you become both deaf and blind?" I tell him, I must think the more, and pray the more, yea, and thank the Lord for eyes and ears enjoyed till I was seventy; and for the prospect of a better pair of eyes and ears, when these are gone. What a mercy to have a never-failing Jesus, when all things else are failing! O my God, I thank thee for the precious gift of thy beloved Son, and for sweetly joining my heart unto him.'[20]

There are a few references to domestic life during these years. A maid who had become insane, although still able and keen to work, was in Berridge's prayers. After two years he was able to praise God for her recovery. We do not read of any contact that Berridge had with his own family apart from two letters dating from this period addressed to a nephew, challenging him about the gospel. I include one of these letters in full to show Berridge's concern for and approach to one of his relatives.

Everton, May 30th, 1780

Dear John

I am glad to hear that you are well in health, and diligent in business, and well esteemed and spoken of amongst your neighbours. Honesty, sobriety, and civility are blessings from God; they are his gifts; but no righteousness of our own can save us. Happy is the man who is brought to a right knowledge of Christ, and a saving acquaintance with him: who is taught of God how to believe in Jesus Christ, to love and delight in him, to pray to him and praise him: to trust in him wholly, and to cast every care and burden upon him. May you be found among those happy people!

Dear John, you will find as well as others, care and troubles enough in the world; and after a few years must be removed from it for ever. Oh think seriously of that other world which is eternal; and read the good Word of God daily, and pray earnestly for the grace of Christ, and for the guidance of his Spirit! Now is your spiritual seed-time; now is the day of salvation. Be diligent whilst the day of life lasteth, for the night of death cometh wherein no man can work. Oh, let the concerns of your soul be your daily thought and prayer! Your body will soon be laid down in the dust, but your soul must live for ever. Take care of the main concern; be wise for your soul, and then you are wise for ever. May the Lord protect you by his providence, and direct you by his grace, and bless you in body and soul.

I remain, your affectionate uncle.

J.B.[21]

During these years Berridge records two large fires in local towns. He thanks Mills, who had sent a gift for those who had suffered in the fire at Potton in 1783. The fire had started through a smouldering haystack and half the town was on fire within twenty minutes. The rich suffered the most and not many believers' houses were affected. A John Miller, whom Berridge considered to be heretical, was given two guineas at Mills' request and Berridge hoped that 'his late calamity may be sanctified'.[22] His curate lost everything, with furniture valued at the sum of £300, and he and his family arrived at Everton with nothing but the clothes they had on because the fire was so rapid. Within a fortnight a house was provided for them at Gamlingay.

Two years later a fire occurred at Biggleswade. Berridge saw it as sent by God. Writing to Thornton he says how 'Potton felt the Lord's fiery ravage some time past; and Biggleswade smarts under it now. One hundred and twenty houses, eight malthouses, and a meeting house, with barns and stables are consumed. The wealthy sufferers had insured three-fourths of their substance. This loss, therefore, will not break their backs, nor does it seem to humble their hearts; but the little tradesmen and poor labourers have lost their all, and are herded together in an old malthouse, and barns; among whom are several of the Lord's dear children, begotten under my ministry. I should like to deal out all my mites privately among these, but for the gospel credit, I must appear a public contributor, which will shorten private relief. A man is taken up on suspicion of firing the town, but alas! sin wants taking up, for sin is the incendiary.'[23] Within a fortnight Berridge was again writing thanking Thornton for the gift received 'which brings comfortable relief to the poor and distressed people at Biggleswade'.[24]

During the early 1780s Berridge put the finishing touches to a hymn-book which he had mainly written in 1773 during his long illness. He wrote to Thornton in October 1784, saying that if he was called to London in the winter he had thoughts of publishing the hymn-book. It was published in 1785.

Although Berridge's physical faculties were deteriorating, the evidence from his letters shows a clear and sound mind. In 1782 he thanked Newton for copies of his own works and for the works of Owen and says, 'I can read them again and again with fresh pleasure.'[25] This same letter contains a most detailed evaluation of Cowper's poetry. He praises his descriptions, his choice of epithets and his imaginative powers, which he thinks may be related to a grain of insanity. His criticisms are made as a lover and a friend. He considered that the poetry did not read aloud very well and that the meaning was frequently as obscured 'as that of a

Hebrew root'.[26] He comments to John Newton on an
unexpected reply that he had received from Cowper concerning his criticisms: 'It is beneath a good poet to heed the
vituperation of a crazy old vicar. My strictures will not hurt
him; I wish his muse may hurt him no more. Poetic fame is a
sweet morsel for the mind to feed upon, and will try to
beguile his heart into idolatry. Indeed, the muses are all
wanton girls, with meretricious hearts, and quickly draw
Helicon-hunters unto their embraces.'[27] Later he thought
that although Cowper's poetry was excellent it was not
likely to sell because 'There is too much gospel for the world
and too little for most believers.'[28]

In 1786 Berridge wrote to Newton supporting his stand
against the new fashion of oratorios. 'The fiddling of
Scripture in a theatre seems to me a profanation of God's
Word, making it a mere carnal amusement; and the matter
is made worse by bringing oratorios into God's house, they
then become a satanical ordinance.'[29] Berridge had penned
a private letter on the matter to Benjamin Mills at the
Tabernacle which had obviously been passed around and
caused a stir. Berridge did not regret the stir as he hoped
the evil had been nipped in the bud. He wished the leaders
in London would take a more positive stand: 'I am sorry to
find you all agree in calling oratorios inexpedient things and
nothing more. Whereas, if they are lawful exhibitions for
God's house, the devil will soon find a way to make them
expedient. For what more expedient to ease a chapel of its
debt, than a lawful oratorio? And what more expedient to
repair a decayed chapel, or to help to support the ministers,
than a lawful oratorio? Jesus Christ is Lord of the sabbath,
and Lord of his house, and no one has a right to appoint
offices or ordinances but himself. All human inventions are
innovations of his authority, neither expedient nor lawful.'[30]

In the autumn of 1788 Berridge began a new task.
Thornton had obviously started a revision of Bogatzky's
*Golden Treasury* back in the early 1770s, as he had sent papers
then to Berridge in order to obtain his views, but now he
seems to have finished it and sent an interleaved copy for
Berridge's revision and comments. These comments and
corrections were not published until a century later, in 1891.
They show that Berridge's mind was still alert and vigorous.

The editor of this work gives his view of Berridge at this time: 'The veteran John Berridge has for thirty years been labouring with voice and pen, as author, pastor and evangelist, in the cause of the gospel. Yet in five years he will have finished his course. Meanwhile, his spiritual eye is not dim, nor is the force of his sanctified intellect abated. He stands, ready for every good work.'[31]

# 20.
# The worn-out servant

Berridge kept mentally alert during his final years even though physically he was growing very feeble. The first-hand evidence, such as letters, the crowds that still attended Everton on Sunday, the comments of friends and associates, his written comments on Thornton's edition of Bogatzky and his ability to keep up his London visiting until the end – all witness to the clarity of his mind even though his memory and eyesight were weakening fast. Abner Brown's second-hand comments, seventy years after Berridge's death, that Berridge suffered delusions in his old age, (for example, that he was made of glass and that his body would swell up and burst), are not supported by any material from the period.[1] Of course, such things could have happened, but it is difficult to believe that a mentally ill man could have sustained a large congregation both at Everton and in London, and even more difficult to believe that his many opponents did not remark on this fact. A reading of Berridge's last sermon in London just nine months before his death confirms the view that Berridge kept much of the communicative and reasoning ability of his younger days. Of course, there were periods of marked physical decline and perhaps his mind was affected, although we have no direct evidence of this apart from the second-hand comment by Brown.

At the beginning of 1789, Berridge set out for his usual trip to London. He wrote from the Tabernacle on 10 January to Thornton, thanking him for twenty pounds which he had sent for the poor, 'who will now be flocking for relief, like sparrows to a barley-stack in winter, and will have the comfort of your silver grains'.[2] On the journey to London he experienced problems with a horse which collapsed at six in the morning: 'We were now eight miles from Stevenage, sitting cold in a chaise. I betook myself lustily to the good old remedy, prayer, and the Lord inclined a wagoner to lend us a horse to Stevenage, and put our rusty one into his team. Is not the Lord wonderful in working? Who would distrust him?'[3] He was also encouraged about his friends' search for a suitable curate who could profit the people at Everton. It was in May 1789 that John Byng records that he met 'many people returning from the evening service' at Everton and that 'to his church does the county flock for instructions and consolations'.[4]

During the next summer Berridge was impressed at the passage of time and thought more of his own death: 'Our years are rolling away fast, and will quickly roll us into eternity. How needful that admonition: "Prepare to meet thy God!" . . . I have been crawling many years on the road to Sion: and sometimes in, and sometimes out, and the Master has somewhat quickened my pace in the summer by a draught of birch wine, as needful at times for a heavy-heeled pilgrim, as the wine of the kingdom. Now being almost through the wilderness, very sick of self, and of a daggling world, I am drawing near to Mount Pisgah: and when I stand on its top, the Lord give an open eye of faith, to see all the promised land, and rejoice in hope of the glory of God!'[5]

His eyes were very poor although his hearing had improved and his legs were stronger. He tells Mills that if the weather was reasonable he hoped to come to London on Tuesday, 28 December. Whittingham records how on this occasion Berridge addressed the congregation after he had been led up the pulpit stairs, presumably because of his poor sight: 'My dear Tabernacle friends, [the tears trickling down his cheeks] I bless my dear Lord that has thus far brought me on my wearisome pilgrimage through the wilderness, and has permitted his old worn-out servant to see your face in the flesh once more, which in all probability will be the last time. Satan said to me as I was coming, "You old fool, how can you think of preaching to that great people, who have neither strength nor memory left?" I said to him, "Well, Satan, I have got a good Master, that has not

forsook me these forty years, and in his strength I'll try."
And, blessed be his name, he has thus far helped me: and if
you'll pray, I'll try to preach once more in my poor way; and
may the Lord make it a blessed opportunity to us all! And I
think you'll say "Amen" to it.'[6] And so the old worn-out
servant with neither strength nor memory was still preaching in London, although with difficulty.

Henry Venn alludes in several letters written in the
autumn of 1791 to a visit which he paid to Berridge, whom
he calls 'the venerable pastor of Everton': 'I lately visited my
dear brother Berridge. His sight is very dim, his ears can
scarcely hear, and his faculties are fast decaying; so that, if
he continues any time, he may outlive the use of them. But
in this ruin of his earthly tabernacle, it is surprising to see
the joy in his countenance, and the lively hope with which
he looks for the day of his dissolution. In his prayer with me
and my children (for two of them accompanied me) we were
much affected by his commending himself to the Lord as
quite alone, not able to read, or hear or do anything; "but if
I have, Lord", said he, "thy presence and love, that suf-
ficeth".'[7]

There are evidences that point to Berridge recovering
enough strength to preach again after this. Firstly there is
an extract from the diary of B. Gilpin recording the visit of
John Warner, who visited Everton shortly before Berridge
died, and secondly there is the sermon recorded at the
Tabernacle in April 1792. Also letters written in the
summer of 1792 indicate that although he was weak, he was
still preaching.

John Warner was searching for spiritual reality and went
to Everton, not long before Berridge died, probably in the
summer of 1792: 'There was a great crowd, and I stood at
the church door. Soon I saw the old gentleman stretch out
his hand, and pull himself up into the pulpit. Oh, how I
stood ready to devour his word! "Brethren," he said, "no
scholarship is required to take you to heaven: Jesus Christ
wants broken hearts, true beggars." My heart was ready to
leap out of my body for very joy. I cannot describe my joy –
it was a true heaven on earth. Afterwards I was told I might
go into his house and refresh myself, where there were many
besides: and, oh, how sweet I found it to converse with them

on the love of Jesus, and the experience of his blessing in the heart!'[8] It is interesting to note that even in extreme old age Berridge could preach with power and that he maintained his practice of hospitality for the many who came from a distance.

This ability is seen in a sermon preached at the Tabernacle on 1 April 1792 which was taken down in shorthand and published as the 'Last Farewell Sermon' after his death. The publisher in a short preface to the first edition thought that this sermon would be acceptable to many of God's people, especially to those who heard it, who would attest that it was an exact copy of what was delivered. The frailty of Berridge renders it even more remarkable and makes one wonder what he was like at the height of his powers. It is surely no accident that Berridge chose as his subject the great 'only' psalm (Psalm 62) which summarized so clearly his own view of the Christian faith since his conversion, for which he had fought in the controversy of the 1770s and which he recorded on his epitaph. There is salvation in the Lord *alone*. Jesus is the *only* rock and will not share his glory with another. Yes, there will be troubles and trials but we must wait upon God *alone* for deliverance and trust him because 'the Lord *only* is my defence'. Berridge spells out the implications of such a theology to trust in the Lord whatever our circumstances.

The full sermon is included in an appendix so that the reader may see how Berridge was careful to set his text in its context, and that his preaching was biblical, simple, expository, practical, experimental, challenging to both sinner and saint, and full of Christ from beginning to end. Berridge would have liked to have said a little more but he closes with a few personal remarks as his strength begins to fail. He applies to his own heart the words 'God is a refuge for me' and prays that God will fix it on his hearers' hearts. He notes that 'I came up to you trembling, but the Lord has carried me through, blessed be his name; and I look to him to carry me home; for I have no feet of my own to walk with. But the Lord can hold me up till I have done my work, and then he will put an end to my labours.'[9]

He prays that God will bless the hearers who gather at the Tabernacle, the preachers, the trustees and the children. A touch of humour occurs in asking for prayer for himself in his lame state: 'I know not whether I shall ever return any more; nor is it needful for me to know; but this I know, if the Lord continues my life, and allows me some measure of strength, I shall crawl up again. In the meantime, think of a poor crawling creature when you are upon your knees, and put up a short petition to the Lord that he would bless me, pardon me, sanctify and prepare me for his kingdom and glory.'[10] And so the many sermons in London were at an end. When he died in the following January the pulpits at both Whitefield's Tabernacle and Tottenham Court Road Chapel, where he had so often preached, were hung with black. Torial Joss preached at Tottenham Court Road, the Sunday after Berridge's burial from the text: 'Behold! an Israelite indeed, in whom there is no guile,' and Matthew Wilks, whom Berridge had helped at his ordination service, preached at the Tabernacle on John 5:35: 'He was a burning and a shining light.' It is a pity that these sermons were never printed.

There are two letters from the summer of 1792 which show Berridge's desires and his relationship with God as his death drew near. Both are to women, presumably London friends. In the first, written on 6 May 1792 to a Miss L., it seems that Berridge was concerned that he write to friends for the last time because of his eyesight:

Dear Lizzey,

Once more I am paying a corresponding visit to you and others, expecting it to be my last on account of my eyes, which are growing so dim, that I can read but little of what I love dearly, the precious Word of God. I now lament the many years I spent at Cambridge in learning useless lumber, that wisdom of the world which is foolishness with God. I see nothing worth knowing but Jesus Christ, and him crucified; for him to know is life eternal. Follow him at all times, and let your heart dance after him, as David danced after the ark. And when he comes into your bosom hold him fast, and turn all other company out. He loves to be alone with his bride. You may find him in the shop, or in the street, if you seek him there; and often whisper in his ear, 'Dear Jesus, come and bless me!' If he sometimes surprises

us with his visit, and comes unexpectedly; yet he loves to
see the doors open, and the bosom waiting for him. Many
kind visits are lost through a gadding heart; therefore keep
at home with the Lord, and let him hear much of your loving
talk, and tell him all your wants, and all your grievances,
and cast all your care upon him, and hide nothing from him.
Lean firmly upon him, and he will cheer your heart in every
trying hour, and bring you safe at last to his eternal home,
where sin and sorrow never come; but where joy and peace
for ever dwell. In this world we must expect tribulation; it is
the Christian's fare, and comes because it is wanted, and
stays no longer than whilst it is wanted. Hereafter he will
make us know, if not before, that he hath done all things
well.

I am very feeble in body, but as well as I should be, and
must suffer my heavenly Physician to prescribe for me. My
kind respects attend you all and Nathan. Peace be with you,
my dear Lizzey, with spiritual health and joy in the Lord.
The Lord give us a happy meeting above. Farewell.

J.B.[11]

In the letter in August written to Mrs E. he thought he
might continue for a year or two longer and it is clear that he
was still preaching although feeling the loss of those who
had supported the work financially. Mills, a trustee of the
Tabernacle, had only recently died and John Thornton with
whom Berridge had always had a very special relationship
and who had greatly helped him, had died in 1790.

You ask me how I do? Eyes very dim, ears deaf, head much
shattered, and spirits very low, yet much exempt from pain.
Here my Jesus shows his tenderness; he knows his old horse
can scarce carry his legs, and he will not overload him. I am
apt to think the Lord may continue me here a year or two
longer, because he has sent me a supply for that time.
Having lost my benefactors, I was thinking what I must do.
'Go on and trust,' was the word. When we are low, Satan
will batter us with unbelief. I dare not argue with Satan, but
cast myself at Jesus' feet, committing soul and body to him,
asking and expecting his assistance; it is not long before it
comes with a loving reproof: 'O thou of little faith,

wherefore didst thou doubt?' The last two Sundays I was
led to church and into the pulpit; my voice was feeble but
hearable, and Christ was precious. Oh, to see Jesus as he is,
and surrounded with his ransomed people, hearts full of
love pouring out hallelujahs, and filling heaven with his
praise! Thanks to my Jesus for putting me in the way of his
kingdom, and for holding me on hitherto; give me, dear
Lord, a safe and honourable passage through the wilderness, and a joyful entrance into Canaan. The Lord bless
you, with great and endless blessings and keep you under
his care. Amen

J.B.[12]

In June 1792 there were published in London five letters
of Berridge under the title *Cheerful Piety: or Religion without
Gloom*. The advert recommended them particularly to young
Christians 'who wish to be serious, but not sad; lively, but
not light and trifling; religious but not gloomy'.[13] These
short essays, three probably written to himself, while the
other two were taken from letters from an earlier period, are
typical of Berridge, being racy and sober at the same time.[14]
They portray the practical workings of Berridge's evangelical theology.

The first letter thanks the Rev. Mr B. for his lectures on
the fall of man and for opening up the problems of the heart
and the disease of sin. It portrays the workings of Satan and
the need for the great Physician. The second and third
letters give detailed descriptions of the civil war in the
breast of a Christian between the old and new man. There is
final victory but only through the grace of God. The fourth
letter is a letter to a Christian friend undergoing sore
trouble. This is a wonderful letter, full of practical sympathy, linked with a frank acknowledgement of our need for
disciplines 'that wean us from this wretched dying world'
and 'teach us to live more constantly by faith on Jesus
Christ'.[15] Berridge reminds us that 'The chastening rod of a
reconciled Father might have been the flaming sword of an
avenging Judge.'[16]

The final letter, addressed to Lady Huntingdon, would
seem to come from a much earlier period, when Berridge
was troubled with pride after his initial great success. It

speaks of his own experience of the house of correction and how his views on his own righteousness were finally removed like rags to be exchanged for a sight of the robe of Christ. We do not know why they were published at this time or whether Berridge was involved. They do, however, give us a hint of the experimental nature of Berridge's preaching. He was surely such an effective preacher because of his knowledge of the workings of his own heart.

In January 1793 Berridge was hoping to go to London but on the very morning agreed for setting out he had a violent attack of asthma. This was on 12 January and clearly his life was immediately at risk. Henry Venn at Yelling wrote to his son John on the 17th and noted that 'My dear brother Berridge is dying: as a letter received last night from Mr Whittingham informs me.'[17] Whittingham says that on Sunday, 20 January although exceedingly weak he came down and sat in the parlour, but had great difficulty getting up to bed again.

Gorham from St Neots saw him on that same day: 'I stood by his chair in his study. He was very ill, but extremely cheerful. He was alarmed at the growing infidelity of the country; yet pleased that a spirit was stirred up against it. He asked, "Have you burned Tom Paine yet at St Neots?" I told him they had. He seemed pleased. He took most affectionate notice of both myself and my wife, who stood by. He then smiled, and said, "I thought my Master would have called me home yesterday, but I must wait his time," or to that effect. He spoke but little more.'[18]

The effort involved in getting back to bed must have hurried the end for Whittingham says that a few hours after he was in bed he was seized with symptoms of immediate dissolution. His face was contracted and his speech was faltering. He continued in this state until three o'clock on Tuesday afternoon when he received his call to wait on his Master above. A letter from Mr Bellman of Potton on that evening says: 'We had a meeting this evening for prayer; an affecting sight! I believe not a dry eye in the place, while we sung, or attempted to sing, a hymn suited to our distressed state, as a people or flock left destitute of an under shepherd. I saw him this morning, but he was not able to speak; nor had he spoken anything since last Sunday. He has been very happy during his illness, being well assured he was drawing very near his beloved Father's house; sometimes using this and the like expression: "Yes; and my children too will shout and say, Here's our father coming.""[19]

The funeral was held on the following Sunday when a huge crowd gathered at Everton. Venn was too ill to preach and had to remain at Yelling and so Charles Simeon of Cambridge preached from 2 Timothy 4:7,8. Berridge's testimony recorded on the tombstone has continued to challenge many people to this day.

> Here lay the earthly Remains of JOHN BERRIDGE
> late Vicar of Everton and an itinerant Servant
> of JESUS CHRIST who loved his Master and his Work
> and after running on his Errands many Years was called
> up to wait on Him above. Reader art thou born again?
> No salvation without new birth.
> I was born in sin Feb 1716
> Remained ignorant of my fallen State till 1730
> Lived proudly on Faith and Works for Salvation till 1754
> Admitted to Everton Vicarage 1755
> Fled to JESUS alone for refuge 1756
> Fell asleep in Christ Jan 1793

# Part II
# Evaluation

# 21.
# Berridge: the preacher and communicator

There is little doubt that few men have been blessed by God in preaching as was John Berridge of Everton. Smyth is certainly correct in his evaluation of Berridge as a preacher when he says, 'Few men have had more reason to know the power and efficiency of a preaching ministry.'[1] Ryle concludes that 'Few preachers, perhaps at this period, were more honoured by God and more useful to souls.'[2]

In considering Berridge as a preacher we must examine the whole of his preaching, both evangelistic and teaching, in country and town, over his thirty-four years as an evangelical preacher. False pictures can easily arise by selection. For example, to overemphasize the part that humour played could easily detract from the content, which was solemn and scriptural. Also if one were to focus attention on the summer months and activities recorded in 1759, one could certainly produce a caricature due to the drama and enthusiasm of that early period which would bear little resemblance to the total picture of a man who consistently over many years preached to thousands, and was judged by his peers to be a great preacher.

Wesley, Whitefield, Venn, Harris and Hill regarded him as an outstanding preacher. The regular winter preaching at the Tabernacle and Tottenham Court Road Chapel for over thirty years, to two of the largest congregations in London, confirm his ability. The great success he had at Everton, where many from the countryside flocked on Sunday, and his open-air work, which attracted large crowds, illustrate not only his evangelistic ability but also his gifts in building up a work and providing food for those on the Christian pathway. What John Wesley called 'a vile custom' and to be

181

rejected (that of a minister continually addressing the same people), Berridge successfully pursued over many years at Everton. It is surely this last point that should stimulate our interest in evaluating his success as a preacher, both as an itinerant evangelist during the week and as a provider of spiritual food to a large congregation on Sunday.

Before we examine the style and content of Berridge's preaching and the response to it, let us consider his own view of preaching. Probably because of his experience at Cambridge he was sceptical about human institutions making preachers. Human ordination is of no avail unless the preacher is divinely called: 'Unless the hand of the Spirit is laid on them all human hands avail nothing.'[3] Human learning and church ordination are ineffective until God makes himself known: 'It seems they have been trying for many years to make good pens at the universities; but after all the ingenuity and pains taken the pens which are made there are good for nothing till God has nibbed them.'[4] As we have seen, Berridge felt, within a few months of his conversion, that anyone could speak if he had the gift of utterance. He clearly felt it was God's prerogative to send preachers; they must be called by him:

> O Lord, stir up thy power
> To make the gospel spread;
> And thrust out preachers more,
> With voice to raise the dead,
> With feet to run where thou dost call,
> With faith to fight and conquer all.[5]

When Lady Huntingdon founded a college at Trevecka in 1768 in order to train evangelical ministers, this provided Berridge with a chance to question the value of such an undertaking: 'The soil you have chosen is proper; Welsh mountains afford a brisk air for a student; and the rules are excellent; but I doubt the success of the project; and fear it will occasion you more trouble than all your other undertakings besides. Are we commanded to make labourers; or to "pray the Lord to send labourers"? Will not Jesus choose, and teach, and send forth his ministering servants now, as he did his disciples aforetime; and glean them up when and where he pleaseth? The world says "No;" because they are strangers to a divine commission and a divine teaching . . . We read of a school of prophets in the Scripture, but we do not read that it was God's appointment. Elijah visited the school, which was at Bethel, and seems to have been fond 'of it, yet the Lord commands him to fetch a successor, not from the school, but as the Romans fetched a dictator, from the plough. Are we told of a single preaching prophet that was taken out of this school? Or do we find any public employment given the scholars, except once sending a light-headed young man, when light heels were useful, with a horn of oil to anoint Jehu (2 Kings 9). That old prophet who told a sad lie to another prophet was of this school, and might have been the master of this college, for he was a grey-headed man.'[6] Although Berridge concludes his letter by saying that he is the most dubious man concerning his own judgement and he was later to preach at an anniversary meeting of the college this quotation underlines his scepticism of man-made institutions. He believed that God sent out the poor unlettered preachers connected with him and that God used the weakest means in order to show that the work was his. He praised God for his own calling to open-air work: 'Thanks be to his name for calling me to preach out of doors. It is the glory of a creature to publish the fame and salvation of God.'[7]

Although Berridge stressed divine ordination he also had practical views for his own kind of preaching life. He viewed his life as hard work and spoke about pursuing his heavenly calling with the same energy as men pursue a worldly career. Most college youths he regarded as impractical and lacking the motivation required for a field preacher. The poet William Cowper reflected on how seriously Berridge regarded preaching when he wrote of John Newton and Berridge as 'labouring always for the souls of men, and not to tickle their ears as I do'.[8] He believed in single-mindedness, in humility mixed with boldness, and in being prepared to take opposition. Itinerant preaching might offend the consciences and scruples of the local clergy but such offence was to be expected. He wrote to Rowland Hill, 'As Paul was, so be thou a fool for Christ's sake; yea the very scum and off-scouring of all things.'[9] The preacher must be

prepared to lose the world's esteem: 'Happy is the man who
has lost it wholly and honestly.'[10] He believed that the
secret of preaching was not the preparation of sermons but
the preparation of the heart and of the man. Secret prayer
and the study of the Scriptures were foremost in this
preparation. His advice was 'Look simply unto Jesus for
preaching food; and what is wanted will be given, and what
is given be blest, whether it be a barley or a wheaten loaf, a
crust, or crumb. Your mouth will be a flowing stream, or a
fountain sealed, according as your heart is. Avoid all
controversy in preaching, talking, or writing; preach nothing down but the devil and nothing up but Jesus Christ.'[11]
Berridge believed that a congregation quickly drank in the
spirit of the preacher: 'Much reading and thinking may
make a popular minister: but much secret prayer must make
a powerful preacher.'[12]

Berridge had simple rules in his travelling. The open-air
preacher must be wise and not preach in working hours.
He must conclude before six in the morning and live as his
host usually lived. He was not to allow people to give him
treats. He was not to rail against opposing clergy. A host
must not be kept up late at night in order that they can
rise early in the morning. An itinerant preacher should
leave immediately after breakfast and morning family
prayer are over. If it is possible he should not dine where
he preaches in order to save the people expense. The
preacher must be prepared to trust God to open the way as
he did for the children of Israel through the wilderness.
Practical and spiritual advice were blended in a letter to
the young Charles Simeon: 'A rural dean or rambling
bishop must be able to preach without notes and have a
great desire to spread the gospel.'[13] Overall the preacher
must feel the need of God's grace throughout the whole of
his life.

> I see it now, and do confess,
> My utter need of Jesus' grace,
> And of his Spirit's light;
> I beg his kind and daily care.
> O Lord my heart and tongue prepare,
> To think and speak aright.

Prepare my tongue to pray and praise,
To speak of providential ways,
And heavenly truths unfold;
To strengthen well a feeble soul,
Correct the wanton, rouse the dull,
And silence sinners bold.[14]

Berridge did not leave printed records of his sermons. We do, however, have reports, an accurate record of Berridge's last sermon preached in London as a frail old man, many sermon outlines which portray clearly the content, if not the manner, of presentation, and sections from letters, which perhaps suggest something of his style.

Whittingham notes that 'The mode of his public ministrations was emphatically original. He evidently observed method in all his sermons, but it was unhackneyed. It was not his custom to range his subjects under general heads of discourse; but when he made the attempt his divisions would be peculiarly natural, and rigidly adhered to. As he rarely allegorized, or accommodated the Scriptures, he was less liable to mistake their meaning. He seldom referred to the original text; but when he did his remarks were pertinent. In his discussion of general topics, his figures were new, his illustrations apposite, and his arguments conclusive. His stature was tall, but not awkward; his make was lusty, but not corpulent; his voice was deep, but not hoarse; strong but not noisy; his pronunciation was distinct, but not broad. In his countenance there was gravity, without grimace; his address was solemn, but not sour; easy, but not careless; deliberate, but not drawling; pointed, but not personal; affectionate, but not fawning. He would often weep, but never whine. His sentences were short but not ambiguous. His ideas were collected, but not crowded. Upon the whole his manner and person were agreeable and majestic. But what transcended all the above excellences and gave him such an ascendancy in the consciences of his numerous hearers, were the doctrines he taught, together with their unbounded influence upon all the powers of his mind, and transactions of his life.'[15] Berridge thus stood in the great tradition of English popular preachers which looked back to Bishop Latimer, with a plain style, boldly underlined points and simple colloquial language.

Berridge aimed at simplicity in order that he might communicate. This aim can be appreciated when his audience is considered. Henry Venn when he came to Yelling (a few miles from Everton) from Huddersfield in the early seventies wrote, 'My audience is many degrees, in point of education and of condition, below my congregation at Huddersfield; so that I am under a necessity of labouring to be very plain; for even the manufacturers about you are rich and learned, compared with the peasants in this country. I find, therefore, it is very profitable to tell them stories.'[16] Whittingham tells us that Berridge laid aside an affected style of elegance and 'was remarkably careful to preach with great plainness of speech; so much so, that if possible, there might not be uttered a word but the meanest of his hearers might understand'.[17] Whittingham illustrates this by a story of Berridge speaking to a ministerial friend at Everton, who had just preached, about some of the people not being able to understand his language. Berridge complimented him on his sermon and after expressing difficulty with the language was asked which expressions might be above the comprehension of his audience. Berridge replied, 'You have endeavoured to prove that God is omniscient and omnipotent; but if you had said that God was almighty and knew everything, they would have understood you.'[18]

Many of his published sermon outlines are partly devoted to the definition and explanation of key terms in his texts. He was pleased with the Olney hymns because 'They are experimental and sound; the language intelligible to all believers.'[19] When editing Bogatzky's *Golden Treasury* he showed his dislike of Latin words, preferring Anglo-Saxon ones. He regarded Latin as a weed and there are many comments to this effect: 'Is not the English word "lightmindedness" as good as the Latin "levity", and better understood by plain country readers?'[20] Another paper was 'chiefly Latin and calls aloud for Bailey's Dictionary',[21] and 'An English author, who cannot write English deserves the stocks.'[22]

Berridge's desire for directness and simplicity in communication is confirmed by Thornton's views that one of his illustrations was more suitable for the newspaper or public entertainment than a sermon. Thornton himself, although he was offended at some of Berridge's expressions, recognized that such language fixed the attention of the audience. Berridge spoke to his audience in terms they could understand and in their own language.

Berridge was also against anything that put the preacher on a different level from his audience. He felt that the increased popularity of travelling by coach separated the preacher from those whom he wished to reach: 'Coaching is an evil that creeps among Methodist preachers. It brings a high head and a low purse; lifts the preacher above his hearers, and keeps the poor at a distance from him. Gospel seldom runs well on wheels. Our dear Master always rode upon his own legs, except once, when he borrowed a hackney to make a state entry into Jerusalem; and then any disciple might have got up behind if he pleased.'[23] His ideas of living in the same way as his host and keeping a barrel of ale ready for the refreshment of a worker show the same feeling for keeping the lines of communication open.

Berridge preached with emotion. He was no detached observer; he was seeking to persuade men of the terror of God and the love of Christ. Whittingham says he would often weep. Howell Harris recorded such a sermon when Berridge was affected all the while. Perhaps some of this emotional intensity can be conveyed by two quotations from letters which surely echo his preaching style.

The first comes from a letter to a Mr Edwards on the death of his wife: 'You have not lost your wife; she has only left for a few moments; left an earthly husband to visit a heavenly Father; and expects your arrival there soon, to join the hallelujah for redeeming love. Are you still weeping? Fie upon you brother! Weeping, because your wife can weep no more; weeping, because she is happy; because she is joined to that assembly where all are kings and priests! Weeping, because she is daily feasted with heavenly manna, and hourly drinking new wine in her Father's kingdom! Weeping, because she is now where you would be, and long to be eternally! Weeping, because she is singing, and singing sweet anthems to her God and your God! Oh shameful weeping! Jesus has fetched your bride triumphantly home to his kingdom, to draw your soul more ardently thither: he has broken up a cistern, to bring you nearer and keep you closer to the fountain: has caused a moment's separation, to divorce your affections from the creature; and has torn a wedding string from your heart, to set it a bleeding more freely, and panting more vehemently for Jesus. Hereafter you will see how gracious the Lord has been in calling a beloved wife home, in order to betroth the husband more effectually to himself. Remember that the house of mourning becomes and befriends a sinner; that sorrow is a safe companion for a pilgrim, who walks much astray until his heart is well broken. May all your tears flow in a heavenly channel, and every sigh waft your soul to Jesus.'[24]

Another example comes in a letter to John Thornton and was suggested as a reading for the collection that Thornton was editing. It shows the personal application that results from the preacher's concern. He takes up Thornton's theme of God of Jeshurun: 'How safe then must they be, who are under the wing of the God of Jeshurun, who find him reconciled to them by the death of his Son, and feel themselves reconciled to him by the power of his grace. He rideth on the heavens for their help, and none can outstep his progress, or obstruct his purpose. Verily, he it is that giveth strength and victory to his people; blessed be God! Reader, is the God of Jeshurun, the God of Israel thy God? Is he, who rideth on the heavens, thy help? Does thy thirst in him alone; and does his grace subdue thine outward iniquities, and thine inbred corruptions? Is he, who rideth on the sky, thine excellence? Does he seem only excellent in thine eyes, and cause thee to excel in virtue? Has he planted thee among his excellent ones of the earth, and made thee to abound in faith and love, and fruits of righteousness? If the Lord is not thy help, alas, thou wilt be slain by sin and prove a ruined soul. If the Lord is not thine excellence, thou art still an apostate spirit, a stranger with God, and to his Christ. Awake, arise, and call on God. His ear is open unto prayer, and thou art yet on mercy's ground: Oh, call upon him speedily, and cry unto him earnestly, that thou perish not!'[25]

Linked with this intensity Berridge pursued fresh thoughts and applications from the Scriptures. Berridge's prayer, which Thornton objected to, that 'God would give us new bread not stale, but what was baked in the oven on that day'[26] showed this desire for immediacy, which was particularly relevant in the light of the repetition and reading of sermons in the eighteenth century. Not only was his approach 'unhackneyed',[27] it was hot off the press, so to speak. He often spoke so much off the cuff that he confessed to Thornton that he ran wild and said many things that were somewhat rash, although there is no sign of this in his farewell sermon. He would speak freely and include personal details from his own heart. One of the preachers engaged at Everton while Berridge was in London was highly praised by the people. Berridge uses his own reaction to this as an illustration in a sermon on envy. 'On hearing him so highly extolled, Envy ... began to operate; and my breast swelling like a toad, I said to myself, I will take care that he shall not supply my place again. My great self could not brook to be outdone by another. I took, however, the sword of the Spirit, and made supplications to my Lord and Master, and the fiendish foe was expelled.'[28]

His sermon outlines are simple, with a strong emphasis on application. He was concerned to bring the challenge of the Scripture to the heart of the listener and thus, after some time in dealing with defining terms, he would apply it. In the outline of Romans 8:32 he notes towards the end: 'If God gives *all* things freely, then he gives repentance. Have you got it: (Acts 5:31). Faith, have you received it? (Eph. 2:8.) A spirit of prayer. Have you obtained it? (Zech. 12:10.) Pardon of sin. Have you found it? (Acts 10:43; 26:18.) Deliverance from its power (Micah 7:19). Holiness. Are you possessed of it? Growth in grace. Do you experience it? God who is spiritual, will also give earthly blessings, even all things belonging to this life as well as godliness. He will give daily bread. Do you obtain it?'[29] The outlines show that his sermons were rooted in Scripture and many of them are simple expositions of Scripture passages.

A distinctive feature of the sermon outlines and his recorded farewell sermon is their experimental nature. His walk with God gave practical knowledge to his preaching.

His was no empty orthodox doctrine – his preaching reflected his own heart's trials and triumphs and therefore struck sympathetic chords of encouragement in his hearers.

Speaking on the preciousness of Christ to the believer he acknowledged that: 'A Christian's passage through the wilderness is attended with difficulty and danger; and a Christian would faint under trials if left to himself, but Jesus never leaves his people; this makes him precious. Believers at times are cold and lifeless, but Christ revives them, this makes him precious. Believers sometimes prove unfaithful to Christ, their hearts ramble into the world, or their feet ramble into sinful ways; then Jesus smites and scourges with a heavy hand; he will not leave his people in sin, but makes it bitter to them and restores them. This makes Jesus precious. And woe be to that professor who turns into sinful paths, and is suffered to continue in them. Whatever trouble we are in, Jesus says, "Call upon me, and I will deliver thee", this makes him precious.'[30]

We can see all these characteristics in the only recorded sermon we have.[31] It was taken down in shorthand during his last London visit. Old and feeble though Berridge was, it is still a joy to read. He first sets the words of his message in their context. We see his experience of trust in Christ when he tells how Satan tries to deflect the soul from trusting Christ alone. There is practical advice on how to trust Christ and the material affords a direct challenge to both saint and sinner. The whole sermon is expository, opening up the meaning of the text, and the centrality of Christ and salvation by faith alone clearly dominate. Also he is not ashamed to confess his weakness and his need to have the words of the text, 'God is a refuge for me' applied to his own heart. Perhaps his friend Henry Venn leaves us a realistic summary of his preaching when he says it was 'practical and experimental'.

It is difficult to consider the type and use of illustrations made by Berridge because of the lack of evidence, although Whittingham says that his figures were new and his illustrations apposite. It is in this area that many think Berridge's own character influenced his preaching. In the opinion of several historians Berridge's own personality came through in racy anecdotes, personal and homely illustrations and humorous applications.

As one would expect because of his audience, agricultural images are often used in his writings. Pride is likened to twitch that is so difficult to remove from the ground. It resembles a hedgehog who rolls himself up in his prickly coat so that we cannot see his claws. Gins and traps for the unwary surround Bible doctrines and the heart is like a horse that is difficult to control:

> When my tongue would pray
> My heart will take a different road,
> And start and prance away.[32]

The Christian's heart needs constantly to be ploughed and harrowed by the Word and the patient in *The Christian World Unmasked* is invited to examine the nature of true faith as a grazier examines a beast minutely at a fair, not taking the salesman's word before he buys it. God is compared to a nursing mother whose breasts cannot cloy. Jesus is the lion-tamer over the heart full of lusts. Satan is pictured as a brilliant salesman, as a horse that is held by a bit, or as fire-balls setting the whole city of the soul aflame. Christians are like plants that need the sun before they blossom and send forth their perfume. His heart is often songless and cold when it should be like the warbling songsters of the sky, who tune their little cheerful throats and sound their hymns abroad:

> In cottage coop'd of human clay,
> Or sick or dull I pensive lay.
> And know not how to rise;
> Dear Jesus, give me vigour meet
> Put wings upon my heart and feet,
> And bear me to the skies.
>
> Or fast I cleave unto the earth,
> Or, like a snail, am creeping forth,
> And linger-langer go;
> Oh, for the pinions of a dove,
> Then I would fly and soar above,
> And sing my sonnets too.[33]

Berridge's gospel invitations show that he preached no superficial message. The gospel is for sinners. Speaking on Matthew 9:28 he says that, 'All men are sinners, and condemned by the Law; but all men do not feel their condemnation, and therefore are not heavy laden with a guilty burden, nor labouring after rest. Yet only such are invited, and only such are accepted. What right have you to come to Jesus Christ, unless you come in his appointed way?'[34] The 'promises in the Bible are free for all who see their need of them'.[35] The miracles show the way to Christ. Those healed were helpless, miserable, quite unable to relieve themselves but believing in Christ and totally dependent on him; those who approached Christ in such a condition were always healed even if they had to wait. Spiritually the case was the same: 'All that seek to Jesus Christ, with a due sense of their misery and helplessness, and with a single trust in his power and mercy, will obtain what they seek. They may wait a while at mercy's gate, and meet with some discouragement; but at length it will be opened. The mourners will be comforted with pardons, and weary sinners will find rest unto their souls. Thus the promises, which are only gazed on by others as a fine picture, prove a heavenly feast to them.'[36] Many hymns echo the same theme:

> All ye that weary are of sin,
> And feel your natures all unclean,
> And labour under guilt;
> Who find within no dawn of hope,
> To Christ your weary eyes lift up,
> His blood for you was spilt.
>
> Go, sinner, go, by sin distrest,
> And Jesus Christ will give thee rest,
> And act the Saviour's part;
> He came to save the lost and poor,
> And such are welcome to his door,
> And welcome to his heart.[37]

Or again,

> His love is to all
> The great or the small,
> Who weary of sin are, and come at his call,
>
> True mourners he makes,
> Invites them and takes,
> With lighter or heavier load on their backs.[38]

There was a strong note of assurance concerning the gospel invitation in Berridge's preaching for Christ had come to call 'sinners – sinners sensible of sin and bruised with it'.[39] Mercy he regarded as God's darling attribute and God would certainly respond to those who sought him. 'Are you seeking for pardon? Ask earnestly for it, ask expecting. He is a God, pardoning iniquity, freely, fully, eternally, and will cast all your sins into the depths of the sea. He delights in mercy.'[40] Berridge promised the love of Christ to those who, prepared by the Spirit of God, sought salvation in Christ alone for their sinful condition.

The theme of Berridge's gospel preaching was regeneration, in contrast to what he considered the normal preaching of morality. 'A moral conduct shall avail him nothing, without a new birth, a new nature from above.'[41] He firmly believed that the preaching of law was important, for that will 'make you feel the scores'.[42] The law was preached before the gospel: 'Fresh ploughing also must go before every fresh seeding; the law before the gospel.'[43] He is blunt in his advice to the young Charles Simeon: 'When you open your commission, begin with laying open the innumerable corruptions of the hearts of your audience; Moses will lend you a knife, which may be often whetted at his grindstone. Lay open the universal sinfulness of nature; the darkness of the mind, the frowardness of the will, the fretfulness of the temper, and the earthliness and sensuality of the affections. Speak of the evil of sin in its nature, its rebellion against God as our Sovereign, ingratitude to God as our benefactor, and contempt both of his authority and love ... lay open spirituality of the law, and its extent, reaching to every thought, word and action, and declaring every transgression, whether by omission or commission, deserving of death. Declare man's utter helplessness to change his nature, or to make his peace. Pardon and holiness must come from the Saviour. Acquaint them with the searching eye of God, watching us continually, spying out every thought, word and action, noting them down in the book of remembrance, and bringing every secret thing into judgement, whether it be good or evil.

'When your hearers are deeply affected with these things (which is seen by the hanging down of their heads) preach Christ. Lay open the Saviour's almighty power to soften the hard heart, and give it repentance, to bring pardon to the broken heart, a spirit of prayer to the prayerless heart, holiness to the filthy heart, and faith to the unbelieving heart. Let them know that all the treasures of grace are lodged in Jesus Christ for the use of the poor needy sinner, and that he is full of love as well as power; turns no beggar from his gate, but receives all comers kindly; loves to bless them, and bestows all his blessings tithe free. Farmers and country people chop at that. Here you must wave the gospel flag, and magnify the Saviour supremely. Speak it with a full mouth, (*ore rotundo*) that this blood can wash away the foulest sins, and his grace subdue the stoutest corruptions. Exhort the people to seek his grace, to seek it directly, seek it diligently, seek it constantly, and acquaint them that all who thus seek shall assuredly find the salvation of God.'[44] It is reasonable to deduce that his advice in such a passage flowed from his own practice.

For the true seeker, he forecasts the loss of the crowd and a thousand woes before Christ is seen. There are many distractions but Christ is all powerful. Not only is Christ the message but he is also the reaper:

> A Christian sergeant sent to list,
> Must fill his speech with Jesus Christ,
> And gather with his name:
>
> O Lord, do thou instruct my heart
> With my own reaping hook to part
> And gather all with thee.[45]

Berridge thus confirms the centrality of Christ to the preacher as well as to the thinker or churchman.

Berridge experienced much reaction to his preaching. Whitefield speaks of his preaching with power in London and also says that it was an honour for the young Rowland Hill to share his reproach. His preaching was stigmatized by the majority. In his open-air work many would laugh and mock.[46] His London work seemed very popular and a fellow minister speaks of 'numerous congregations that at all times crowd round him, and hang upon his words with pleasure'.[47] Venn says his word was greatly owned in London and the very large congregations he built up at Everton continued long after his death. However, only a few, comparatively speaking, were interested and on the whole the main response was from the poor. The world hated Jesus and Berridge thought it would hate every true disciple: 'If you dare be zealous for the Lord of hosts expect persecution and threats but heed them not.'[48] If a preacher met with success he must 'expect clamour and threats from the world, and a little venom now and then from the children'.[49] In the early days his house was often being threatened with destruction but he was comforted by what he considered the Lord's insurance - Psalm 91:10.[50]

Although a preacher who was greatly blessed, Berridge was conscious of the limitations of preaching. Crowded and attentive congregations he regarded as encouraging sights, but he thought his age was characterized by hearing rather than by praying. Preaching did not automatically lead to a spirit of devotion. 'Much preaching and hearing is among the Methodists, and plenty of ordinances is a great blessing, but if they do not bring us much upon our knees, they suckle the head without nourishing the heart.'[51] Preaching must lead to Christ; it was no ego trip for selfish purposes. Berridge himself seems to have been a model for humility in spite of his great success, and this walk with Christ and communion with him which he stressed must surely have underpinned his preaching ministry.

# 22.
# Berridge: the thinker and theologian

We have seen how serious a student Berridge was during his twenty years as a scholar at Cambridge, and how avid he was in absorbing the learning of his day. Berridge was recognized in his day as a man of 'considerable learning'.[1] Conversion, however, changed Berridge's whole attitude to books and scholarship. This man 'of considerable intellectual power and much reading'[2] came to regard human wisdom with suspicion. 'Human wisdom he thought might, sometimes, be made useful, but was more often injurious to a child of grace.'[3]

Berridge, after his conversion, looked at his time at university from a different perspective. He had gone there hoping to receive light and instruction from human wisdom but he had found that he had departed 'more and more from the truth as it is in Jesus'.[4] He might have been able to throw off the errors of Socinianism, but he seemed alone in his struggles concerning the relationship between works and faith in salvation, towards the end of the period at Cambridge. He came to regard his time there as a waste of time, 'learning useless lumber, that wisdom of the world which is foolishness with God'.[5]

Conversion for Berridge meant a totally new view of knowledge and this was fundamental to a man of his background. A true knowledge of Christ did not come through human scholarship. 'The Saviour's little child and the apostle's fool instruct us how to seek heavenly wisdom; not by drawing it from human brains or heathen folios, but by meekly going unto Jesus as a little child to be taught, or as a fool to be made wise.'[6] Before we look at some of the main themes of Berridge's theology we need to explore some of the implications of his new attitude to books and learning.

After his conversion Berridge never placed spiritual value on human knowledge. As an evangelist he joined the apostle Paul in regarding the wisdom of the world as foolishness because it did not have 'the least tendency to make men wise unto salvation'.[7] He thought that the more human knowledge increased so did immorality and infidelity. Ancient nations, like Egypt, Greece and Rome, were evidence that reaching a high pitch of human learning could lead to slavery. Solomon's book Ecclesiastes 'was left on holy record to direct us what to think of human science'.[8] Those who laugh at Solomon's conclusion that all is vanity will weep at the end of their lives. The pursuit of human knowledge has some benefits, for it 'keeps men out of mischief, trains them up for civil occupations, and oft produceth notable discoveries, which are useful to the world; but never can lead the heart to Jesus Christ, nor breed a single grain of faith in him. They who know most of human science, and have waded deepest in it, know the most of its vanities, and find it but vexation of spirit.'[9] In spiritual matters the scholar 'must go empty unto Jesus, and see himself a fool in heavenly science'[10] if he wishes to come to a knowledge of the truth.

Berridge also in the beginning held Christian books at bay. This was shown in his restriction on the selling of Wesley's literature amongst his flock, thinking that those who read many books normally neglected the Bible. He maintained a similar attitude himself throughout his life although not to an extreme. It must be remembered that except for periods of illness Berridge was itinerating from Monday to Friday and had little leisure to read. He was, however, grateful to John Newton for sending him his publications as well as other books, such as the writings of John Owen, which he read several times with pleasure. He was concerned for Newton when Newton was engaged on research into church history because it might chill his spirit and deaden his soul. Berridge warned: 'Much writing is pernicious. Besides, you must read over many dry and barren histories; you must bring to light many controversies, foolish or noxious, which had better lie buried fifty fathoms deep.'[11] He did, however, use certain books for evangelistic purposes.

Berridge maintained a library, for Venn records that Berridge gave many valuable books to his son. He wrote *The Christian World Unmasked* during illness but wished in retrospect that the controversial books had remained on the shelves. Towards the end of his life he was engaged at the editor's request on revising Thornton's edition of Bogatzky's *Golden Treasury*. Six years before his death he wrote to Thornton that he needed nothing except the Scriptures; this was probably because of his poor eyesight. However, the tract that Thornton had sent was so savoury that he read it with profit and he proposed to obtain twelve copies for his lay preachers the next time he was in London. He published two hymn-books. He evaluated Cowper's latest book of poems. Thus he was not anti-books, but opposed the reading of books if it meant lost time with the Scriptures, for 'One grain of godly fear is of more worth than a hundred thousand head-fulls of attic wit, or full of philosophic, theologic or commercial science.'[12]

Berridge's conversion meant a radical change in approaching truth. He afterwards placed his reasoning powers under the revelation in the Scriptures. We never find, as we do in his opponents in the Calvinism controversy, arguments based on reason and Scriptures.[13] His approach was 'What saith your Bible? How readest thou?'[14] A firm reliance on God's Word without human props was the pathway for the Christian, in comparison with the man who 'cannot rest upon God's naked Word, nor seat his heart upon the solid chair of promise, without some human stool beside'.[15]

Some felt that his approach gloried in ignorance. John Wesley strongly rejected this approach and replied to the criticisms of Rutherford, that Methodists taught that Christianity rejected the aid of human learning: 'Mr Berridge thinks it does; but I am not accountable for him, from whom, in this I totally differ.'[16] Robert Robinson, the Baptist minister at Cambridge whom Berridge had encouraged to itinerate around the Cambridge villages, used to say of Berridge, 'I know how to estimate his good qualities, without making myself a simpleton.'[17]

However, Berridge never spoke lightly of the gift of reason, but reason had to be informed by grace if there was to be knowledge of God. In the context of writing to a friend mentioning that a maid was losing her mind he says, 'What a mercy to have full use of reason, and reason preserved, and reason improved and illumined by grace!'[18] Independent reason and the human knowledge that it established tended to make men vain and thus drive people further from God. However, 'Bible knowledge, fetched in by prayer, and watered with meditation, makes the mind humble and serious.'[19] He wrote to Rowland Hill: 'Make the Scriptures your only study, and be much in prayer. The apostles gave themselves to the Word of God and to prayer.'[20] In recognizing that God reveals himself through a prayerful, meditative study of Scripture, Berridge saw the true place of reason. Since the Fall man's mind was darkened and thus God must open the understanding.

> Some of their reason boast,
> And haughty is its sway
> And some in learning trust
> To find the gospel way;
> I would not pertly these despise,
> Yet want to see with better eyes.
>
> Thy reason may judge right
> Of worldly things and men,
> But spiritual truth and light
> Are far beyond thy ken;
> Here reason takes her proper road,
> When she cries out for help to God.
>
> All seem to understand
> The gospel mighty well;
> And think in gospel land
> No darkness sure can tell;
> Yet gospel truth no man can find,
> Till Jesus opens his dark mind.[21]

One of the evidences of true faith for Berridge was a new attitude towards the Bible. It would surely become a 'sweet companion'[22] for those who were true Christians. His converts were encouraged to read the Scriptures for themselves. Through the Scriptures a new perspective was gained:

> His Word, with prayer devoutly read
> Will plant new eyes within your head.[23]

Several telling images tumble from Berridge's pen showing how he regarded the Scriptures. They were 'the precious store-house, and the magna carta of a Christian. There he reads of his heavenly Father's love, and of his dying Saviour's legacies. There he sees a map of his travels through the wilderness, and a landscape too of Canaan. And when he climbs on Pisgah's top, and views the promised land, his heart begins to burn, delighted with the blessed prospect, and amazed at the rich and free salvation. But a mere professor, though a decent one, looks on the Bible as a dull book; and peruseth it with such indifference as you would read the title-deeds belonging to another man's estate.'[24]

The promises in the Scriptures 'are real bank-notes of heaven, and the true riches of believers, who do not live on stock in hand, but traffic with this paper currency. Where divine faith is found, it takes the notes to Christ's bank, and receives the cash.'[25]

Berridge's approach was not bathed in obscurantism, for he demanded a serious approach, realizing whose book it was: 'Read the Word of God with care, and in its native language, if you can; but read it too with prayer; and not with prayer only, but with heart dependence upon Jesus, while you read. Put your eyes into the Saviour's head, while you look upon his book; and when his head directs your eyes, you will have light enough.'[26] Berridge wrote comments on the grammatical construction of the original languages in his own Bible where he thought fit and in *The Christian World Unmasked* he occasionally refers to the original languages when emphasizing a point.

Berridge saw a constant need of the Holy Spirit's guidance, particularly in the light of the 'gins and snares' that are scattered in the Scriptures to catch arrogant scholars:

'Every fundamental doctrine meets with something which seems directly to oppose it, and these seeming contradictions are the traps which are laid. A lofty scribe, who depends upon his own subtlety, and cannot pray sincerely for direction, is sure to be taken in these snares; but a humble praying soul escapes them, or, if his foot be caught, the snare is broken, and his soul delivered.'[27]

The Word of God must be appropriated in the individual life and heart. This spiritual tillage of the heart, as he called it, consisted in a 'diligent use of the means of grace, prayer, hearing and reading the Word and holy meditation'.[28] The Word lived and must be eaten.

> According as my wants require,
> Adapt the Word as food and fire,
> To nourish and to warm;
> Let every page afford new wealth,
> Convey some life and godly health,
> And guard my steps from harm.[29]

Berridge saw Christ throughout the Scriptures. Besides those who are normally thought of as types of Christ, such as Moses interceding for the people, he sees even a complex character like Samson as an illustration of Christ: 'Samson was a type of Jesus, who, for the love of a harlot (and we are no better), was willing to part with this strength, to be bound by his own nation (Judg. 15:11) and delivered up to his enemies; to be blindfolded and made sport with, and to be put to death; yet by his death (like Samson) destroying his enemies.'[30] It was because Christ was real that he found 'substantial food' in the Scriptures.[31]

There is a consistency in Berridge's view of Christ as the only way to God from the time of his conversion right through until his death. As we have seen when observing his theological development in the 1760s and in the Calvinism controversy, this 'fled to Jesus alone for refuge' theology was clarified and continually stressed. The choice of Psalm 62, what one might call the 'only God' psalm, in his last sermon in London restated the supremacy and sufficiency of Christ in his understanding of salvation. Christ alone is the rock and is thus worthy of all honour. It must be noted that his

struggle back to orthodox views concerning the person of
Christ in his days at Cambridge did not of itself lead to his
view of Christ as the only Saviour of men. Trust in Christ
alone became experimental for Berridge and it was his heart
experience of a reliance on Christ, and not upon his own
works or any religious forms, which formed the basis of his
view of Christ. The theme of his preaching was not the
unique and supreme position of Christ in theory but the
need to have Christ as Lord: 'Where Christ is really
precious, he is precious above all things. He deserves our
whole heart, and will bear no rival. He that loveth anything
more than me, is not worthy of me; earthly relations, riches,
honour, pleasures, or his own life (Matt. 10:37). Where
Christ is precious the heart cries out with David, 'Whom
have I in heaven but thee?' (Ps. 73:25.) Hence Christ is seen
to be precious only by a few, and of course only few
believers. Among professors not many seem willing to deny
themselves, to part with sinful tempers and sinful pleasures
for Christ's sake. Where sin of any kind is precious, Christ
cannot be so. What is it makes Christ truly precious? Not
merely hearing of his salvation and asserting to it, but
receiving it.'[32]

When discussing the divinity of Christ in *The Christian
World Unmasked*, Berridge stressed that 'If Jesus Christ is
not truly God, he cannot save me.'[33] Many pages are given
over to the scriptural evidence for Christ's divinity,
although he thought that some things taught about his
human nature and his mediatorial office could seem to be
contradictions, if taken in a wrong sense. These traps catch
modern scribes but the Holy Spirit's guidance is promised
to all those who seek it earnestly. He saw the Scriptures as
clearly teaching that Jesus is the Creator and Sustainer of
the universe, having the same attributes as the Father,
given divine titles and worshipped as God and is the Judge
of all men. For Berridge, unlike those who would seek to
divest these expressions of their plain meanings, the truth
was plain in the Scriptures: Jesus Christ was truly man and
truly God.

> His person soareth out of sight,
> A mystery, magnified by Paul.

A child, and yet the God of might,
A worm and yet the Lord of all.[34]

Berridge stressed that Christ was not only a Saviour, but
also a Surety. We saw the development of this theme after the
problems of his own inner failures during the sixties,
culminating in his contribution to the Calvinism controversy. Imputed righteousness was a glory of the gospel, for
all blessings flowed from Christ. Christ has not only died for
his children; he also lived for them. He says, 'Christ, by the
appointment of God, was constituted for us, wisdom, righteousness, etc. St Paul is not here speaking of what Christ
worketh in us, by his grace, but of what he hath wrought for
us, as our legal Surety. The four capital blessings mentioned
in the text were procured for us, without any contrivance or
concurrence of our own; and therefore the conclusion in the
next verse is weighty – "Let him that glorieth, glory in the
Lord".'[35] Berridge saw suretyship, the principle of taking on
the responsibilities of another, not as dishonouring the law,
but increasing reverence for it. There are many hymns
working out the devotional and experimental implications of
Christ's suretyship. In one of these Berridge views the rose of
Sharon and the lily of the valley in the Song of Songs as the
surety's payment of the debt:

Coupled in song we see
The rose and lily are,
And fancy out to me
My Surety's office clear;
One shows his blood to wash me whole,
And one his robe to clothe my soul.

Lord, bring the sweetening rose
To make my conscience clean;
And give me lily-clothes
To hide my rags within;
So shall thy blood and righteousness
Bring gospel peace and heavenly dress.

Completely thus array'd
And sweetly cheered on,

No danger shall I dread
No duty shall I shun;
The rose and lily when combin'd
Afford a peaceful loving mind.[36]

Faith in Christ was not an empty and vague notion for
Berridge. The centrality of Christ's person and work was the
foundation of biblical Christianity. The life of faith was one of
trusting wholly on Christ as Prophet, Priest and King: 'I must
read the Word of God with care, yet not rely upon my own
ability to make me wise unto salvation, but wholly trust in
Jesus, as my Prophet to open my dark understanding, and
direct me by his Spirit into all saving truth. I must watch
against sin, and pray against it too; yet not rely upon my own
strength to conquer it, but wholly trust in Jesus as my King, to
subdue my will, my tempers, and affections, by his Spirit; to
write his holy law upon my heart, and influence my conduct to
his glory. I must be zealous of good works – as zealous to
perform them, as if my pardon and a crown of glory could be
purchased by them; yet wholly trust in Jesus, as my Priest, to
wash my guilty conscience in his purple fountain, and clothe
my naked soul in his glorious righteousness, thereby receiving all my pardon and my title to eternal life.'[37] Berridge
never swerved from his discovery at his conversion of the
sufficiency and centrality of Christ alone, although he only
gradually worked out some of the implications of such a view.

We have already seen his views on the sovereignty of God
in his illness of the late sixties and the Calvinism controversy. It followed therefore that Berridge's view of
conversion should be radical and heaven-orientated. He
stressed that conversion was a work of God that produced
changes in the true believer. Repentance and reliance on
Christ was not necessarily a speedy event for 'when the
heart is conscious of its misery, it will try a thousand legal
tricks to shake its pitched shirt off'[38] but when the one who
changed water into wine and who caused Lazarus to live
speaks, the miracle of regeneration occurs.

In Laz'rus we view
A sinner's sad case,
Bound hand and foot too,

And bound on his face.
No arm may release him
And give a new birth.
Till Jesus says, "Loose him!"
And then he comes forth.[39]

It is little wonder that Berridge looked for evidence of the
Spirit's work particularly in the light of his disappointments
in the sixties, as well as the successes. We saw how false
were John Fletcher's claims that Berridge's teaching was
Antinomian, particularly as Berridge looked for practical
fruit:

Does heavenly love inspire your breast,
And find you sweet employ?
Is God's dear Word your savoury feast,
And Christ your song and joy?[40]

He expected real tokens of the Spirit's presence in
quickening, strengthening, witnessing and bringing heavenly joy. The Spirit's sealing would be a reality bringing
assurance and joy. A person's attitude towards the Scriptures, prayer and God's people would be different. There
would be some evidence of victory in a true believer possessed of the Holy Spirit: 'Does your faith overcome the lust
of the flesh, making you victorious over your palate, and over
outward pollution, and inward uncleanness? Does your faith
overcome the lust of the eye, and keep your heart from grasp-
ing after more wealth, more preferment, or more honours?
. . . Does your faith overcome the pride of life, and prevent
you being charmed with a lofty house, rich furniture, genteel
equipage, and splendid raiment? Does it make you sick of
earthly vanities, and draw your heart to things above?'[41]
Even before he had adopted Calvinist views and within
six months of his own conversion, Berridge wrote in his
letter to a Nottingham clergyman of the need of the Holy
Spirit to bring conviction of sin. As a preacher he deeply felt
the importance of God's Spirit. Nothing availed without the
Spirit: 'He has many voices to call dead sinners by, the voice
of his Word, of his servants, and his providences; but all
these avail nothing, without the voice of his Spirit. His Word

is but a dead letter without the quickening Spirit; his
servants are but barking dogs, who growl, yet cannot bite,
unless he set them on; and his providences are but claps of
thunder, alarming for a time, yet quickly over, except he
rides himself upon the storm. When he takes the work into
his own hand, and the voice of his Spirit accompanies the
voice of his Word, or his servants, or his providences, then a
sinner hears and starts from his grave, like Lazarus, and
lives. And having thus received life, he feels his condemnation and his ruined nature, and crieth after Jesus.'[42]

The irresistibility of the Spirit and his personality and
work are taught in several sermon notes. As a Christian
thinker he felt his desperate need of light from above.
Speaking of William Cowper's sad state he says, 'How dark
and feeble is a Christian's understanding without the light
and comfort of God's Holy Spirit!'[43] In days when the
doctrine of the Holy Spirit is much discussed as if it were
special to our day it is interesting to note that to Berridge
knowledge of him was 'a rule given us to measure our
Christianity by. Do ye know the Spirit? Some may think
themselves good Christians, because they are staunch
churchmen, stout dissenters, or hymn-singing methodists,
or decent moralists; but do ye know the Spirit, his work on
the heart?'[44] As is normal for Berridge, it was the practical
implications rather than speculative concerns of doctrine
that gripped his heart and exhortation. He saw the sealing
of the Spirit in terms of assuring the believer that he did
indeed have saving interest in Christ. Although he believed
that Pentecost was unique he stressed the outpourings of
the Spirit in the hearts of God's people, without which there
was no living worship or approach to God:

> Come, breathe thine influence, Holy Ghost
> And light and heavenly love impart;
> Bring down a gracious Pentecost,
> And kindle fire in every heart.
>
> Without thy breath we are but clay,
> Our harp is on the willow hung,
> Devotion droops and dies away
> On fainting heart, and faltering tongue.

Thy heavenly unction let us feel,
And give us faith, and faith's increase,
The blessings of the covenant seal,
And bring the year of sweet release.

Our spirit unto God unite,
And keep us meekly in his fear;
Thy holy law within us write,
And make the treacherous heart sincere.[45]

In one sermon outline he summarizes the work of the Holy
Spirit as being to open the understanding and to teach
gospel truth, to quicken and to comfort and strengthen the
soul. As in other areas of his theological thinking, he spoke
here not only from his understanding of Scripture, but from
experience informed by the Word. His theology and experience are well expressed in the hymn which Berridge based
on the Scripture, 'As many as are led by the Spirit of God,
they are the sons of God':

An earthly heart I have,
And earthly made by sin!
No good, but sensual, it will crave,
And sweetly drinks it in.

No joy it finds in God;
And when my tongue would pray,
My heart will take a different road,
And start and prance away.

No converse can we find,
With him, our God, we call;
No will or power lodg'd in the mind
To walk with God at all.

Such is man's nature now,
Sunk and bemir'd in earth!
And what can raise his fallen brow,
And give him heavenly birth?

Who can the spirit turn,
And unto God unite,
And make the heart with fervour burn,
And in its God delight?

Thou, Holy Spirit, must
The mighty work perform,
Awake the sleeper from his dust,
And wing the grovelling worm.

Oh, let thy breath inspire
All needful power and will
And make my soul to God aspire,
And with his presence fill.[46]

There was a large streak of realism in Berridge's thinking.
As a Christian he had both feet on the ground and was able to
help and encourage others because of the realistic appraisal
(some might say pessimistic) that he made of his own heart.
Many of his devotional hymns are given dramatic warmth
through the confession of the failure of his own heart and it is
in this area of the psychology of the Christian life, with its
doubts, tensions and little faith, that he has much to teach.
Berridge certainly rejoiced in the grace of God and the victory that was in Christ. Thus, 'A Christian's work is to live
out of himself, and to live upon Christ.'[47] However, he
regarded the life of faith as a continual fight, with opposition
from the enemy, and often God allowed faith to ebb in order
to make the Christian humble and prayerful.

The main trouble of the believer is his heart. In *Cheerful
Piety* he maps out the activities of 'inbred foes' and how the
heart is a theatre for speculative sins. He is ashamed of
'inward masquerades'[48] but looks forward to the peaceful
realms above. A Christian is often going astray until his
heart is broken. Berridge loved the picture of the heart as
the ground and Christ as the husbandman, and spoke of the
continual need to break up the ground that the Word might
enter. Berridge has many things to say about the pressing
need for heart knowledge by the Christian and the need to
give one's heart to Christ. He is the only one who can deal
with such an awful and deceitful thing.

It is exceeding prone to stray,
And wilder than a beast of prey;
No human fetter can it bind,
But thou canst tame and make it kind.[49]

Here was no dry theology but the very issues of life.

Berridge was no preacher with plenty of style but little content. The power of his preaching was obviously based on a deep experimental grasp of the Christian faith. His own experience of an inadequate methodology at Cambridge led him to emphasize the study of the Scriptures, meditation and prayer, above all else. Such a study combined with an analysis of his own heart underpinned the great communicative gifts he possessed.

# 23.
# Berridge: the churchman

Berridge had a practical love for all those, whatever their denominational affiliations, who followed the Lord Jesus Christ in sincerity and truth. However, he made a clear distinction between those who preached and lived the truth and those who were following a false gospel. This position could be difficult to sustain as a minister in a state church seemingly committed to the idea of territorial and sacramental Christianity. Berridge was pessimistic about the future of the national church and the solutions he adopted to such problems as succession in evangelical parishes, itineration in other parishes, fellow clergy who were not believers, a liturgy which was ambiguous and the founding and sustaining of independent congregations were largely pragmatic and were made subservient to his mission, as he saw it, of preaching the gospel.

Berridge's concern that the local church be a place of fellowship and outreach was expressed in the following hymn:

> Give peace in the fold
> And fellowship sweet,
> And make young and old
> Lay down at thy feet;
> The elder ones bleating
> With lustiest praise,
> And lambkins repeating
> The wonders of grace.
>
> Some strays we yet lack
> Which in the world roam;

Lord, whistle them back,
And fetch them safe home.
And thousands which lost are,
And never yet found,
Allure them to feast here
On mercy's fair ground.[1]

Berridge also thought that it was usual for new local congregations to decline in spiritual life and desires. This was seen in the early church itself. In a letter to Lady Huntingdon he used the picture of the latter rain to describe the need for revival in such situations. Such a condition occurred at Everton after the initial interest of the early sixties:

My Lady,
You complain that every new work, after a season, becomes a lifeless work. And was it not in the beginning as it is now? Do not the Acts and Epistles show that the primitive churches much resembled our own? In their infancy we find them of one heart and soul, having all things common; but presently read of partiality in the distribution of their church-stock, then of eager and lasting contentions about circumcision, coupling Moses with Jesus, and setting the servant on a level with his Master. And Gentile churches were much on a footing with Jewish. The Corinthians soon fell into parties about their leaders, into errors about the resurrection, and into many gross immoralities. The Galatians seemed ready at first to present Paul with their own eyes, but grew desirous at last of plucking out his. The Ephesians had been much tossed with winds of doctrine. The Colossians had fallen into will-worship, etc. and the Thessalonians had some of our gossips among them, who would not work but sauntered about picking up news and telling tales. St Paul's labours were much employed in Asia, and many churches were gathered there; yet I hear him complaining in a certain place, 'that they in Asia were turned aside from him'. The General Epistles, which were written late, unanimously show that errors and corruptions had broke into all churches during the apostles' lifetime; and the seven epistles dictated by Jesus in the Revelation confirm the same.

Scripture mentions a former and a latter rain; between
which there must of course be an interval of drought and
barrenness. The former rain falls just after seed-time, when
there is plenty of manna coming down from above, plenty of
honey flowing out of the rack, and plenty of joyful hosan-
nahs raising up to Jesus. After this rain comes the interval,
during which most of the stony and thorny grounds sheer
off, taking a final leave of Jesus; and the good grounds are
scarcely discernible, so barren they appear and full of
weeds, and so exceedingly cold and swampy. Now one soars
up into the cloud of perfection, crying out, 'I am a queen!'
and becomes the devil's goddess. Another falls asleep and
snores hard in election; God's truth, indeed, is often made
the devil's cradle. A third drops plump into a pond, and
then keeps roaming day and night about the devil's
washpot. A fourth gets bemired in the world, and lies quite
contented, though nearly choked in the devil's quagmire. At
length the Lord ariseth in just indignation to chastise and
vex his people, continuing his plagues till he has broken
their bones and humbled their hearts, causing them to see,
and feel, and loathe their backslidings, and raising up a sigh
and a cry in their hearts for deliverance. Then comes the
latter rain to revive and settle; after which they learn to walk
humbly with God.

J.B.[2]

Berridge's attitude towards the established church was
pragmatic in that it provided him with a base for his
operations. He thought that Christianity was better before
the establishment of churches began and spoke of a 'fanciful
alliance'[3] between state and church. Although he accepted
the situation as it was without any real theological criticism
of the state-church concept, he believed that if the
downward movement continued and God did not intervene
the church's candlestick could be quite removed and she
would become 'a sister to the African and Asiatic
churches'.[4]

Although he accepted the principle of establishment he
was more concerned about the establishment that the Holy
Spirit brings: 'I regard neither high church, nor low church,
nor any church, but the church of Christ, which is not built

with hands, nor circumscribed with peculiar walls, nor confined to a singular denomination. I cordially approve the doctrines and liturgy of the church of England, and have cause to bless God for a church-house to preach in, and a church revenue to live upon. And I could wish the gospel might not only be preached in all the British churches, but established therein by Christ's Spirit, as well as by a national statute; but from the principles of the clergy, and the leading men in the nation, which are growing continually more unscriptural and licentious, I do fear our defence is departing and the glory is removing from our Israel. Perhaps in less than one hundred years to come, the church-lands may be seized on to hedge up Government gaps, as the abbey-lands were two hundred years and fifty years ago.'[5]

Ten years later he expressed the same ambivalence towards the established church in a letter to John Thornton: 'By birth and education I am both a churchman and a dissenter – I love both, and could be either, and wish real gospel ministers of every denomination could embrace one another. And though I do think the best Christianity was found before establishments began; and that usually there are more true ministers out of an establishment than in it; and that establishments are commonly of an intolerant spirit, and draw in shoals of hirelings by their loaves and fishes; yet I am very thankful for an establishment which affords me a preaching house and an eating house, without clapping a padlock on my lips, or a fetter on my foot.'[6]

In *The Christian World Unmasked* he painted a bleak picture of what he considered the unreality of worship in the majority of the national churches, where the service was drudgery, there was lack of spiritual food, and many leaders were in danger of serious doctrinal error and, like Eli's sons, would 'kick at the sacrifice, and, in a mighty rage of zeal for the Father, would strip his dear Son of divinity, and trample on his blood'.[7]

Berridge had to meet the challenge of being schismatic right at the start of his evangelical preaching. Within six months of his conversion, in his letter to a Nottingham clergyman which was later published as *Justificaion by Faith Alone*, he set forth his conviction that schism is essentially a matter of belief; it is about departing from the doctrines of a church and not departing from its walls. He had been the true schismatic in his unconverted state. Justification by faith alone was clearly taught in the articles of the Church of England but many clergy had departed from the doctrines, articles and homilies of the national church. Although such a departure had been going on for fifty years he seems to have been more optimistic in those days of revival that more clergy would be converted and would rediscover the true gospel than he was to be later: 'But you will say, perhaps, that these Methodists are schismatics. Let us therefore examine the matter. A schismatic is one that dissents from and divides an established church; at least this is the general notion of a schismatic. Now I ask, what do you mean by a church? Or, what is it that makes one church differ from another? It is the doctrine. The Church of England differs from the Church of Rome, not by its steeples, bells, or vestments, but by its doctrines. Schism, therefore, consists in departing from the doctrines of a church and not from the walls of a church. In the time of Stirbitch fair, one sermon is always preached in the open fields to the people at the fair, and preached by some fellow of a college, or clergyman at Cambridge. Now I ask, would you call this clergyman a schismatic? No, surely, and yet he preaches in the open fields, and upon unconsecrated ground. It is plain, then, that schism doth not consist in preaching out of the walls of a church, but in preaching contrary to the doctrines of the church.

'And now, dear sir, let me lay open my sin and my shame unto you, I solemnly subscribed to the articles of our church; and gave my hearty assent and consent to them. Amongst the rest, I declared that, "We are accounted righteous before God, only for the merits of our Lord and Saviour Jesus Christ by faith, and not for our own works and deservings, and that we are justified by faith only," as it is expressed in the eleventh article. But though I solemnly subscribed this article, I neither believed nor preached it; but preached salvation partly by faith and partly by works. And oh, what dreadful hypocrisy, what shameful prevarication was this! I called and thought myself a churchman, though I was really a dissenter and a schismatic; for I was undermining the fundamental doctrine of our church, and the fundamental doctrine of the gospel, namely justification by faith only, and yet, dreadful as my case was, I fear it is the case of most of the clergy in England.'[8]

Berridge is not surprised to find that those who are convicted of sin and converted are often forced to leave the established church in order to find food for their souls. However, he did not consider it a fundamental issue for people to leave the established church, as the Wesleys did. Many of the congregations that he founded were to follow that path, but what was important to him was spiritual life. He had an excellent relationship with nonconformist ministers and congregations and enjoyed and stressed the oneness they had in Christ. Joshua Symonds, who was pastor of the Bunyan Meeting in Bedford from 1766–1788, wrote of visiting 'my dear and good friend the Rev'd Mr Berridge'.[9] Berridge wrote to Thornton asking for help for a nonconformist minister in financial trouble. He preached regularly in one of the main nonconformist chapels in London and spoke of the Tabernacle as 'that old bee-hive, which has filled many hives with her swarms'.[10] He took part in the ordination of one of its ministers. He wrote to Lady Huntingdon not to think ill of dissenters, for the students that she was trying to prepare for the ministry of the Church of England would be regarded by the authorities as dissenters because of the doctrine that they preached. 'Dissenters may appear wrong to you. God hath his remnant among them, therefore lift not up your head against them for the Lord's sake; nor yet for consistency's sake, because your students are as real dissenting preachers as any in the land, unless a gown and band can make a clergyman. The bishops look on your students as the worst kind of dissenters; and manifest this by refusing that ordination to your preachers which would be readily granted to other teachers among the dissenters.'[11]

One area where Berridge was deeply pessimistic about the established church was the question of evangelical succession in a parish. The solution of evangelicals buying livings, in order to control the type of clergy inducted to them, which was to come with Charles Simeon's ecclesiastical statesmanship or politics, does not seem to have occurred to him. Perhaps this was because of his stress on spiritual reality rather than on organizational solutions. The circumstances in which he moved called for immediate preaching action and he remained pessimistic about the future of evangelical congregations in the Church of England.

C. Smyth criticizes Berridge's evangelistic work for failing to create the type of organization necessary to carry on the work and this is certainly true if one thinks of the Church of England. The problem of who follows in leadership either illustrates Berridge's weakness in his general view of the church and its organization or else confirms his suspicion of all external forms and conviction of the need for the direct working of God.

When Lady Huntingdon wrote that God was sending many labourers into the Church of England he agreed but raised the problem of succession. He considered that this increase was 'with a view, I think, of calling his people out of it; because, when such ministers are removed by death, or transported to another vineyard, I see no fresh gospel labourer succeed them, which obliges the forsaken flocks to fly to a meeting. And what else can they do? If they have tasted of manna, and hunger for it, they cannot feed on heathen chaff, nor yet on legal crusts, though baked by some staunch Pharisee quite up to perfection.

'What has become of Mr Venn's Yorkshire flock? What will become of his Yelling flock, or of my flocks at our decease?'[12] This blunt rhetorical question shows Berridge's pessimism, for indeed the large Christian congregation that Venn had built up at Huddersfield had left the church when a non-evangelical vicar arrived and built a nonconformist chapel with Venn's financial support. He criticized John Thornton for offering a new living to Dr Conyers, because he thought that the congregation that Conyers would be leaving at Helmsley would be given over to wolves. He was equally gloomy about the continuance of evangelical life at Everton after his own death.

The work at Everton did in fact continue under the leadership of Whittingham who, although he seems to have obtained a living for himself in the late 1780s, apparently returned to help before Berridge's death and continued until 1807, when he moved to Potton as vicar. It would seem that the new vicar appointed by Clare College after Berridge's death was in agreement with the same type of preaching being maintained although there is no suggestion that he was an evangelical himself. Large congregations were maintained and in 1795 the churchwardens reported that the church building was 'very fully crowded with a numerous congregation by persons who do not belong to the parish'.[13]

Some, however, did make the break at Berridge's death, with many of those from Sandy (about three miles away) going to join the Baptists at Blunham before opening and founding their own church in Sandy. An independent Baptist congregation at nearby Potton also dates from this time.

At the bottom of Berridge's pessimism on the problem of succession in his own church was the distinction he made between converted ministers, a small minority, and unconverted ministers who formed the vast majority. Speaking of succession, he says that 'Whenever a gospel clergyman comes, and meets with success, at his removal, I never see a gospel clergyman succeed him, and of course his flock must become dissenters to get food, for awakened sinners cannot live upon chaff.'[14]

It is little wonder that soon after his conversion Berridge was sending out ordinary working-class men to preach the gospel in the villages around Cambridgeshire if they had what he called the 'gift of utterance'. He had a very low view of the majority of clergy, considering that many were only in the establishment for the money and could not preach without their tithes. The doctrines of grace were a great offence to them and he counselled his workers not to reply when railed at by local clergy. He considered that the majority were preaching the soul-destroying doctrine of faith and works as he had done himself before conversion.

As we have seen, he was looked upon as a dangerous character by the majority of clergy and there were very few clergy for miles around who had any sympathy with his message. Perhaps one reason for his poor image in the nineteenth century is that later evangelicals in the Church of England were to soften the clear distinctions drawn by

Berridge. C. Smyth, summarizing Berridge's own logic on
the distinction he draws between converted and unconverted ministers, says that once this distinction was granted 'It
was difficult not to be impatient of church order, and it was
difficult not to despair of preserving continuity of gospel-
teaching in any parish.'[15]

Berridge's attitude to his church's articles can seem
confusing and vacillating in the light of his explicit teaching
on the need for personal faith in Christ to be right with God.
Although he felt that the doctrinal statements in the Prayer
Book about the plan of salvation were correct, he was fully
aware that sacramentalists apppealed to the Prayer Book in
their teaching on baptismal regeneration, and did so with
justification. He could declare, 'I cordially approve the
doctrines and liturgy of the Church of England'[16] and wish a
student from Cambridge would leave his scruples about the
articles and liturgy at Everton when he returned to his
college, and yet he could argue against oratorios being sung
in Christian congregations on the grounds that no one has
the right to appoint offices or ordinances but the Lord
himself. 'All human inventions are innovations of his
authority, neither expedient nor lawful.'[17]

His attitude to infant baptism shows something of the
tension that Church of England evangelicals have lived
with. In *The Christian World Unmasked* he sets the issue in the
context of his evangelical preaching when challenging the
notion that because the patient lives in a baptized country
he is himself a Christian. 'But, you say, we sojourn in a
baptized country. True; the country swarmeth with
baptized rakes, baptized worldlings, and baptized infidels.
A watery profession, without the Spirit's baptism, will never
wash the heart from pride, and subdue it to the gospel
doctrines; and legal righteousness will set the heart still
more against them.'[18] When challenged later that he was
reviling church baptism he makes a long reply which shows
what his attitude was in the early 1770s: 'No, sir; not at all. I
only meant to keep you from relying on baptismal water,
without the Spirit's baptism. I have no doubt that infant
baptism is attended with the same blessing now, as infant
circumcision was formerly. Both the ordinances are of God's
appointment, and introductory rites into his visible church

on earth. The Jews were saved as Christians are, by faith; the gospel-covenant belonged to them, as well as to ourselves; only the introducing rite was different. And if Jewish children were received into the church's fold by circumcision, why not Christian children too by baptism? Nothing is said to forbid them. Jesus encouraged the bringing of little children to him, and rebuked his disciples when they sought to prevent it. And how can little children now be brought to Jesus, but by baptism?

'I believe, as anciently was taught, that baptismal water, through the grace of Christ, does wash away the guilt of original or birth-sin; and that baptised children, who die before they can discern between good and evil, and of course are not guilty of actual sin, will be saved; but that children dying unbaptized are left to God's uncovenanted mercy. And what that is no man can tell.

'Long before the law was given, God declares to Abraham that an uncircumcised child shall be cut off from his people: he hath broken my covenant (Gen. 17:14). These are awful words, and should be well attended to. The covenant here spoken of is not the Sinai covenant, but the covenant of grace. Circumcision was the outward sign of this covenant to Abraham, as baptism is to us. The outward rite is different, but the covenant the same. And therefore this awful threat against neglecting infant circumcision may cast a further look to the sister-rite of infant-baptism.

'I would hate no man, and do condemn no man, for thinking differently in this matter; yet, I feel a tender brother's love for many, and can lay them on my heart, though they do think differently; yet surely it behoveth every parent to act very cautiously. No harm can possibly arise from baptizing an infant; but harm may arise from neglecting baptism. Such neglect may be considered as contempt; so it was considered formerly, and so it may now.'[19]

There are arguments here which do not seem consistent with his gospel message and it seems that Berridge recognized this to some degree in his last paragraph. He was greatly aware of the false gospel that sacramentalism could be if relied upon for grace.

Baptismal water I have had,
And hold the water needful too
Yet sure I need the Spirit's aid
To wash my heart, and make it new.[20]

Towards the end of his life he was more blunt and seemed willing to face up to this issue more directly: 'I do not much prize our Church Catechism; it begins so very ill, calling baptism our new birth, and making us thereby members of Christ, children of God, and heirs of the kingdom of heaven. Mr Stillingfleet should have spoken more fully and pointed about this weighty matter; for all carnal churchmen fancy they are new born, because baptized, and quote the Catechism as a proof of it, and the carnal clergy preach accordingly, and quote the same authority. The acting as sponsors is now become a mere farce, and a gossiping business: and the promising for infants, what they cannot engage for themselves, may suit a covenant of works, but not a covenant of grace.'[21]

There was one area where Berridge differed radically from other evangelical incumbents, with the exception of Grimshaw, and that was his belief and practice of itinerant preaching in other parishes. It is this view which is at the root of many of his ideas on other church issues and it is for this continual practice over many years that he was regarded as 'eccentric' in the eighteenth-century connotation of 'going beyond one's true sphere of duty'. He certainly deviated from normal belief and practice in holding it to be not only his right, but his obligation to preach what he understood to be the truth to all who would hear, whether the particular vicar of the parish welcomed him or not. Smyth sums up by saying, 'No Anglican incumbent of his day defied Church Order more violently than John Berridge, or with as much impunity.'[22]

Nineteenth-century evangelicals, writing two or three generations later, would join in the condemnation although they generally gave excuses for Berridge's approach. Abner Brown recalls Charles Simeon saying that he thought that Berridge was right in preaching from place to place as 'He lived when few ministers cared about the gospel, and when disorder was almost needful. I don't think he would do now as he did then; for there are so many means of hearing the gospel, and a much less need of disorder. To do now as he did then would do much harm.'[23]

Cecil wrote in 1798: 'I love consistency. If you think you have a general call to evangelize and to go about proclaiming the glad tidings of salvation, then you cannot conscientiously enter the established church. Now I don't call Mr Whitefield or Mr Berridge inconsistent characters. They entered the church in the simplicity of their hearts; God afterwards called them to another line. . . But to promise regularity while at the same time a man intends to be irregular, cannot be done with a good conscience.'[24]

John Venn excused his father's preaching in 'unconsecrated' places by saying that he did not encourage it in others. Berridge does not need any excuses for his behaviour; he acted consistently in this matter throughout his life and was sorry when his friend Venn succeeded in stopping the young Charles Simeon from adopting his own practice. Berridge wrote with passion to John Thornton hoping that he might influence Venn against discouraging Simeon (who was helping Venn at Yelling) from itinerant preaching: 'Yelling church is well attended under Mr Simeon's afternoon ministry. A brave Christian sergeant he is, having the true spirit of an evangelist; but his feet are often put in the stocks by the Archdeacon of Yelling, who is doubtless become a vagabond preacher as well as myself, a right gospel hawker and pedlar, but seems desirous of having the trade to himself. Through mercy he is grown as scandalous as I could wish him, yet he wants to fasten the shackle on Simeon, which he has dropped from himself. Oh, worldly prudence, what a prudish foe thou art to grace!'[25] The whole history of evangelicalism in the Church of England might well have been different if Charles Simeon had followed Berridge in breaking with traditions.

Berridge felt strongly that what was called irregularity was actually regularity in the eyes of God. He wrote to David Simpson who had asked for advice about itinerant preaching: 'If you are invited to go out, and feel yourself inclined to do so, take a lover's leap, neck or nothing, and commit yourself to Jesus. Ask no man's leave to preach Christ; that is unevangelical and shameful. Seek not much advice about it; that is dangerous. Such advice, I found, comes the wrong way, heels uppermost. Most preachers love a smug church, and a whole skin; and what they love they will prescribe. If you are determined to be evangelically regular, i.e. secularly irregular, then expect, wherever you go, a storm will follow you, which may fright you, but will do no real harm. Make the Lord your whole trust, and all will be well.'[26]

Berridge indeed thought that the major difficulty would come from evangelical ministers. He wrote to Charles Simeon, 'The chief block in your way will be from prudent Peters, who will beg and entreat you to avoid irregularity. Give them the same answer that Christ gave Peter (Matt.16:23). They savour of the things that be of men; heed them not.'[27] Rowland Hill's adopting of itineration was a thrill to Berridge: 'The more scandalous you grow, I mean evangelical scandalous, the more I must love you.'[28] A 'riding pedlar' or 'a recruiting sergeant' was glorifying God, whatever the world or the religious establishment or evangelical brethren might think. For Berridge obedience to declaring the gospel was a matter of obedience to God, not men. He was indeed under obligation.

Berridge's motivation was extremely simple: 'Must salvation give place to a fanciful decency and sinners go flocking to hell through our dread of irregularity?'[29] The 'parish way of going unto Jesus Christ'[30] was based on decency and good works, a theology that was bereft of spiritual truth and power. Satan was so much in the pulpit that 'some people fancy that the devil sure is dead, and that hell-fire is quite burnt out'.[31] Christendom was not true Christianity. A man must be born again, not by forms and ceremonies or his own righteousness, but by the Spirit of truth producing a new heart and mind. It was the simplicity of the need and the failure of the established church to meet that need that motivated Berridge: 'If every parish church were blessed with a gospel minister, there would be little need of itinerant preaching; but since those ministers are thinly scattered about the country, and neighbouring pulpits are usually locked up against them, it behoves them to take advantage of fields, or barns, or houses, to cast abroad the gospel seed.'[32]

In order to understand Berridge's churchmanship we must come to grips with his understanding of the gospel itself. He took advantage of the freedom given by his position as a Church of England vicar (which was probably greater than he would have enjoyed if he had opted for the nonconformist alternative) for spreading of the truth as he saw it. Such a policy may have been inconsistent and have created problems for both establishment and nonconformist positions, but, as in other things, Berridge was not typical; he was his own man. Many were thankful for his itineration, whether or not they agreed with him on matters of church organization.

# 24.
# Berridge: the shepherd and friend

The gifts of evangelism and those of shepherding the flock are not necessarily found in the same person. Berridge, in holding responsibility for a particular flock and also engaging in itinerant preaching and church founding, exercised both of these functions. As his Christian experience deepened he became more useful in his shepherding role. He comforted and warned in his inimitable way over the normal pastoral concerns of depression, death, lack of assurance, the attacks of Satan and sickness. His letters show he was a great encourager to his fellow believers. There was nothing cold and remote about Berridge: he was a man who entered into the concerns and feelings of others.

In the early days, with all the calls for preaching in other parts of the country, Berridge was convinced that these roles must not be separated as long as he had a responsibility in a particular area. Lady Huntingdon had asked him to preach at her chapel at Bath but he believed he had been disciplined by God for not concentrating on his own area. Berridge thought that a wide-ranging commission was nearest to that of the apostles and was highly honoured, but in his own case there was a congregation to care for as well as the weekly circuit around the area. By 1767 he was determined to keep close to his own fold and, with the exception of his winter preaching in London, he seems to have remained faithful to this conviction.

Like other evangelical clergy Berridge used his house for meetings and hospitality. The serious people of the parish came to the house about seven o'clock on Saturday evenings and on Sunday his house and table were open for the many travellers. We have seen that in the early days he was constantly visited by those enquiring concerning their spiritual state and he encouraged people to meet together in societies, although not ones with strict rules, because he saw the need for mutual care. 'The decay of true religion in a kingdom is greatly owing to the decay of religious societies. Preaching kindles the fire of grace, but societies nurse and keep the flame alive.'[1]

As with preaching, visiting depended for its effect on the quality of the shepherd's communion with God. 'Much secret prayer will solemnize your heart, and make your visits savoury as well as your sermons. The old Puritans visited their flocks by house row; the visits were short; they talked a little for God, and then concluded with prayer to God. An excellent rule, which prevented tittle-tattle, and made visits profitable.'[2] Berridge had the gift of turning conversations to spiritual ends and Whittingham notes that many who met him remembered the conversation years afterwards. He had a real love for the believers in the area and when he spoke about some only paying occasional visits to Everton in the mid-eighties because they were attending more local meetings he looked forward to meeting them above: 'I shall meet them all by and by, and a blessed meeting it will be when sheep and shepherds will give to Jesus all the glory of it.'[3]

In his pastoral advice, which we can glean from his letters, there is the same openness and honest confrontation with the issues as in his preaching. There is no hint of easy mechanical solutions to spiritual problems but a desire to have a right attitude and of waiting for the Lord's direction. Berridge confronts a young man perplexed about the direction of his life with the fact that his present perplexing experiences will be for his good: 'How can you tell what others feel, unless you have felt the same yourself? How can you sympathize with a prisoner, unless your own feet have been fast in the stocks? How can you comfort those who are cast down, unless you have been often at your wit's end? Expect nothing but conflicts, day after day, to humble and prove you.'[4] In discussing assurance in one of his sermon notes he confirms that it 'may be higher or lower at various seasons',[5] and that the Christian in this life will not always abide on the mount but must come down to the battle.

Although assurance may thus vary, 'Believers may have assurance of their acceptance with God, when they are wrestling with tears and supplications, as when they are exulting with joy. A man's assurance may be as true, though not so joyous, when lying on the earth through a sense of sin, as when lifted up to heaven by a foretaste of glory.'[6] To someone doubting the reality of his own profession Berridge counselled the evidence of the Word and the Spirit. It is not 'the strength of faith but the reality of it'[7] on which salvation depends. Writing to a woman in London on the same subject he agreed that 'Good frames are desirable things, and to be sought after, yet we are apt to judge of ourselves too much from our frames, and too little from the Word of God.'[8] In his farewell sermon he directed the people to trust Christ: 'If you cannot with full assurance, do it with some assurance, with a little faith, and expect more.'[9] The subjective enjoyment would follow the objective exercise of faith for 'The faith producing heavenly peace, and the peace produced, are both the gift of God.'[10]

Much of his advice came from his own experience concerning the goodness of God in all circumstances: 'Afflictions have been to me some of my greatest mercies.'[11] Samuel Wilks, who held a high office in the East India Company, experienced troubles, but for Berridge these very difficulties were encouragements: 'The Lord has led you through a variety of scenes, but he knows what he does, and does all things well. Sitting safely on the beach is very sweet after a stormy voyage; but I fancy you will find it more difficult to walk closely with Jesus in a calm than a storm, in easy circumstances than in strait. A Christian never falls asleep in the fire or in the water, but grows drowsy in the sunshine. We love to nestle, but cannot make a nest in a hard bed.'[12]

To a fellow preacher in London Berridge speaks of the wonder of heaven and the need for continual discipline while here on earth: 'Here below we are often meeting and parting but above we shall meet to part no more. And oh, what a meeting! when this noisy world and the roaring lion will be far removed, and the body of sin be wholly broken down; when the soul will be all peace, all love, all joy, and become all eye to gaze on Jesus, and from his sweetness and fulness drink eternal pleasure in. No fretful look, nor envious eye, nor jarring note is there; for every vessel is quite full, and every harp is well in tune and every string rebounds with purest thankfulness. But we must remember, brother, that daily tribulation comes before this blessed meeting: bitter herbs and bitter draughts are needful food or physic for a sickly stomach.'[13]

As he visited sick believers he would perhaps sing one of his hymns asking for spiritual gain in the trial:

> Support his heart and hold his head,
> And sanctify the rod;
> Purge out the dross which health has bred,
> And draw his heart to God.
>
> Bestow a calm and patient mind,
> With strength to suffer pain,
> And in the furnace let him find
> Some rich and solid gain.[14]

He counselled the believer in great bodily weakness to look to the future:

> Afflicted soul, lift up thine eyes
> To Jesus' glorious throne;
> Thy mourning days, and pensive sighs
> Will all be quickly gone.[15]

Again experience underlines his advice towards the end of his life to a lady not to argue with Satan: 'I dare not argue with Satan, but cast myself at Jesus' feet, committing soul and body to him. . .'[16] Berridge quickly turned enquirers to the positive aspects of their own lives. He wrote to one full of deep troubles: 'If you see no family so afflicted as yours, can you find any family so blessed? All of one heart and one mind seeking after Jesus.'[17] His counsel constantly centred on the need for spiritual perspectives and on the continual need of Christians for discipline from a loving Father who has their best interests at heart.

As a shepherd he was not prepared to comfort those who needed challenge, nor console those who needed to exercise faith. His funeral hymns challenge the non-committed

about their state before God and the transitory nature of
life.

> Pray cast a look upon that bier,
> A corpse must preach today,
> It tells the old, and young, and fair,
> Their house is built of clay.
>
> The funeral knell you heard today,
> By tolling tells your doom;
> The hours are posting fast away,
> To lodge you in the tomb.
>
> But are you wash'd in Jesus' blood,
> And thus prepared to die?
> His blood alone gives peace with God
> And ripens for the sky.[18]

However, for the Christian death is a joyful prospect and
Berridge himself continually looked forward to seeing his
Master:

> O happy soul, who safely past
> Thy weary warfare here,
> Arrived at Jesus' seat at last
> And ended all thy care!
>
> Adieu vain world, the spirit cries,
> All tears are wip'd away;
> My Jesus fills my cup with joys,
> And fills it every day.[19]

His consolations and advice to friends whose partners had
died are spiritually motivated even though the bluntness
may shock our twentieth-century sensibilities. To his dear
friend and benefactor John Thornton he wrote that now the
rib was gone he must lean firmer on the staff. Berridge
thought that Thornton would now be able to assess what
was really needful in terms of life-style and seek more
communion with God. He concluded this section of his
letter with a typical challenge: 'What a mercy, you need not

fly to worldly amusements for relief, and run away from yourself to find comfort! Along with plenty of this world's husks, the prodigal's food, God has bestowed a pearl on you which createth an appetite for spiritual cheer, and bringeth royal dainties into the bosom. May this season of mourning be sweetened with a sense of the Lord's presence, bringing many tokens of fatherly love, and sanctifying the visitation, by drawing the heart more vigorously unto God, and fixing it on him!'[20]

A few days earlier he had written to John Newton and his wife rejoicing at 'the gentle dismission and blessed translation of Eliza, no longer your niece, but the Lord's bride, trained up for wedding at your own house and church, and solemnly espoused Oct 6.'[21]

To Lady Huntingdon, grieving her daughter's death, he stressed that he could not soothe her or flatter her and wished her to think on what it meant for her daughter to be with Christ. Lady Huntingdon remained upset for some time and although Berridge felt for her he wanted her to face the issues: 'I find your heart was sorely pained, and I pitied you but durst not soothe you; for soothing, though it eases grief for a moment only makes Lady Self grow more burdensome, and occasions more tears in the end. A little whipping from your Father will dry up your tears much sooner than a thousand lullabies from your brethren. And I now hope you will be well soon.'[22]

In a letter quoted in chapter 21 he chided a fellow believer for his grief. How could he grieve over his wife's present state when she had arrived at her Father's house? Such trouble and weeping was shameful and Berridge prayed that God would comfort him and give to him a triumphant entrance into God's kingdom. After reading such a letter, so full of the joys of heaven, we see the continual desire of Berridge's pastoral advice – a renewing of the mind according to the purposes of God.

We can infer from his letters that exhortation as well as challenge played a prominent part in his shepherding. His letters are full of positive encouragements to his correspondents. The one letter to Whitefield that we possess reveals a warmth, openness and affection which speak of a genuine relationship. Both men suffered from the same physical difficulty of asthma and were to die from asthmatic attacks. Both men had been experiencing difficulties and Berridge quickly added a word of encouragement: 'These thorns often seem to us a mere dead weight, but prove an excellent ballast, and keep every ship from oversetting. When we get into port, we shall drop our ballast, this house of correction. Oh, for a safe passage and a happy landing! To be met and welcomed by Jesus, and embraced in the arms of this faithful and unchangeable Friend. Come, my brother, let us trudge on. Whilst I creep, do you run, and the Lord direct our feet, and quicken our pace, and prosper our work continually.'[23]

Writing to a fellow worker in Essex, he sympathized with his many troubles and shared his own experiences: 'Be not discouraged at your trials; Jesus will help you out, and help you through.'[24] Cornelius Winter acknowledged that the letters Berridge wrote him concerning guidance were of a great help. Berridge was always encouraging his younger brethren to work and preach. It was through Berridge's recommendation that Cornelius Winter first preached at the Tabernacle. The letters to Rowland Hill are full of exhortations to wait on the Lord only and to praise God for his success. It was Berridge, aged forty-eight, and in the midst of great success, who sought out Rowland Hill at Cambridge and sought to encourage his work and witness amongst the students and later in itinerant preaching. A typical example of exhortation to Hill is the following: 'My dear Rowly, give up yourself wholly to Jesus, and freely employ body and soul, and sustenance, in his service. Work while the day lasteth, for life, health, are uncertain, and what your hand findeth to do, do it with all your might.'[25] It was through Berridge that the Baptist minister at Cambridge, Robert Robinson, was encouraged to preach in the surrounding villages. Lay preachers and Sunday preachers in the area were encouraged both practically and by example. His encouragement to a friend who was a curate at Lakenheath and threatened with expulsion by his vicar was to ponder the sovereignty of God and leave matters in the hands of God: 'Be not anxious, be not fretful, be a little child, and your Lord will direct your paths.'[26]

Berridge was grateful for John Newton's writings and sermons. There are gems of encouragement and stimulus in their correspondence. After Newton's early publications Berridge wrote, 'It is pleasant to behold the improvements of a Christian. May your heart keep pace with your understanding.'[27] Fifteen years later Berridge compliments Newton in a typical Berridge fashion: 'All ministers should preach about Jesus, but only his secretaries are fit to write about him.'[28] When Newton moved to London Berridge was wishing him well: 'I hope you find some refreshing seasons in your new barn floor, and some grain beating out of the straw. Present my very kind Christian respects to Mrs Newton; and if you could peep into my bosom, you might see how much you are loved and esteemed by J.B.'[29]

He encouraged John Thornton in all his activities and indeed they seem to have had a special relationship. Berridge, as others, was deeply impressed with the generosity of this very rich man who gave so much of his wealth away. Because of Thornton's benevolence Berridge confessed an inclination to make a little Christ of him. However, he was aware that if he trusted a benefactor rather than God, Christ would remove the benefactor. He counselled Thornton: 'As you keep abounding in good works, may you also grow rich in faith and abound in sweet humility, feeling yourself nothing, and living as a pauper daily on heavenly alms.'[30] After receiving a gift for the relief of those in Biggleswade affected by a fire, Berridge reminded Thornton of spiritual riches: 'The Lord has rewards of grace to give, and such you are seeking, being blest with a supernatural ambition of coveting the best things. Most of the wealthy prove bankrupts or beggars at last, spend all, or leave behind, live rich and die poor, regale their palate here with the choicest wines, and cannot gain a drop of water hereafter to cool their tongue. But God is making you wealthy for both worlds. Providence provides the nether springs for you, and grace is preparing the upper.'[31]

Sometimes a warning note is present, as illustrated in a letter to a Mr Adams who had just married a believer well known to Berridge. After congratulating him Berridge shows his concern that he really is a Christian and then moves on to warn him concerning his business: 'If your family should increase, I hope that will not induce you to enlarge your business immoderately. The cares of the world are as fatal as its pleasures. The former, like cancers, eat up the heart; the latter, like syrens, bewitch it. You will remember for what purpose labour was appointed, not for the sake of thriving, but of eating. "In the sweat of thy face shalt thou eat bread." And "they that will be rich", are willing, are desirous to be rich, trade with this view, though ever so honestly, "fall into many snares". Labouring for bread to eat is part of the curse; therefore make it not a greater curse than God intended.'[32]

Berridge's exhortatory style is seen in a letter to Samuel Wilks. He quickly passes from his own inadequacy to the faithfulness of Jesus. It is little wonder that the recipients kept letters like these.

Everton,
April 8th, 1774

Dear Sir,

I received a kind letter from you in town, which I laid in a drawer along with some others, and intended to call upon you before I left London; but a cold, attended with much feebleness of body, prevented my going out some weeks. When my cold was somewhat removed, your letter had wholly escaped my memory, and did not occur to my thoughts till it presented itself to my view on rummaging the drawers to pack up my things for my journey. Well, dear sir, though you have had a very forgetful preacher you have a kind remembering God, a faithful Jesus, who watches over his vineyard day and night, lest any should hurt it. And what a mercy it is, that your beloved partner and yourself are both looking and drawing the same way. The Lord draw you both near to his side, and keep you there. Troubles you need and troubles will sprout up every day from within and without; but a sweet view of Jesus will make rough ways smooth, and rough winds calm. Our business is to follow Christ with the heart as well as life, in the affections as well as actions, and to cultivate a closer acquaintance and stricter union with him. The nearer our union is, the sweeter will be our communion; and the end both of tribulation and consolation is to drive us or lead us nearer to Jesus. Old pilgrims, I find, are apt to talk of past attainments, and to nestle in them; by which they soon become dry-skinned, and footsore, and formal. Oh, dear sir, let us be ambitious of the best things, and daily covet more of the true riches; pursuing our heavenly calling as men pursue a worldly one, with all our might. No traffic so sure and so gainful as Christian traffic; and no laziness so shameful as Christian laziness. The Lord help us to gird up our loins, and trim our lamps! The Lord make us watchful and prayerful, looking and longing for the coming of the Bridegroom!

I feel a Christian affection for you; but you must not be jealous when I tell you honestly, I find a stronger affection for your wife. My love for you is brotherly; for her, is fatherly; and none but a spiritual father knows what affection he bears to his children. The Lord bless you both. Grace and peace be with you, and with your affectionate servant, for Christ's sake,

J.B.[33]

These short glimpses from his letters give us some feel of his concern for believers, his desire for their spiritual growth and development and his ability to raise people from the mundane to spiritual issues and to the Lord himself. There is little doubt that Berridge had unusual views about some issues, but his strength as a shepherd lay in feeding on Christ and not in special teachings, kinds of churches or special seasons of encouragement. His openness and frankness in dealing with fundamental spiritual problems must have endeared him to those who sought his advice and his testimony to the goodness and greatness of his Saviour reinforced pastoral concern with a living witness.

# 25.
# Berridge: the hymn-writer

Berridge was a pioneer in his attitude towards the place of hymns in the established church. Hymn-singing was well established amongst nonconformists and an outstanding feature of Methodist societies was their fondness for hymns. The established church on the whole limited congregational singing to the metrical versions of the Psalms and it was left to the evangelicals in the Church of England to introduce hymn-books in the latter part of the eighteenth century. Not that all evangelical clergy agreed with the practice, and some, like William Romaine, objected strongly to the very principle of the place of poetry, as human compositions, occupying such a prominent place in public worship.

Berridge's own collection for congregational use[1] was one of the first of several such collections to be published by evangelical clergy in the next thirty years.[2] Although this collection may have contained a few originals it mainly consisted of the hymns of John and Charles Wesley, many of which Berridge had revised for his rural audience in the interests of ease of understanding. Due to Berridge's theological changes in the sixties he was to regret the publication of this collection as some of the hymns contained perfectionist and Arminian sentiments which he later came to oppose. He gives the reasons for his dissatisfaction with his first collection in the preface to his own hymn-book published much later: 'I was not wholly satisfied with the collection I had published. The bells, indeed, had been chiefly cast in a celebrated foundry, and in ringing were tunable enough, none more so, but a clear gospel tone was not found in them all. Human wisdom and strength, perfection and merit, give Sion's bells a Levitical twang and drown the mellow tone of the gospel outright.'[3] He therefore gave up its use.

In the preface to the 1785 hymn-book Berridge confirms the low state of much public worship at that time: 'Psalm-singing is become vulgar business in our churches. This tax of praise is collected chiefly from an organ, or a solitary clerk, or some bawling voices in a singing loft. The congregation may listen if they please, or talk in whispers, or take a gentle nap.'[4] Because few would own a hymn-book the hymns, like the psalms, would be sung line by line. Berridge's own view on what makes a good hymn is seen from his comments on the *Olney Hymns* written by his friends John Newton and William Cowper: 'They are experimental and sound; the language intelligible to all believers; and the sense sufficiently closing at the end of each line: a very needful thing in public worship, where many are destitute of a hymn-book.'[5] After the withdrawal of the 1760 collection the congregation presumably carried on the usual practice of singing line by line which, because of illiteracy, would not have been dropped even when some possessed books.

Not only must hymns combine orthodoxy with devotion, they must be sung in a way which unites rather than divides. In the preface to the 1760 hymn-book he wrote against ostentation and signs of overt enthusiasm: 'Avoid all waving of the hand, or tossing of the head, or beating with the foot, in singing: leave these affectations to the mouth-singers. Aim not to make as great a noise as you can in singing; but rather seek after softness and sweetness than loudness: and let no one strive to be heard above the rest, for this springs from pride, a pride to be distinguished from the rest.'[6]

Berridge actually turned to writing hymns as a form of diversion during his long illness in the early seventies. Writing in 1785 he says, 'Ill health some years past, having kept me from travelling or preaching, I took up the trade of hymn-making, a handicraft much followed of late, but a business I was not born or bred to, and undertaken chiefly to keep a long sickness from preying on my spirit, and to make tedious nights pass over more smoothly. Some tinkling employment was wanted, which might amuse and not fatigue me.'[7]

It seems that a good number, if not the majority, of the

songs published in 1785 as *Zion's Songs or Hymns composed for
the use of them that love and follow the Lord Jesus Christ in sincerity*
were written within six months in 1773. Berridge wrote in
the preface that 'Twelve years ago these hymns were
composed in a six months illness, and have since laid
neglected by me: often threatened with the fire, but have
escaped that martyrdom. Fatherly mercy prevented that
literary death; for authors can seldom prove cruel to their
offspring, however deformed.'[8]

Although it was not his forte, towards the end of his life
Berridge was willing to add about ninety stanzas of verses to
Thornton's revision of Bogatzky's daily readings, and perhaps he enjoyed this trade more than he realized. Concerning the 1785 hymn-book he asked a blessing from God in a
typical manner: 'What is water in the hymns, turn into wine,
by giving them a charge to enliven the hearts of thy
children, and to stir up the wills of aliens to seek thy
salvation. Only attend them with an unction of thy Spirit,
and whatever be the hymns, thy glory shall be promoted by
them.'[9] He offered them to the reader supposing that he will
find in them that which is common to all hymn productions:
'some things to blame, and some to commend'.[10]

It is difficult to understand why Berridge published this
collection of his own hymns in the light of what he himself
said was his motivation for writing the majority of them.
Perhaps the publication of other collections encouraged him
to do it or perhaps he found challenge and encouragement
in rereading the struggles through which he had come and
thought that they might encourage others on the same path.
There is little doubt that the hymns are intensely personal
and contain much autobiographical material. 'Berridge's
hymns reflect, to an extent displayed by no other writer
except Joseph Hart, the conflicts and other experiences of
his own soul.'[11] Although very helpful to the biographer in
showing Berridge's experimental theology and method of
thinking, the hymns on the whole seem more suited to
private reading rather than public singing.

Perhaps another motive for their publication was that
they spoke of issues which were avoided to some extent in
other collections. These hymns were not published for
nominal Christianity but for those who drew their supplies

from Christ: 'Where human pageantry appears in any shape, Jesus Christ is veiled by it; and much of this is found among us. Human wealth, human grandeur, human litera- ture, all naturally producing human loftiness, have almost buried Jesus in Great Britain. The power of godliness is gone, and the form is scampering after it. The Head of the Christian body is dishonoured and rejected; and the members can have no life apart from the Head. These hymns are likely to please no one, who is pleased with himself. They are designed to set a man at variance with himself, and to show that his worst foes are lodged in his own breast. Nor yet will they satisfy a Laodician professor, who is neither cold nor hot, and seemeth to be rich, but is poor, having an head full of knowledge, and a heart full of mammon, talking bravely of the doctrines of faith, but a stranger to holiness and the life of faith. My kindly readers must be such as feel they have no spiritual supplies in themselves, nor ability to lay up stores for a future supply, and therefore live as daily pensioners on the Saviour's bounty: having vital union with him by faith, producing conformity to him; and centring all their hope in him, while receiving all supplies from him.'[12]

Berridge seems to have borrowed the occasional line from other sources and it is strange that he did not acknowledge his sources. Whittingham was unaware of this as he states, 'The hymns which he composed during a cessation from public labours occasioned by illness, are perfectly original.'[13] The borrowings only came to light afterwards. J.C. Philpot acknowledged that Berridge had borrowed from Erskine's *Gospel Sonnets*, a fact he was completely unaware of when he wrote his preface to a new edition of the hymn- book, and he concluded, 'I cannot think the plagiarism to be so extensive or its confession so indispensable, as to nullify either that originality, or that honesty which I have pointed out as characteristics of his hymns.'[14] Gadsby hints at a wider plagiarism: 'They were not all strictly original, as some were made up from Allen and Batty, Cennick, Erskine etc,'[15] whereas R. Butterworth sums up his own research by concluding that 'The borrowings and adaptations from Methodist sources are very few, not extending beyond one hymn and an occasional line.'[16]

Although the hymns have been largely ignored by evangelical writers they must have had a certain appeal, for up to the time of Philpot's revised edition in 1842 there had been at least six editions and reprints. Ryle makes no excuse for ignoring the hymns: 'The hymns I shall leave alone. The vicar of Everton was no more a poet than Cicero or Julius Caesar; and although the doctrine of his hymns is very sound, the poetry of them is very poor, while the ideas they occasionally present are painfully ludicrous.'[17] J.C. Philpot, after speaking of the value of the hymns says, 'Berridge has few poetic ornaments. His rhymes are often false, his metre limping, his language slovenly and ungrammatical, and his expressions rude and coarse. But there is a heavenly unction which buries all defects. . .'[18]

However these hymns are judged, it is this recognition of their spiritual insight that demands our attention rather than their value as poetry. Berridge never claimed to be a poet, although he did know how to communicate, and it is perhaps the unusualness and directness of many of these hymns that mean that they will have only a limited appeal. William Wileman, who published the notes from Berridge's study Bible, thought that Berridge, 'as a writer of hymns for public worship, must not be judged by the refined taste of the poet, nor will his productions bear a rigid comparison with the loftier strains of Watts, or the more stately stanzas of Toplady. His pithy quaintness, so often considered a defect, only serves slightly to veil the rich and mellow experience of divine truth interwoven with every line.'[19]

The hymns were written for all believers. This was important for Berridge, with his negative views on controversy, as we have seen. In the preface he expresses this point as follows: 'My heart, I think, is open to embrace every one of every sect, who truly loves and follows Jesus Christ. The whole household of faith are my brethren, and some care had been taken not to give any of them a needless offence. In matters, which are not fundamental, let everyone see with his own eyes, and judge for himself, as God enables him. The hymns are upon a catholic plan, not intended to depreciate any set of Christians, but to sink the creature to his real standard of worthlessness and helplessness, and to exalt the Saviour in the hearts of his people, that they may trust in him, love and obey him. Man's emptiness and Christ's fulness are my general topics, but diversified in a variety of cases; and these topics are not suited to the relish of depraved nature, which loveth gilding and varnish to hide a base metal.'[20] J.C. Philpot, although he himself left the national church, acknowledges that 'From all taint of national churchmanship Berridge is singularly free.'[21] The hymns are clearly meant to be sung by those who have a commitment to Christ. Something of the appeal to Christians of all denominations is seen in the experience of Hymn 210:

O Lord, with shame I do confess
My universal emptiness,
My poverty and pride;
I cannot keep thee in my sight,
Nor can I think one thought aright,
Unless thy Spirit guide.

I cannot from my idols part,
Nor love the Lord with all my heart,
Nor can myself deny:
I cannot pray and feel thee near,
Nor can I sing with heavenly cheer,
Unless the Lord is nigh.

Since life divine in Adam fell,
On spiritual things we cannot dwell,
The heart is turn'd aside;
And none can raise to life the dead
But he, who rais'd himself indeed,
And for dead sinners died.

On him almighty help is laid,
An all-sufficient Saviour made,
And stands within my call;
Though nothing in myself I am,
But deaf and dumb, and blind and lame,
Through him I may do all.

Then let this mighty Jesus be
An all-sufficient help for me,

> Creating power and will;
> Thy grace sufficed saints of old,
> It made them strong, and made them bold,
> And it sufficeth still.'[22]

In his poetry, as in his preaching, Berridge strove for simplicity. He writes, 'The thoughts are easy and free, flowing from the heart; and the language simple and plain, yet neat and elegant. And nothing sure can be more unsuitable than humble prayer uttered in pompous expressions.'[23] Through Berridge's comments on Thornton's revision of Bogatzky's *Golden Treasury* we learn that he often felt that the imagery and language of poets went beyond truth. One extract was good, 'but your poets torment me sadly. They soar up to the moon and show the flight of fancy, rather than the fight of faith. I would clip their wings, but can scarce lay hold of their tails, so high do they soar.'[24] He changes a line in a hymn by Charles Wesley, with the comment: 'Mr Charles Wesley in his poetry, often soars above all hyperbolics.'[25] Philpot thought that simplicity in the hymns was a great strength, as 'Mock sorrows and mock joys, as if conscious of imposture, aim at high-flown expressions; reality gushes forth in the simplest.'[26] This simplicity is seen in the first of his hymns written for the Lord's Supper:

> The table now is spread
> With guests around the board;
> Dear Jesus, bless the wine and bread,
> And heavenly peace afford.
>
> Yea, let the Lord appear
> With looks divinely mild,
> And whisper in each humble ear,
> I love thee well, my child.[27]

In dealing with the crucifixion the language is direct and powerful:

> His back with hardy stripes is hew'd,
> Till flakes of gore, and streams of blood

Besmear the frighted ground:
A scornful and a smarting crown
His holy head is thrust upon,
And thorns begird it round.[28]

Much of Berridge's imagery is drawn from the Scriptures, but the agricultural and rural world naturally breaks through. He compares himself to a bird:

Of Christ I chirp and sing,
And when he casts an eye,
I flutter up with brisker wing,
And warble in the sky.[29]

In a world where the horse was vital people understood the following entreaty:

Lord, draw me by the secret touch,
Or backward I shall start;
For sure I want entreating much,
So fearful is my heart.[30]

Or, speaking of the heart,

No joy it finds in God;
And when my tongue would pray,
My heart will take a different road,
And start and prance away.[31]

There is little in these hymns of the originality of expression that marks Berridge's letters. The overall impression is one of directness and simplicity.

Most of the hymns are meditations on a scripture and relate Christ to the text. Berridge says that 'Some text of Scripture also has been taken as a subject for each hymn, with a view to keep my thoughts from rambling, and to explain Scripture with reference to Christ. He is the *end of the law*, which was *a shadow of things to come*; and *Christ is that body*, to which the shadow belongs. Accordingly he is shadowed forth by patriarchs, prophets, and kings of Israel, and by a vast variety of types and similitudes; and must be sought in the book of Proverbs as well as in Leviticus, the clearest book of the Jewish gospel.'[32]

The story of Daniel in the lion's den brings the thought of Jesus the lion-tamer who brings help in the time of trouble.[33] The defeat of Israel at Ai challenges the Christian in terms of failure because of idols in his heart.[34] Zechariah's promise of a change of clothes speaks of the dress of Christ:

> Christ's soldiers too, if Christ-like bred
> Have regimental dress,
> Tis linen white, and faced with red,
> Tis Christ's own righteousness.[35]

Many of the hymns reveal a passion for communion with Christ and it is this motivation that underlined Berridge's approach to understanding Scripture. J.C. Philpot thought that Berridge was unrivalled in this area: 'In the simple breathing forth of his desires after communion with his Lord he has, I think no rival. There is no dry theoretical statement what communion is; no boasting for himself, because he has had it; no flogging of others, because they have had it not; but there is a pressing after it in his own soul, as the only thing desirable, loved for its own sake, valued for its own sweetness, mourned after when lost, rejoiced in when found.'[36] Many of his hymns reflect the passion and concern of a man who wanted to live in the joy and presence of his Lord. Perhaps a couple of verses will illustrate:

> For thee my heart will pine,
> Though much from thee it roam;
> And sure I would be only thine,
> And keep with thee at home.[37]

> I would be near thy feet,
> Or at thy bleeding side,
> Feel how thy heart does beat,
> And see its purple tide,
> Trace all the wonders of thy death,
> And sing thy love in every breath.[38]

The hymns are experimental, with an emphasis on heart knowledge and honesty. They reflect Berridge's own spiritual autobiography. The blindness of the human heart to spiritual concerns, the need of the Spirit's awakening, the wonder of the grace of God in Christ for the new believer, the reality of communion with God and the struggles of grace and nature in the believer are all dealt with in a subjective manner by Berridge. There is something to challenge and comfort the Christian whatever his stage or state. Jubilation mixes with lamentation, challenge joins with comfort as Berridge echoes the variety of Christian experience. How often have Christians been saddened, as Berridge was, by the behaviour of others, only to be more grieved at their own lives:

> Yet chiefly, Lord I grieve
> For my untoward heart;
> How full of doubts I live,
> Though full of grace thou art;
> What poor returns I make to thee,
> For all the mercy shown to me!
>
> And must I ever smart,
> A child of sorrows here?
> Yet, Lord, be near my heart,
> To soothe each rising tear;
> Then at thy bleeding cross I'll stay,
> And sweetly weep my life away.[39]

Christians so often get distracted by legitimate concerns to their own spiritual loss:

> Too long, O Lord, my soul has fed
> On graces, duties, frames,
> Yet these are not my heavenly bread,
> Though lovely things and names.
>
> Thou art my gospel bread and food,
> Thou art my joyous feast;
> To eat thy flesh, and drink thy blood,
> Is gospel health and rest.

> Thy life and death are my repast,
> The precious fruit of grace;
> And when this dainty food I taste,
> I live, and love, and bless.[40]

We thus see something of Berridge's theology in these hymns: his dependence on the merits of Christ alone for acceptance with God and a frank recognition of the evil of his own heart. Berridge would certainly have been concerned about some of the statements in our modern hymnbooks. From a study of the notes he made in Thornton's revision of Bogatzky's *Treasury* we see that he disagreed with hymns for general use that contained statements of positive confession. He changed a line, 'I shall behold thy blissful face' to 'I long to see thy blissful face' with the comment: 'I cannot bear to see positive assurances put into the mouth of every reader. They are not fit for general reading or singing. They distress weak Christians and feed the presumption of carnal professors.'[41] He changed a line, 'For ransom'd thou art' to 'If ransom'd thou art' commenting, 'Can every reader say, "For ransom'd thou art"?[42] He thought a line 'Our souls are all on flame', was not suitable for general use. 'Could the composer of this hymn say always, "My soul is all on flame"? Then why did he publish that, which was neither fit for his own, nor for any other's general use? It should have been a closet hymn, in a precious hour.'[43] He criticized Thornton, saying, 'Many of your hymns were composed on a pinnacle of the temple, or on the top of Jacob's ladder, and do not suit a lame pilgrim, who is only two rounds from the bottom.'[44] He offered an alternative:

Original:

> The Lord is ours, and we despise
> The rage, tho' hell itself should rise;
> The Lord is ours; the thought imparts
> Immortal transport to our hearts.

Berridge:
> If Christ is ours, we may despise
> All rage, tho' hell against us rise;
> His love, experienced, will impart
> Immortal transports to thy heart.[45]

Something of Berridge's concern for honesty and the disinclination to make promises can be seen in his approach to another hymn, over which he wrote, 'I dare not sing the following hymn, unless it be altered, yet my alteration may not please.'

Original:
> 'My God, my King, thy various praise
> Shall fill the remnant of my days;
> Thy grace employ my humble tongue,
> Till death and glory raise the song.
>
> The wings of ev'ry hour shall bear
> Some thankful tribute to thine ear;
> And ev'ry setting sun shall see
> New works of duty done for thee.

Berridge's alteration:
> 'My God, my King, thy works of praise
> Demand thanksgiving all my days;
> Oh, let thy grace employ my tongue,
> Till death and glory raise the song.
>
> Grant, Lord, that ev'ry hour may bear
> Some thankful tribute to thine ear,
> And every setting sun may see
> New works of duty done for thee.[46]

Such changes show that Berridge believed that hymns should be truthful and not mislead the nominal Christian or present problems to sensitive Christians by speaking of mountain-top experiences as if they were the norm. His own hymns reflect these concerns and he was careful to indicate that they were composed for the use of those who love and follow the Lord Jesus Christ in sincerity. A Christian who reads the hymns will be well repaid for his trouble.

# 26.
# Berridge: the Christian

Although Berridge was an outstanding preacher and communicator, this public role tells us little about the real struggles and secrets of his relationship with God. Success turns the heads of most people and until his illness in the late 1760s there is a suggestion that Berridge thought of himself as indispensable. This illness reinforced the best features of his character, made him appreciate the true nature of the human heart and led him to stress a personal walk with God before all else. Berridge certainly put his whole strength into his private life and lived, particularly in his later years, with the constant challenge of combining a realistic view of his own heart with a growing appreciation of the grace of God. The vital truths of the gospel that he continually preached were not dead doctrines; they had vital implications for daily living.

> The man who walks with jealous care,
> And fix'd on Jesus keeps his eye,
> And watcheth daily unto prayer,
> Shall find the Lord's help ever nigh.
>
> His inbred foes with rage may rise,
> And kindle war within his breast,
> But Jesus Christ will send supplies,
> And make him rule and give him rest.[1]

Whittingham testifies how real eternal issues were to him and how he lived in their light: 'His daily walk was close with God. He delighted himself in the Lord, and maintained almost constantly delightful fellowship and communion

with him. His enjoyments of a religious character were rich
and sublime; and, not contented with inferior attainments in
grace, he pressed with increasing ardour, as long as he lived,
toward the mark for the prize of the high calling of God in
Christ Jesus. And that he might realize more and more the
pleasantness and peace that are found in the ways of
heavenly wisdom, he walked circumspectly, carefully weigh-
ing every circumstance that tended to abate the fervour of
his spirit in serving the Lord. Hence the various graces of the
Holy Spirit shone with remarkable brightness in all his
deportment. Warmed with the love of God, which was
abundantly shed abroad in his heart, he was always alive to
those subjects which related to the excellence and
importance of heavenly things. He was not fond of conversing with any of his friends on the common concerns of life;
and, if the conversation happened at any time to take such a
turn, he would with admirable dexterity divert it into a
religious channel, making it subservient to the introduction
of some instructive and edifying observations. When anyone
called on him, and appeared desirous of spending the time
in conversing about matters of indifference, he would show
by his silence that he was not interested in what was said;
and at length would arrest the ear of the visitor by relating
matters of the greatest moment, or which concerned the
welfare of the soul for time and eternity. His devout mind
could not feel any pleasure in trifling and unimportant
conversation. His soul was strongly imbued with the mag-
netic influence of divine grace, and was restless when
diverted by any circumstance from its proper tendency, until
it gained its destined point of the heavenly compass. Thus
alive to God, and daily cultivating a more heavenly state of
mind, he was blessed with rich foretastes of future felicity,
and animated by a good hope of possessing the inheritance
of the saints in light. His citizenship was in heaven, and his
conversation was habitually there; hence he longed, especially in the last years of his life, to be with his Lord and
Master, often exclaiming, "When shall I see his face?" The
Saviour was very precious to him; he highly exalted him, and
spoke of his kingdom, and talked of his power with great
delight.'[2] Such a testimony shows the reality in his private
life of the Christ and the doctrines that Berridge preached.

Holland, preaching a memorial sermon in London, said
that Berridge 'was in an especial manner favoured with
nearness to and communion with his God'.[3] In one of
Berridge's sermon outlines the last section of application
reads: 'Your daily business is to draw nigh to God for more
light of his countenance; more comfort of his love; more aid
of his Spirit. And the more your hearts are purified, the
more communion you will have with God.'[4] This was a
matter that Berridge himself was very serious about, particularly in the rush of a hectic preaching life:

> O Lord, thy Spirit's aid impart,
> And fill me with devotion's fire;
> Create anew my earthly heart,
> And heavenly breathings there inspire!
> Bid heart and flesh cry out for thee
> And thou my joyful portion be!
>
> Let incense smoking from my breast
> In praise and prayer ascend thy hill;
> And where I rove, or where I rest,
> Do thou, my God, surround me still;
> My heavenly intercourse increase
> Till as a river flows my peace.[5]

Enoch showed that true spirituality lay in walking with God,
not in outward forms and ceremonies:

> No pattern more plain
> Or striking than this,
> To show unto man
> What godliness is,
> Not merely rehearsing,
> A hymn or a prayer,
> But with God conversing,
> And feeling him near.[6]

In these issues Berridge believed that God allowed no
monthly or weekly store but poor lepers were fed daily at his
gate.[7]

Whittingham reminds us that Berridge often stressed this

theme of personal communion with God in the latter part of his life. In 1788 he wrote from London, expressing his weariness and looking forward to being at home at Everton with the Word of God for his companion 'and leisure enough for musing and prayer. Never am I well, but when at home with Jesus.'[8] He wrote to young Cornelius Winter, whose thoughts were disturbed over what actions he should take in his personal life: 'It is want of communion with God that makes our thoughts run a gadding.'[9] A letter to Lady Huntingdon published in *Cheerful Piety* finished with a paragraph showing his desires: 'I am now removed out of the book of Proverbs which I have long studied, into the book of Canticles; but am got no further than the first chapter, verse the second: "Let him kiss me with the kisses of his mouth." I seem to want nothing now but a closer union with the dear Redeemer. The world at times strives to divert my attention from the chief object of my affections; but my soul is ever panting after him, yea, my heart and my flesh cry out for the living God (Ps.42:1,2). Come Lord Jesus, come quickly! The Lord strengthen your union and communion with the Prince of peace. Amen.'[10]

As a Christian he lived in the reality of God's care for him. Of course, there were times when he was dejected and depressed, questioning the purposes of God, but after his serious illness in the late sixties and early seventies he recognized the need for discipline and began to live out the practical implications of the sovereignty of God. The Calvinism debate, which he entered with *The Christian World Unmasked*, was not an intellectual game but a matter of heart knowledge painfully learnt in the school of Jesus. As a Christian he evidenced both close communion with God and restfulness in him. Berridge wrote a lovely hymn in this period when he became utterly convinced of the need for the Christian to trust completely in the purpose of God for his life:

> Oh give me children, or I die,
> Was Rachel's fond and peevish cry,
> To Jacob vented forth;
> Her wish was granted to her cost,
> The children came, and Rachel lost
> Her life, to give them birth.

Poor Rachel tells us with a tear,
How vain all earthly wishes are,
How fatal oft they grow!
Though harmless things are only sought,
Yet if pursued with eager thought,
Death may attend them too.

How things may prove, or good or ill,
No man with all his wit can tell,
And wishes must be vain;
What seems desirable at first,
Of all bad things may prove the worst,
And slay the heart with pain.

This wishing trade I fain would leave,
And learn with sweet content to live
On what the Lord shall send;
Whate'er he sends, he sends in love,
And good or bad things blessings prove,
If blessed by this friend.

Then let no care perplex me now;
My only wish and care be thou,
Be thou my whole delight;
Bid every sigh of rising thought,
And every pant of breath go out
For Jesus day and night.[11]

All who knew Berridge commented on his humility and
what a grace this was in the light of temptation to pride
because of his success. Whittingham calls it the most
prominent feature of his character: 'During all the years of
my acquaintance with him, notwithstanding his unabated
popularity, I never saw him betray the least symptom of
vanity on any occasion.'[12] Whittingham goes on to say how
Berridge mixed easily in the company of the poor and
unpolished lay preacher. He had a realistic picture of his
own frailty and boasted in his Lord. If friends wrote praising
him he gently rebuked them. To Samuel Wilks he wrote, ' I
received your very friendly letter, and thank you for it; but is
it not rather too profuse of honour conferred – upon whom?

Why, truly, on a miserable sinner, like yourself. One toad
may croak to another, but, sure, it would raise a smile on
your face to hear one toad compliment another, and speak
very handsome things of his toadship. I do not love hard
words, yet am much afraid of kind ones; they have procured
me many a whipping. Sweet words are to the heart what
sweetmeats are to the stomach; unwholesome, producing
sickliness. Children may bear such sweet things, but elderly
people cannot digest them.'[13]

He had a clear view of the sinfulness of his own heart and
this understanding, particularly after his move away from
Wesley, reinforced the continual need for broken-
heartedness and humility. In one hymn he expresses his
desires in a simple form:

> Jesus, cast a look on me,
> Give me sweet simplicity,
> Make me poor and keep me low,
> Seeking only thee to know.
>
> Weaned from my lordly self,
> Weaned from the miser's pelf,
> Weaned from the scorner's ways,
> Weaned from the lust of praise.
>
> All that feeds my busy pride,
> Cast it evermore aside,
> Bid my will to thine submit,
> Lay me humbly at thy feet.
>
> Make me like a little child,
> Of my strength and wisdom spoil'd,
> Seeing only in thy light,
> Walking only in thy might.[14]

Whittingham speaks of his love for all those who loved his
Lord, whatever their denomination and whatever the form
of worship to which they adhered; thus 'he despised no one
because his sentiments on some subjects did not accord
with those which he himself entertained'.[15] Although he was
thus unsectarian, (and this was also shown by his preaching

at the Tabernacle in London and in his attitude to giving),
Whittingham points out that he held firmly to the essentials
of true Christianity in those with whom he had fellowship:
'Repentance toward God, and faith toward our Lord Jesus
Christ, and holiness of heart and life he inculcated, as
absolutely necessary to the attainment of the heavenly
felicity.'[16]

Although a humble man, Berridge was in Ryle's words 'a
man of extraordinary courage and boldness'.[17] It was surely
no easy thing to exchange the leisured life of a senior fellow
of a Cambridge college for that of a despised Methodist
preacher. From the early days onwards he encountered the
opposition of the local clergy and squires when preaching
throughout the area and met a mixed response from the
villagers. His prayer was for meekness and boldness to be
joined together:

> O Lord, give me an heart upright,
> An heavenly courage for the fight,
> And zeal that is alert,
> Not raving mad, but meekly bold,
> And not seduc'd by fear or gold
> My Saviour to desert.[18]

J.C. Ryle quotes an anecdote recorded in the *Churchman's
Monthly Penny Magazine* which related the story of how
Berridge resolved never again to be ashamed: 'In one of the
villages in which he was known as a preacher of the new
doctrines, which were then beginning to excite a great
sensation in different spots in England, he was exposed,
when passing through it, to the hootings and revilings of the
mob to an extent which frequently chafed his excitable
spirit. This village was composed nearly exclusively of a
long, straggling street, and, as it is to be seen in many
similar hamlets in England and elsewhere, was surrounded
on one side by a narrow lane, which jutting off at one end,
joined it again, by a much wider circuit than that made by
the street, at the other. On one day in which Berridge was
about to pass through this village, his spirit quailed within
him, in anticipation of the rough reception he would
certainly meet with from the bigoted inhabitants. He felt as

if he could not encounter it, and accordingly turned into the narrow lane of which we have spoken just at the moment when a pig-driver of his acquaintance entered the street with his noisy charge. It was their hap, each pursuing his own course, to meet again at the farther end of the village, when the pig-driver, who not only knew Berridge, but knew his principles, and knew the truth, looked up in his face with a most peculiar expression, and said: "*So you are ashamed on't.*"

'The saying went to his heart. "Yes," he said, 'I have been ashamed *on't*; I resolve, in the strength of God, to be ashamed of it no more, but henceforth to press after it, firm unto the end." A resolution which, undertaken by a resolute mind in the fear of God, was, perhaps, never more faithfully carried out in the future progress of a long and devoted life.'[19]

A refreshing characteristic of Berridge was his spiritual honesty and openness when discussing his own spiritual life and actions. He described in *Cheerful Piety* how spiritual pride invades the mountain-top experience or how quickly his heart set up idols: 'When I have been enlarged in prayer, how has pride and the devil clapped me on the back and said, "Well done; you have been very great today." How abominable is this, to attribute an enlarged frame, in any respect, to self? How often have I been pleased with flowery words and fluency in prayer more than spirituality! Again, how often have worldly objects and creature-comforts been set up in the heart; and have not the affections too frequently bowed down to them? Or when a near relation, or a beloved prattling child it may be, have been called away by the superior owner, how often has the heart whispered, and the tongue been ready to blab out, "You have taken away my gods and what have I more?" What is this but speculative idolatry?'[20]

Towards the end of his life he wrote in a similar vein to John Thornton, saying that he could do no religious act without pride skulking at his elbow and affecting him by both her smiles and frowns. An affected audience stirred up his pride but so did a sleepy one. He concludes on this theme: 'Henceforth if you ask my real name, it is Pride, and such an odd mysterious evil is it, I can even be proud of loathing my pride.'[21]

He also wrote about his half-heartedness in serving God:

> So base and crafty is my heart,
> It fain could act a double part
> And serve the Lord by half.[22]

He faced up to the reality of a sometimes hypocritical heart when preaching Christ: 'Often is my tongue describing him as the fairest of men, whilst my heart is painting him as the Witch of Endor; and many big words have I spoken to his credit; yea and frequently beseeching people to trust him with their *all*, whilst my own heart has been afraid to trust him with a groat.'[23] His openness and honesty about the evils of his own heart and the continual need for grace would take a chapter to describe; there are so many references to them. Perhaps a hymn quoted in full will show his openness and spiritual honesty:

> How damp and earthy is my heart!
> How apt through sloth to gather rust!
> From Jesus Christ it loves to start,
> And like a child, roll in the dust!
> This hour, perhaps, is heavenward bound,
> The next, is burrowing under ground.
>
> I cannot hold my heart, I feel:
> All tricks I try, but all in vain;
> It slips my hand much like an eel,
> And slides into the mud again;
> And there would lay and famish too,
> In spite of all that I can do.
>
> But oh, my Lord, thy check it fears,
> And pays obedience to thy Word,
> Thy soft commanding voice it hears,
> And hearing springs up to the Lord,
> Shakes off its dust, and claps its wings
> And soars aloft, and sweetly sings.
>
> If thou wilt take my heart in hand,
> And lodge it near thy bleeding breast,

It must and will adoring stand,
And cling and clasp the Saviour fast;
Forget its kindred to the earth,
And triumph in its heavenly birth.[24]

There are many such hymns describing his heart as 'gadding', 'foolish', 'evil', 'starved', 'treacherous', 'roving', 'earthy' and 'corrupt'. It is little wonder that Berridge earnestly recommended to his Christian friends study of the soul, the devil and the snares of the world.

After Berridge gained more understanding of the spiritual demands of God's law he continually cried both, 'O wretched man that I am!' and 'God be merciful to me a sinner. As a result Christ became far more precious to him. Whittingham said that 'No one. . . could be more sensible of his own helplessness and insufficiency for the performance of spiritual services than he was.'[25] In one poem he described himself as full of inconsistency, extremely changeable and indeed a motley wretch. He wrote that he was daily praying to know more of his own blindness, helplessness and vileness. Henry Venn wrote that Berridge loathed himself for the inexpressible corruption he felt within. Berridge simply had a very low view of his own spirituality and a correspondingly high view of the greatness and loveliness of Christ. He spoke of learning to prize the grace of election as he learnt to loathe himself. He knew that God looks on the inward whereas man judges from outward appearances. Whittingham roundly declares, 'He never spoke of himself but in language the most depreciatory.'[26] This was not false modesty for Berridge knew that the 'stupid ass of Everton', as he called himself, with the often hypocritical heart, was the real John Berridge. He was what he was in his Christian life through the grace of Jesus Christ alone:

Keep Jesus' grace in sight,
And feed upon it well;
Be strong in Jesus' might,
And thy own weakness feel;
Then sing and boast along with Paul,
I nothing am, and Christ is all.[27]

In an age when few people cared about the common people Berridge's life of continual giving stands out. He was a man of great kindness and unselfishness. He had a clear philosophy of giving. He saw Jesus Christ as his banker and felt it shameful 'that the London Bank, or even a private bank, would have more credit than the Lord's bank'.[28] He confessed, 'I scatter my mites about, because I am trading for another world. What silver and copper is left behind me, will profit nothing; but what is given for Christ's sake will find a gracious recompense. The world could call me a fool for this traffic, but they will see and own hereafter, that I carried my goods to the best market.'[29]

Although he acknowledged in a letter that he had a liberal nature as a child so that relatives had said he was likely to become a beggar, he praised God for giving him this gift. 'God has given me a free heart to dispose of my substance, and I am no more indebted to myself for this liberality than a nightingale is for her wings or voice.'[30]

His response to needs was: 'I make no feasts, but save all I can to give all I can. I have never yet been worth a groat at the year's end, nor desire it.'[31] He supported preachers who travelled from town to town in the area. His house was always open for travelling Christians and on Sunday besides the use of his field and stable he provided 'food and liquor for poor pilgrims who come to church from afar'.[32] With his help barns and houses were rented for preaching and those who lodged him always gained. Whittingham says that 'He invariably left half-a-crown for the homely provision of the day.'[33] He sold plate and books which he did not need and by 1773 had sold his inheritance from his father in order to meet the demands he felt. He had compassion for the many poor locally and during his period at Everton there were to be many economic difficulties in the area. Added to this those who became Methodists were often penalized and they usually applied to Berridge for help. He wrote in 1773: 'The flocks in every place are very poor, and often distressed, on account of their religion. Labouring men have been turned out of work; and some, who are unable to work, through sickness, lameness, or old age, have been deprived of parish collection, or received a very scanty one, because they are Methodists.'[34] In this work he was greatly helped by John Thornton.

His open purse as well as open heart sometimes led to problems and at various times we find Berridge writing to London friends requesting help. He returned home from preaching to find a Baptist minister from Northamptonshire had called requesting a loan to discharge some debts. Unable to help himself, he immediately sat down and wrote to Thornton: 'Had I seen Mr Wildbore, I would have given him a guinea, but could not lend him ten pounds. I have many demands upon me and am often in the deep myself, with my chin under water, but the Lord keeps my nose above it, which is enough, quite enough to keep me from sinking, but not enough to save a brother from drowning. Had I Mr Thornton's heart and purse, I would not lend Mr Wildbore a groat, but send him ten pounds immediately, and thus refresh my own bowels, by relieving his wants. I know your poor's bag is a deep one; but how far exhausted at present, I know not; yet if a ten pound bill lies skulking in some corner of the bag, I do wish and pray you would drag him out and send him to Oundle.'[35]

In the early years he was often imposed upon but he was frightened of becoming too suspicious in these matters: 'When Jesus opened mine eyes, my heart was so enlarged that I gave away money and books without discretion: and was frequently imposed on, chiefly by the borrowing people, who all forgot to repay me, excepting one. Upon my own credit I once borrowed twenty pounds for a person, paid the interest for two years, and then was forced to pay the principal. These impositions are everywhere met with by benevolent people, and are trials for benevolence for every virtue must be tried; and where benevolence is not rooted in the heart by grace, such trials overset it. I suppose such impositions are intended also to teach us caution. They have made me cautious, but I am afraid of growing suspicious, for we are apt to run into extremes; and it is better to be imposed on sometimes, than turn away a real needy person unrelieved from our door.'[36] Problems there were but Berridge was a model of unusual kindness and self-sacrifice.

As a Christian Berridge exercised his mind, and his literary remains are saturated with good sense. His struggle

with Wesleyan theology, his comments on the poetry of
Cowper, his thoughts about Lady Huntingdon's college at
Trevecka and the future of those trained there, his grap-
pling with the succession problem in the Church of England, his ideas for successful communication with his rural
audience and his counsel and encouragement to friends
show that he was no weak-headed fanatic. He might hold
unusual views, but he had his reasons.

One area which may cause concern was his occasional
recourse to letting his Bible fall open for guidance in
matters where he could see no direct scriptural principle on
which he could base his actions. It was certainly no habit
with Berridge for in 1770 he wrote to Lady Huntingdon
saying how he used this method concerning whether he
should have a wife or not and commenting that he had only
used the method on three or four occasions in the last
twelve years 'on matters that seemed important and dubious, and have received answers full and plain. Was not this
the practice of the Jewish church? God gave laws and
statutes to them as well as to us; but when dubious cases
arose they consulted the oracle, which gave directions how
to act ... I believe perplexed cases are often sent on
purpose to teach us to enquire of the Lord. But leaving the
oracles of God we make an oracle of man; a dozen wise
heads are consulted, and their sparkling opinions usually
prove as various as the colours of the rainbow. . .'[37]
Berridge said that he tried consulting people, only to be
perplexed. He argues that the lot must only be used on very
important issues and the seeker must have a hearty desire
to know God's will. God must not be trifled with or made
the object of an amusing game and most matters are either
plainly resolved by the Word or require only common faith
and waiting. That such guidance was very rare in his life
can be seen from the flyleaf of his Bible where he notes the
passages of Holy Writ that were given him when in trouble
or perplexity and these passages were all marked distinc-
tively in the text.

> '1 Chronicles 17:1,2. June 22 1758, when I began
> to itinerate, and when my squire and Potton vicar
> complained of me to the bishop.

Revelation 3:8,9,10,11. July 24 1758 when my squire complained to my college.
Job 11:16,17,18,19 – also Isaiah 54:7,8,9,10 – Psalm 91:14,15,16. After a long illness much wanted to humble my heart, greatly lifted up.
Jeremiah 1:19. Often given, as fresh troubles came.
Jeremiah 16:2 given when I consulted the Lord about marriage.'[38]

From this it would seem that he only used this approach once after his concern over marriage. This particular passage is confirmed in a letter of 1774 when Berridge speaks of God having 'turned his old ass out of door again, which confirms a sweet passage given me in my illness (Job 11:16-17)'.[39]

Thus such guidance was rare and restricted to the early part of his evangelical life. In letters to friends he stressed that servants must be guided both by providence and the Word. He wrote to a confused young man: 'Pray frequently and wait quietly, and the Lord will make your way plain. Jesus trains up all his servants to waiting, and if you are called to the ministry, he will exercise your soul beforehand with sharp conflicts. Joseph must be cast first into a pit by his own brethren, then into prison by his master, before he rules the kingdom, and David must be hunted as a flea upon the mountains, before he gets the sceptre.'[40]

God will sometimes allow us to make mistakes to humble us and stop us growing headstrong. 'It is good for us, I know, to have our well-meant views frequently perplexed and overturned, else we might grow headstrong, and fancy ourselves wise enough to be the Lord's privy counsellors, yet able to out-counsel him. We had rather sit with Jesus at the council-board than follow him with a string on our nose, to turn us round, or turn us back, at his pleasure.'[41] His letters to Rowland Hill during 1770 are full of encouragements concerning guidance. He advised him to 'ask no counsel, take no counsel but of the Lord: so shall you walk more evenly, than if you had the whole congregation of gospel divines at your elbow every moment to advise you'.[42] Berridge was very aware that one could not sincerely live off the convictions of another.

For all his faults, and Berridge was more aware of the divided nature of his own heart than most great men, he was truly a Caleb-type man. The quality and strength of his personal life formed a substantial basis for his public work. The clarity and simplicity of his walk increased towards the end of his life; he had indeed learnt lessons in the school of Christ. Perhaps one historian exaggerated in saying of Berridge that 'A more single-minded, devoted man never lived,'[43] but the reality of Berridge's walk is a challenge to any disciple of Christ.

# Select bibliography

**Primary Sources**
Works by John Berridge in order of publication.

*A Collection of Divine Songs, designed chiefly for the religious societies of churchmen, in the neighbourhood of Everton, Bedfordshire*, London, February 1760.

*Justification by faith alone: being the substance of a letter from the Rev. Mr Berridge in Cambridge to a clergyman in Nottinghamshire, giving an account of a great work of God wrought in his own heart*, 3rd ed., 1762.

*The Christian World Unmasked. Pray come and peep*, 1773.

*Sion's Songs and Hymns: composed for the use of them that love and follow the Lord Jesus Christ in sincerity*, London, 1785.

*Cheerful Piety: or Religion without gloom: exemplified in selected letters on the most important truths of Christianity*, London, 1792.

*The last farewell sermon preached at the Tabernacle, near Moorfields April 1 1792 to which is added a short account of Mr Berridge's death, in a letter from a friend*, London, 1793.

*Evangelical Magazine 1794*, 'An Interview with the late Mr Berridge.'

*The Works of the Rev. John Berridge, with an enlarged memoir of his life: numerous letters, anecdotes, outlines of sermons, and observations on passages of Scripture; and his original Sion's Songs*, ed. Rev. Richard Whittingham, London, 1838.

*The Works of the Rev. John Berridge*, 2nd edition with additions, London, 1864.

Letters in the following magazines

*Congregational Magazine*

*Arminian Magazine*

*Methodist Magazine*

*Gospel Magazine*

*Churchman's Monthly Penny Magazine*

*Wesleyan Methodist Magazine*

*Bedfordshire Magazine*

*Proceedings of Wesley Historical Society*

*New Methodist Magazine*

*Gospel Herald*

Unpublished letters, Ryland Library, Manchester.

**Other primary sources**.

Baker, *History of St John's College*, ed. J.E. Major, 1869.

*Bedfordshire Magazine*, vol. 18, no. 137, 1981, extract from the diary of B.Gilpin.

Beynon, *T. Howell Harris, Reformer and Soldier*, Caernarvon, 1958.

*The Bletchley Diary of the Rev. William Cole*, 1765–67, ed. F.G. Stokes, 1935.

Brown, A. *Recollections of the Conversation Parties of the Rev. Charles Simeon*, London, 1863.

Bogatzky, C. *Golden Treasury, a reprint of John Thornton's edition of 1775 with notes hitherto unpublished by John Berridge*, ed. Charles P. Phinn, London.

Dyer, G., *Memoirs of Robert Robinson*, London, 1796.

*Evangelical Magazine 1793*, 'Biography of the late Rev. John Berridge.'

Fletcher, J. *Works*, London, 1829.

*A Fragment of the true religion, being the substance of two letters from a Methodist preacher in Cambridge to a clergyman in Nottinghamshire*, London, 1760.

Gadsby, J. *Memoirs of the Principal Hymn-Writers and Compilers of the 17, 18 and 19th centuries*, London, 1882.

Green, *The Principles and Practices of the Methodists Considered in some Letters to the Leaders of that Sect. The First addressed to the Rev. Mr B.*, London, 1760.

Jay, W. *Memoirs of the Life and Character of the late Rev. Cornelius Winter*, London, 1807.

Seymour, A. *The Life and Times of Selina Countess of Huntingdon*, London, 1839, 2 vols.

Sidney, E. *The Life of Rowland Hill*, London, 1834.

Smith, E. *Two Centuries of Grace. History of the Baptist Church Waterbeach*, 1903.

*The Torrington Diaries*, Vol iv.

*The Life and a selection from the letters of the late Rev. Henry Venn*, London, 1853, 7th ed.

*The Journal of John Wesley*, ed. Curnock, London, 1938, vols. IV and V.

Wesley, *Letters*, ed. Telford, London, 1931 vol. IV.

**Secondary Sources – books included that make some evaluations of Berridge or related topic.**
Abbey, C.J. and Overton, J.H. *The English Church in the Eighteenth century*, London, 1886.

Ayling, S. *John Wesley*, London, 1979.

Balleine, C.R. *A History of the Evangelical Party in the Church of England*, London, 1951.

Bullock, F.W. *Evangelical Conversion in Great Britain 1696–1845*, St Leonards on Sea, 1959.

Bulter, B. *The Story of the Cambridge Baptists*, Cambridge, 1912.

Butterworth, R. 'The Rev. John Berridge and His Hymn Book 1760 and 1785', *Proceedings of the Wesley Historical Society*, vol. XI, 1918.

Carpenter, S.C. *Eighteenth Century Church and People*, London, 1959.

Dallimore, A. *George Whitefield*, vol. 2, London, 1980.

Dimond, S.G. *The Psychology of the Methodist Revival*, Oxford, 1926.

Elliott-Binns, L.E. *The Early Evangelicals: A Religious and Social Study*, London, 1953.

Green, V. *Religion at Oxford and Cambridge*, London, 1964.

Guthrie, T. Introduction to *The Christian World Unmasked*, Edinburgh, 1853 ed.

Holland, W. *The Christian's Warfare and Crown*. A sermon occasioned by the death of the Rev. John Berridge. Preached at Bartholomew Chapel Bartholomew Close on Sunday evening February 3rd 1793 by the Rev. W. Holland, published in *Works*.

Hunt, A.L. *David Simpson and the Evangelical Revival*, London, 1927.

Knight, H. *Lady Huntingdon and Her Friends*, New York, 1853.

Knox, R. *Enthusiasm; A Chapter in the History of Religion, with special reference to the 17th and 18th centuries*, Oxford, 1950.

Lloyd-Jones, D.M. *Preaching and Preachers*, London, 1971.

Loane, Marcus L. *Cambridge and the Evangelical Succession*, London, 1952.

Marshall, D. *John Berridge. The Forgotten apostle of Bedfordshire*, *Evangelical Library Bulletin* No 36 Spring 1966.

Overton, J.H. *The Evangelical Revival in the Eighteenth Century*, London, 1886.

Overton, J.H. and Relton, F. *The History of the English Church from the Accession of George I to the end of the Eighteenth Century 1714–1800*, London, 1906.

Philpot, J.C. Preface to *Zion's Songs*, new edition, London, 1842.

Poole-Connor, *Evangelicalism in England*, London, 1951.

Ryle, J.C. *The Christian Leaders of the Last Century*, London, 1869, reprinted as *Five Christian Leaders*, Banner of Truth, London, 1963.

Stothard, D. 'John Berridge of Everton' *Wesleyan Methodist Magazine*, 1906.

Skevington, Wood A. 'John Berridge and the Everton Revival', *The Evangelical Library Bulletin Spring 1960*, No 24.

Skevington Wood, A. *The Inextinguishable Blaze*, Exeter, 1960.

Smyth, C.H. *Simeon and Church Order: A Study of the Origins of the Evangelical Revival in Cambridge in the Eighteenth Century*, Cambridge, 1940.

Southey, R., *The Life of Wesley*, vol. 2, 1820.

Stephen, L. *A History of English Thought in the Eighteenth Century*, 2 vols, London, 1881.

Tile, F. *The History of Methodism in Cambridge*, London, 1966.

Trevelyan, G.M. *Illustrated English Social History, vol. 3 The Eighteenth Century*, London, 1951.

Tyerman, L. *Wesley's Designated Successor*, London, 1882.

Tyerman, L. *The Life and Times of John Wesley*, vols. II & III, London, 1880, 1890.

Tytler, S. *The Countess of Huntingdon and her circle*, London, 1907.

Vaughan, E. *Some Account of the Rev. T. Robinson*, London, 1815.

Vulliamy, C.E. *John Wesley*, London, 1931.

Walker, E. 'John Berridge of Everton' *Bedfordshire Magazine*, vol. 4, no 30, 1954.

Wright, T. *Toplady and Contemporary Hymn-Writers*, London, 1911.

# Appendices

# Appendix 1
# The last farewell sermon

'Trust in him at all times; ye people, pour out your heart before him: God is a refuge for us' (Ps. 62:8).

This psalm is a very precious one, full of gospel manna; containing directions for the church how to walk with God.

The psalmist says, 'Truly,' in good truth, 'my soul waiteth upon God; for from him cometh my salvation.' And does he not give a good reason why his soul waited upon God? It was because all his salvation came from him. And where should a sinner look but to him that has purchased salvation for sinners, and brings it to them who find their need of it?

He then says, 'My soul, wait thou only upon God.' He hath put in another word 'only'; it is but a very little one, but it is very emphatical, for it is a common case with people to make Christ half a Saviour, relying upon him and upon themselves, saying they are to be saved by faith and works. 'No,' says David, 'that will not do for me; I must have all my salvation from the Lord.'

'He only is my rock', the rock on which my heart shall rest – that is, on Jesus. And if he is not your only rock, my brethren, you will find that the rock which you trust in will slip away from you. Jesus will not suffer his glory to be diminished, nor let any steal one jewel from his crown, for he is worthy of all the honour that we can give him, and he is jealous of his honour. Do you be jealous of his honour too, and show that you are desirous of giving him all the praise that he deserves, and give him all that you can, you will never give what he deserves; you will always be defective in this to all eternity, for while we are giving to him our best praises, our obligations to him increase every day.

269

He then says, 'I shall not be greatly moved, while the Lord only is my rock, and my salvation. I find him to be as he says; he is my defence from time to time; I shall not be greatly moved.'

The word 'greatly' is often of use to the children of God, who fall into doubts at times, ready to fear they shall fall from their confidence. 'No,' says David, 'make the Lord all your rock, and build upon him all your salvation, then though you may be shaken at times and find your confidence beginning to totter, yet you shall not be greatly moved; the Lord will come again and lift you up, and cause you to rejoice in him.'

But David is so pleased with the words that he hath uttered, that he repeats them over again, and he could not repeat them too often. 'My soul', says he, 'wait thou only upon God.' Before he told you what was his daily use, and now he exhorts and encourages himself to go on with this waiting. Do not be afraid of your being disappointed: continue waiting and looking for the Lord; for he will never let them fail through trust in him.

Now if David encourages himself in trusting in the Lord, we have also the same reason, for our hearts at times are ready to sink, and to think that we shall be wrong at last; therefore, take David's words: 'My soul, wait thou only upon God; for my expectation is from him.'

But Satan may say, 'Where will you look and go?' What says Peter? 'Unto him who has the words of eternal life.' So we may say to our souls, when they are beginning to doubt, 'Where would you go? Where would you find salvation in any other? Christ only has the words of eternal life.'

Then he adds, 'The Lord only is my defence.' I find him so while I am trusting in him; though I am often afraid, yet he is better to me than either my fears or my hopes.

Then he adds, 'I shall not be moved.' Thus, by exhorting and waiting upon the Lord he gets more strength. He drops the word 'greatly', which he began with when he said, 'I shall not be greatly moved,' and now he speaks courageously, 'I shall not be moved.' The Lord is my defence; he holds me up, carries me on, and at length he will bring me to himself in glory.

Then David goes on to the words in my text, 'Trust in the

Lord at all times, ye people.'

Now he exhorts us what to do – good advice, the best advice; and such as all the children of God are taking, and never find themselves disappointed: 'Trust in the Lord', make him your confidence for all things – not only for all things, but at all times. When people are in peace and prosperity they do not seem so much to see their need of trusting in the Lord as they did; but they are ready to drop their confidence when the Lord has given them what they want of worldly things. Now this is a shameful practice and the Lord often takes away what he had given them, because they make a bad use of it. Has the Lord given you outward peace and prosperity? Trust in him to preserve it; for none can preserve it but he who gave it.

But are you brought into worldly trouble, and in great distress, and know not which way to look? You have no friend, perhaps, to go to, and your heart is ready to say, 'What must I do now? All have forsaken me.' No, there is one that never forsakes his people. But you can see no way how you are to be relieved. What of all that? Has the Lord no better eyes than you? He can make a way for you, no doubt, if you trust in him. But you say, 'What am I to expect?' Why, that relief which you want. Therefore, however difficult your worldly affairs may be, and though you have no friend at hand to help you, yet there is one above always at hand; go to him; he will not despise the poor and destitute, but will hear their cry, and will help them.

If he bids you come to him, and trust in him at all times, it is your business to go to him at all times; and the more distressed your circumstances are, the more fit for God to take care of. Supposing your bosom is full of guilt, and you find trouble on account of it, in this case you say you cannot go to Christ; whereas it is the only reason that you should go. Sinners will not go to Christ while they are at ease; but when they know themselves to be in a lost state and condition, and when they can find no help anywhere else, then Jesus says, 'I am come to save the lost.' Go your way to him. He bids you trust in him at this time, when under a sense of your lost estate. If you see yourselves ruined, however deplorable and wretched your case be, it is not too hard for Christ; for he receives all that come to him – not with frowning looks, no, but with a smiling countenance. 'Come unto me, all ye that are weary and heavy laden; and I will give you rest.'

What are you to do, but to trust in him in this time of sin and misery? Go to him just as you are. Do not be running to some of your lusts; nor imagine that you can do anything to prepare your way; but go and cast yourselves at the feet of Christ, saying, 'Lord, I am come as a ruined sinner; I know none can help me but thee; and thou hast ordered me to trust in thee at all times; I am come, Lord, at this time.'

But perhaps, when you are dying, your adversary the devil may tell you, 'Now you are sick, and lying upon a dying-bed, it is too late to come now; why did you not come sooner? There was mercy to be had then; but you have overstayed your time. Christ has been calling by his Word, and by his ministers, but you would not hear them; and now he has sent the summons to you to remove you out of this world; and you would be glad of salvation when you can have no more comfort here.' Well, when these words, or words like these, are brought to your hearts, remember from whom they come: they come from the adversary of your souls. Oh, he does not love to see a sinner, burdened with sin, looking unto Christ!

But Satan may say, 'Did you ever hear of a sinner, so great as you are, to come to Christ, and be received by him?' 'Yes,' tell him; you read of a cross-thief, as bad as yourself, that railed on Christ when on the cross, and when he went to Christ he must naturally think, 'Will he show mercy to me?' He asked for mercy, and he received it. Go you and try; that is the only way to deal with Jesus. Mind not what the adversary tells you. If your grief is great, confess it, and tell the Lord all your trouble; and at the same time tell him, for he loves to be told of his Word with confidence and modesty, tell him when you go, though your heart is discouraged and Satan distresses you and unbelief terrifies you, yet you have got his word, 'Trust in me at all times.' 'I come at this time; it is late, indeed, but it is in the time of life; I come to thee, Lord, and beseech thee to help me. Show thy mercy towards a poor sinner who is come at last. I am now come, and desire to partake of that mercy held forth to sinners; Lord, send me that mercy, and I will shout the loudest of thy children above.'

There is nothing which the Lord delights in more than to hear his people, when they come to him, plead his Word, and hold it fast. Though Satan wants to take it away from you, never give it up. Die with your souls deceived (if that is possible) in the hands of Christ. Tell Satan, 'Though I am as vile as any in the world, yet the Lord has taught me to put my trust in him; I will go to him, and endeavour by his grace to trust in him at all times.' 'Ah, but,' says Satan, 'what a poor feeble faith is thine! What hast thou to depend upon? Sometimes hoping, and sometimes doubting, dost thou expect that the Lord will look upon thy little faith?' 'Yes', tell him. 'The Lord does not so much look at the greatness of our faith, when we go to him, as at the reality of it. Though faith is weak when we come before the Lord, yet he will receive it. He never sent any away for the weakness of their faith, but he often reproves his people because they do not believe more strongly. Go to him, and tell him your condition, and when you call upon him expect an answer. Nothing pleases the Lord more than when a poor tempted and troubled soul comes to him, as Abraham did, against hope, believing in hope. You are ready to think his was a poor hope from time to time, for about twenty-five years; but he believed in hope. And what is said of this believer in God? That he gave glory to him.

The Lord is never more glorified than when we go to him, relying upon his Word, notwithstanding providences, and everything else make against us. Yet, even then, says the poor soul, the Word is for me; for Christ invites sinners to come, whoever they are.

Though Abraham against hope believed in hope, yet the Lord did not look upon this as a poor testimony of his faith. We see, by his not hearkening to what he felt within him, nor to the temptations which the devil cast in his way, that he only looked at the Word of God, relying upon his word and promise, though all providences made against him, he thereby gave glory to God.

And so it will be with us. When we find many things make against us, if we have but a word of promise to rely upon, and hold it fast, then we are giving glory to God. What says the tried old soldier Job? 'Though he slay me, yet will I trust in him.' Well said! Though the Lord seems, by his providence and dealings with me, to cast me off, and to take no notice of me, I do not mind that. The Lord says, 'Trust in me at all times.' Go to him; lie at his feet; tell him you are come, merely relying upon his word of promise, and that you have nothing to encourage you but his word. Put your trust in him and you will find that the Lord in due time will come and bless you.

I might mention many other times in which we might trust in the Lord, but they are comprised in this little word 'all', and a precise word it is: 'Trust in him at *all* times.' When you are full of fears then you shall bring the little word 'all' unto him, and say, 'I have nothing to encourage me to come unto thee but that precious little word, "all".' 'Trust in the Lord at *all* times.'

Satan is very crafty. He will tell poor souls, 'Why, what do you mean by trusting in the Lord? What right have you to do so? Are you a child of God? Are you one of the elect? You are doubting of it every day. What have you to do to trust in the Lord? Give him this answer: 'Though I am afraid about my adoption, and cannot say I am one of the children of God, this I can say, "I am one of the people."' What does my text say? 'Trust in the Lord at all times, ye people.' You may go with this to the Lord. Though you cannot satisfy yourself that you are an adopted child, you may say, 'I am one of the people, and will lie at thy feet till thou dost show me that I am thine adopted child.'

Many are often discouraged in themselves, because they know not their election. Seek for it, wait upon the Lord, wait his time and in due time he will make it manifest. For your encouragement the Lord has given you these words in our text, 'Trust in the Lord at all times, ye people.' Are you not one of the people? May you not plead this with the Lord, who commands all his people to trust in him? Why, then, go to him as one of the people, and expect to receive his salvation.

Take notice; it is not said in my text, 'Trust in him at all times, *my* people,' but '*the* people'. Thereby he gives a general order. Go to him, then, as one of the people and expect his help.

But let us notice the next words in my text: 'Pour out your hearts before him.' This is a precious command. Many times the children of God are so burdened with grief, with sin and worldly cares, that they know not how to bear them; and their bosom is so full of sorrow, so that they sit down and mourn over their hard lot. The devil dearly loves to see a child of God sit down and say, 'What a sad condition I am in! I dare not go to the Lord, I am so miserable.' Well, suppose you are; where would you go? You cannot be worse for it. Others are running about, from post to pillar, desiring to know what they shall do; their trials are so great, they know how to be delivered out of them; and they go and ask one neighbour and another, till they tire them all out. What does the Lord say to them? He gives good advice. Instead of making your neighbours your counsellors, go to him, who is the chief Counsellor, able to tell you what to do, and willing to relieve you at all times. Go to him and say, 'Lord, I am come, with a heart laden with grief, and with worldly cares, and know not which way to turn myself: what must I do?' The first thing which he tells you to do is 'Pour out your hearts before me.' You have been pouring them out before your neighbours, and what have you got there? Why nothing! Then 'Come and pour them out before me.'

The word 'pour' plainly signifies that the heart is full of grief, and almost afraid to empty itself before the Lord. What does he say to you? 'Come and pour out all your trouble before me.' He is never weary with hearing the complaints of his people; therefore you should go, and keep nothing back; tell him everything that hurts you, and pour all your complaints into his merciful bosom. That is a precious word: 'Pour out your hearts before him.' Make him your Counsellor and Friend; you cannot please him better than when your hearts rely wholly upon him. You may tell him, if you please, you have been so foolish as to look to this friend and the other for relief, and found none; and you now come to him, who commands you to pour out your heart before him.

But perhaps your heart is burdened not only with worldly cares, but with sinful lusts and corruptions. A sore burden indeed! And you are afraid and ashamed, perhaps, to go and tell the Lord all your trouble. But you need not be afraid of going, when he commands you. He knows everything in your heart: all worldly cares, all sinful burdens, and when the heart is quite full, he says then, 'Pour out all before me.' Here is great encouragement for you. Take the encouragement which the Lord offers; go and tell him your grief and burdens.

'Ah!' says the poor soul, 'I have been to the Lord again and again; but I find I am sinning against him daily, and I am ashamed to go to him. Now my conscience accuses me, and the devil tells me I am impertinent, how shall I appear before Christ to pour out my heart before him?' Go and pour out your heart before him till that crafty devil leaves you. You have the best reason in the world to go to the Saviour. He that knows what you are, what burdens you are bearing and what sins you have committed, even he says, 'Come and pour out your hearts before me.'

But I may add, further, does not the Lord command us in his Word and in his prayer to say, 'Forgive us our trespasses'? And does not this plainly intimate that trespasses are to be forgiven daily? Where are you to bring them but to the Lord? Go, therefore, and tell him you are come, according to his word, to acquaint him with your sins and trespasses. 'Ah, but,' you say, 'I have gone so often already that I am ashamed to go.' What does the Lord say to Peter? 'If thy brother trespass against thee seven times a day, thou shalt forgive him.' And Peter had not a little forgiven him.

Go to Christ every day for pardon. If you keep your guilt in your bosom it will only make it rankle. Tell him you are weary and ashamed of yourself, and you are come to tell him all your grief, and to beg that he will come and deliver you from guilt, and save you more and more from the power of sin. Whatever burden, therefore, you have upon your heart, the Lord would not have you suffer it to rest there; for if you do it will make you feeble by and by. But when you find your breast full of trouble, remember his kind word to you: 'Come, poor soul, and pour out your burdens before me.' Pour out your whole hearts, and let him know everything that distresses you.

But what follows in the last words of my text: 'God is a refuge for us'? Oh, these are precious words! We may look round about us again and again, for a place of refuge, for a person to apply to for help, and we shall find ourselves frequently, if not continually, disappointed. Therefore the Lord tells his people for their comfort that God is a refuge for them. Are you poor? The Lord is rich. Can you find no refuge in your fellow creatures, and have you nowhere to fly to? Go to the Lord.

It is very strange, when the Lord has all things in his hands, and all love in his heart, and advises his people to come to him, telling them that he is a refuge for them, they so often delay to come; they had rather find refuge from a fellow creature than from their God. They who have learned to trust in the Lord know what precious words these are: 'God is a refuge for us.' Come, and try, and you shall find him so too.

The devil will often be telling you that are the people of God, 'There is no help for you, even in your God. You have been seeking for help a long time but have found none. What will you do now?' Why, tell him, you will go to him that says, 'God is a refuge for us.' But the devil will say, 'You are so poor and so despicable a creature; what, can you think that Christ will take any notice of you? Why, your own brethren are ready to overlook you and the world despises you and yet you think Christ will take notice of you?' Tell the devil, 'Yes, he never fails them that trust in him.' Whatever your circumstances may be, though you may look all around you, this and that way, and find no place to flee to, no refuge for your souls, yet God, the faithful God, says he is a refuge for you. Trust him; go to him accordingly; look unto him at all times. Let your condition be what it may, be it ever so deplorable and wretched, yet the Lord tells you, when you go, 'I am a refuge for you.'

Be sure, if you forget every other part of the sermon, carry this home with you: 'God is a refuge for me.' Therefore, though I find no help in myself, nor in creatures, yet there is help enough in God; all my help is laid upon him; and he tells helpless creatures, 'I am a refuge for you.'

Hear it, ye poor burdened sinners, and thank him for his kind word. Go to him, to have his promise fulfilled time after time. Yet a little while, and he will bring you to his kingdom, where you shall live and reign with him for ever.

Are you sick, and in great distress, and without any friend

to apply to, ready to say, 'What must I do now?' Why, my text tells you what you are to do at all times. Whatever your case is, whether sick, poor, naked, or wretched, come to the Lord; he says, 'I am a refuge for you.'

'But,' you say, 'Lord, I have been sinning against thee, time after time.' 'I know it,' says Christ, 'but if you come, weary of sin and desirous of gospel rest, you shall find that I am a refuge for you.'

But, you say, you come so often that you are ashamed to come. That may be a good argument to keep you from your fellow creatures; you have been knocking often at their doors and they are ready to say, 'You came to my house the other day.' 'Well,' say you, 'may I not come every day?' No, you find no such help from man. But Christ never complains of your coming too often, but is better pleased with those that are oftenest knocking at his door, and looking to him for the help which he has promised.

And you that are poor in spirit, who cannot find relief in yourself, nor from your fellow creatures, go to Christ and he will be ready to help you. 'God is a refuge for you.' Oh think of that word whenever troubles enter into your mind. Repeat them again and again, and shame the devil out. Tell him, 'Though everything looks black, yet "God is a refuge for me."' Are you to believe the devil or God? Keep these words always in your mind, for all of you will be in such circumstances at times as not to know where to go, nor what to do; then these words come sweetly into the bosom: 'God is a refuge for me.' He loves to help the helpless, to heal the poor wounded soul, and to save the guilty sinner; while he is doing this he is acting the part of a Saviour, and brings glory to himself. But I might add that no one knows the compassion which is found in the heart of Jesus but himself; therefore, when you go to him do not entertain any unkind thoughts of him, for he invites all sinners to come to him, all poor and wretched sinners, and he that invites us to come has blessings to dispose of. Keep the last words of my text evermore in your mind; they will be of use to you, living and dying, sick or well; whatever circumstances you are in, you may find the want of such words as these: 'God is a refuge for us.' Take heed, when you go to him, to do as David did: plead his word with him. This is one part of the Christian's

duty which he often neglects. David says, 'O keep my soul
and deliver me.' What then, David? 'Why,' says he, 'for I
trust in thee.' He pleaded the Lord's word, and so may you.

The promises in the Bible are free for all who see their
need of them, and the Lord has told thee, if thou trustest in
him thou shalt never be confounded. But perhaps you are
thinking, 'If I trust in the Lord, I shall be confounded.' And
suppose you are, you will be no worse than before; you will
lose nothing by your trusting, even though it should not be
fulfilled. But remember that the Lord will never suffer his
promise to fail: 'Faithful is he that hath promised.' Though
you may often doubt of his performing, yet he never did, nor
ever will fail. Therefore, 'Trust in the Lord at all times, ye
people; pour out your hearts before him' in every time of
trouble.

I do not know a more precious verse in the Scriptures than
my text: 'Trust in him at all times, ye people.' Though at
present you may not know whether you belong to the family
of God, yet trust him, you are of the people; here hang till he
gives you better support. And when you find your poor
bosom laden with cares and grief, whatever causes your
distress, the Lord knows very well that if you keep it back it
will make you worse; therefore do as the Lord says, 'Pour
out your heart before me'; tell me all your grief; make me
your Counsellor and Friend, and you shall find what a
Counsellor I am; and I will remember to comfort you in the
worst state that you can be in.'

In health and in sickness, in life and in death, this will
apply to Jesus: 'He is a refuge for us.' What could you wish
for more? Go, then, unto him; doubt no more; cast away
your doubts and fears; trust in him. If you cannot with full
assurance, do it with some assurance, with a little faith, and
expect more. Remember, the Lord loves to increase what he
has given, and to build you up in faith and holiness.

I would say a little more, but I find my strength begins to
fail. I am glad and I am thankful that the Lord has held me
up hitherto, blessed be his name. When I begin to totter,
and when I experience infirmity, I am ashamed that I
should ever entertain a doubt of him. May these words be
impressed upon my heart: 'God is a refuge for me' and may
he fix it on all your hearts.

And now I conclude my subject. I came up to you trembling, but the Lord has carried me through, blessed be his name, and I look to him to carry me home; for I have no feet of my own to walk with. But the Lord can hold me up till I have done my work, and then he will put an end to my labours. Thanks be to his name for calling me to preach out of doors. It is the glory of a creature to publish the fame and salvation of God.

I must now speak a little by way of taking leave.

Lord, I beseech thee to pour thy blessing constantly upon this congregation; thy power and glory, let it be made manifest among them. Open the eyes of those that are spiritually blind, deaf and dead. Comfort the mourner. Strengthen the weak to go on their way. Build up thy church in their most holy faith. May this house be filled with thy presence. Bless every hearer that attends here from time to time, and may the Lord delight in them to bless them, and may they excel in his blessed service. May this ever be an house for God, kept from error, kept in union, going on their way, looking and longing for the coming of their dear Lord.

Bless all the ministers that labour here, occasionally and statedly. Fill their mouths with thy truth. Warm their hearts with thy love. Keep them evermore in the faith, zealously disposed to exalt the honour of the dear Redeemer, and to promote the salvation of sinners.

And may the Lord bless the trustees. Lengthen out their days. We bless thee that they have been faithful and true to their trust. Give them, Lord, the comforts of thy Holy Spirit. Enable them to go forward yet for a while, and bless their labours; and may they see that the people honour them for what they have done. May there never be wanting faithful men to succeed them, nor faithful ministers to labour among them. And as one of the trustees has been lately removed from them, the Lord direct them in the choice of another. Be gracious to their partners in life; impress their souls with thy precious love; strengthen them, quicken them, and build them up; may the Lord delight in them and water their souls from time to time, causing the seed of grace, that has been sown in their bosom, to bring forth fruit to life eternal.

The Lord remember all the children for good, causing

them to receive a blessing from the Lord and righteousness from the God of their salvation.

And now, Lord, I must take my leave of this chapel, which I have visited. Oh, keep them continually in thy fear, and bless them abundantly with all spiritual blessings! May they evermore delight in the Lord, and the Lord delight in them to heal them.

I know not whether I shall ever return any more, nor is it needful for me to know; but this I know – if the Lord continues my life, and allows me some measure of strength, I shall crawl up again. In the meantime, think of a poor crawling creature when you are upon your knees, and put up a short petition to the Lord that he would bless me, pardon me, sanctify and prepare me for his kingdom and glory. Amen and Amen.

May the peace of God, that passeth all understanding, keep your hearts and minds in the knowledge and love of God, and in the fellowship of his Son, Jesus Christ our Lord. And may the blessing of God Almighty, the Father, the Son and the Holy Ghost, be among you and remain with you always. Amen.

# Appendix 2
# Sincere obedience

The following extracts from the writings of Berridge and Fletcher will help the reader to judge for him/herself the approach of the two men. I first quote Berridge on sincere obedience and follow with Fletcher's attack.

'Sincere obedience is nowhere mentioned in the gospel as a condition of salvation. But if it were a condition, sure it would have been expressly mentioned, because of its high importance. Yet the Bible is not only silent in this matter, but asserts the contrary. St Paul declares roundly, "We are saved by grace through faith; not of works, lest any man should boast (Eph. 2:8,9). The reason added, "lest any man should boast," plainly shuts out all works of sincere obedience as a condition. For though these works are often small enough, yet if the condition is fulfilled by them, such is human vanity, they would afford a ground for boasting. Therefore to dig the whole cankered root of merit up, and give all the glory of salvation unto God and the Lamb, the apostle says absoutely, "It is of grace, not of works." Works have no share in the covenant of grace, as a condition of life. They are only the fruit of salvation freely bestowed, and the genuine evidence of a true faith, which works by love'.[1]

'"Sincere obedience is nowhere mentioned in the gospel as a *condition* of salvation,' and page 36 1.4: "Works have no share in the covenant of grace as a *condition* of life." I grant it,

---

1   *The Christian World Unmasked*, p.33.

if by salvation in the first proposition, and by life in the second, Mr Berridge means *initial* salvation and life *begun* in the world of grace. For undoubtedly the "free gift is come upon all men to justification," or salvation from the damning guilt of original sin, and consequently to some interest in the divine favour previous to all obedience and works. Again and again have I observed, that as by one man's disobedience many (*oi polloi*, the multitudes of men) were made sinners; so by the obedience of one many (*oi polloi*, the multitudes of men) shall to the end of the world, be made righteous, i.e. partakers of the above-mentioned justification, in consequence of Christ's atonement, and the talent of free grace, and supernatural light, which enlightens every man that comes into the world (Compare Rom. 5:18,19 with John 1:4,5,9). Far from opposing this initial life of free grace, this salvation "unconditionally begun", I assert its necessity against the Pelagians, and reality against the Papists and Calvinists, who agree to maintain, that God has absolutely reprobated a considerable part of mankind. But Mr Berridge's propositions are Antinomianism unmasked, if he extends their meaning (as his scheme does) to finished salvation, and to a life of glory, unconditionally bestowed upon adulterous backsliders. For sincere obedience, or the good works of faith, are a condition (or, to use Mr Berridge's word, "a term",) indispensably required of all, that stay long enough upon the stage of life, to act as moral agents. "Every branch in me that beareth not fruit he taketh away" (John 15:2). "Be not deceived, neither fornicators, . . . shall inherit the kingdom of God" (1 Cor. 6:9. See Ezek. 18 and 33). "If the penitent thief had lived, (says our church) and not regarded the works of faith, he should have lost his salvation again." As for the argument taken from these words, "He that believeth (not, with the heart unto righteousness) hath everlasting life," (i.e. has a title to it, and hast of a life of glory, shall have the enjoyment of it "if he continue in the faith rooted and grounded") it is answered at large in my Fourth Check.[2]

---

2   J. Fletcher, *Works* Vol. I pp.429–430.

# References

Unless otherwise stated, all references from the *Works* are taken from *The Whole Works of the Rev. John Berridge*, ed. Richard Whittingham, 2nd edition, London, 1864.

## Chapter 1

1. J.C. Ryle, *Five Christian Leaders*, Banner of Truth, London, 1963, p. 148.
2. M. Loane, *Cambridge and the Evangelical Succession*, Lutterworth, London, 1953.
3. C. Smyth, *Simeon and Church Order*, Cambridge University Press, Cambridge 1940.
4. J. Overton, *A History of the English Church 1714-1800*, London, 1906, p.149.
5. *Works*, p. vi.
6. C. Abbey & J. Overton, *The English Church in the Eighteenth Century*, London, 1878, vol. 2, p. 178.
7. Letter to Lady Huntingdon, *Works*, p. 503.
8. S. Tytler, *The Countess of Huntingdon and Her Circle*, London, 1907, p.110.
9. A.L. Hunt, *David Simpson and the Evangelical Revival*, Charles Tynne, London, 1927, p. 111.
10. *The Torrington Diaries*, Methuen, 1970, vol. IV, p. 105.
11. Letter to Lady Huntingdon, 10 March 1759, J. Wesley, *Letters*, ed. Telford, Epworth, 1931, vol. IV, p. 58.
12. 'An Interview with the late Mr Berridge', *Evangelical Magazine* 1794, p. 76.
13. *The Life and a Selection from the Letters of the late Rev. Henry Venn*, London 1853, p. 218.
14. J. Fletcher, *Works*, London, 1829, vol. I, p. 444.
15. William Jay, *Memoirs of the Life and Character of the late Cornelius Winter*, London, 1809, p. 66.
16. *Ibid.*, p. 86.
17. *Works*, p. xxix.
18. *Works*, p. xxxi.
19. Hymn 112, *Works*, p. 240.
20. Letter to John Thornton, 2 July 1785, *Works*, pp. 414-5.
21. Letter to Benjamin Mills, 23 November 1790, *Works*, p. 436.
22. Hymn 112, *Works*, p. 240.
23. L. Tyerman, *The Life and Times of John Wesley*, London, 1880, vol. 2, p.310.
24. A. Skevington Wood, 'John Berridge and the Everton Revival', *Evangelical Library Bulletin no. 24, Spring 1960*, p. 2.

25.   D. Marshall, 'John Berridge, The Forgotten Apostle of Bedfordshire', *Evangelical Library Bulletin, no. 36, Spring 1966*, p.2.

26.   Berridge produced two hymn-books. The first, *A Collection of Divine Songs*, (1760), was mainly a collection of works by other writers, which he later withdrew. *Sion's Songs and Hymns*, mainly containing original hymns, was published in 1785, although most of the hymns had been composed some fifteen years before during the time when he was incapacitated through illness.

27.   *The Christian World Unmasked. Pray come and peep*, first published 1773.

28.   C. Bogatzky, *Golden Treasury - A reprint of John Thornton's edition of 1775 with notes, hitherto unpublished, by John Berridge*, ed. Charles P. Phinn, London, 1891.

29.   *Cheerful Piety - or Religion without Gloom: exemplified in select letters on the most important truths of Christianity*, London, 1792.

30.   *The Works of the Rev. John Berridge, with an enlarged memoir of his life; numerous letters, anecdotes, outlines of sermons, and observations on passages of Scripture, and his original Sion's Songs*, by the Rev. Richard Whittingham, London 1838.

31.   *Gospel Gems - A Collection of Notes from the Margins of the Bible of John Berridge, Vicar of Everton 1755-1793*, ed. and pub. William Wileman, London, 1882.

32.   Letter to Samuel Wilks, 16 August 1774, *Works*, p. 386.

33.   Letter to John Newton, 17 September 1782, *Works*, p. 407.

34.   Ryle, *Five Christian Leaders*, p. 116.

35.   H. Knight, *Lady Huntingdon and her Friends*, New York, 1853, p. 123.

36.   *Works*, p.iv.

## Chapter 2

1.   *The Journal of John Wesley*, ed. N. Curnock, Epworth, London, 1938, vol.7, p. 338.

2.   John Venn, *Annals of a Clerical Family*, Macmillan, London, 1904, p. 99.

3.   *Works*, p. xxv.

4.   Letter to John Thornton, 14 January 1774, *The Congregational Magazine 1845*, vol. IX, p. 27.

5.   W. Lecky, *A History of England in the Eighteenth Century*, 1879, vol. I, p.363.

6.   Abbey & Overton, *English Church in the Eighteenth Century*, pp. 39-40.

7.   *Christian World Unmasked*, 1853 ed., p. 215.

8.   *Ibid.*, p. 216.

9.   *Justification by Faith Alone, Works*, p. 355.

10.   *Christian World Unmasked*, p. 18.

11.   Letter to C. Simeon (undated), *Works*, p. 439.

12.   Letter to Lady Huntingdon, 26 April 1777, *Works*, p. 517.

13.   *Christian World Unmasked*, p. 160.

14.   T. Scott, *The Force of Truth*, London, 1836, p. 18.

15.   *Christian World Unmasked*, p. 207.

16.   Hymn 7, *Works*, p. 203.

17.   *Christian World Unmasked*, p. 85.

18.   *Ibid.*, p. 87.

19.   *Ibid.*, p. 206.

20. *Ibid.*, p. 213.
21. *Ibid.*, p. 215.
22. *Ibid.*, p. 223.

**Chapter 3**
1. *Evangelical Magazine 1793*, p. 8.
2. *Ibid.*, p. 9.
3. Hunt, *David Simpson and the Evangelical Revival*, p. 68.
4. *Works*, p. 352.
5. *Evangelical Magazine 1793*, p. 9.
6. *Ibid.*, p. 15.
7. *Works*, p. xix.
8. G.Dyer, *Memoirs of Robert Robinson*, London, 1796, p. 54.
9.   E. Walker, 'John Berridge of Everton,' *Bedfordshire Magazine*, vol. 4, no.30, 1954, p. 246.
10. *Works*, p. x.
11. Smyth, *Simeon and Church Order*, p. 159.
12. *Works*, p. xi.
13. *Ibid.*
14. *Ibid.*
15. *Ibid.*
16. *Ibid.*, p. 352.
17. Ryle, *Five Christian Leaders*, p. 121.
18. *Works*, p. xi.
19. *Works*, p. 352.
20. Ryle, *Five Christian Leaders*, p. 121.
21. Epitaph.
22. Dyer, *Memoirs of Robert Robinson*, p. 54.
23. G. Dyer, *History of the University*, quoted in *Works*, p. xliii.
24. *Justification by Faith Alone, Works*, pp. 345-6.
25.   G.R. Balleine, *A History of the Evangelical Party in the Church of England*, Longmans, London 1908, p. 98.
26. Preface to *Gospel Gems*.

**Chapter 4**
1. Epitaph.
2. *Gospel Gems*, p. 14.
3. Sermon Notes, *Works*, p. 556.
4. *Christian World Unmasked*, p. 219.
5. *Ibid.*, pp. 89-90.
6. *Congregational Magazine 1842*, p. 221.
7.   *A Fragment of the True Religion. Being the Substance of Two Letters from a Methodist Preacher in Cambridgeshire to a Clergyman in Nottinghamshire*, London 1760, p. 2.
8. *Works*, p. xiv.
9.   J.Green, *The Principles and Practices of the Methodists Considered in some Letters to the Leaders of that Sect. The First addressed to the Rev. Mr. Berridge*, London, 1760, p.10.
10. *Works*, p. xvi.

11. Marshall, 'John Berridge, Forgotten Apostle of Bedfordshire', p. 3.
12. *Justification by Faith Alone, Works*, p. 346.
13. *Works*, p. xiv.
14. Hymn 275, *Works*, p. 304.
15. *Christian World Unmasked*, p. 64.
16. *Ibid.*, pp. 83-4.
17. *Gospel Gems*, p. 11.
18. *Justification by Faith Alone, Works*, pp. 346-9.
19. Hymn 127, *Works*, p. 245.
20. Hymn 153, *Works*, p. 254.
21. *Works*, p. xvi.
22. *Christian World Unmasked*, p. 169.


**Chapter 5**
1.   *Works*, p. 554.
2.   Hymn 58, *Works*, pp. 222-3.
3.     A.C.H. Seymour,  *The Life and Times of Selina Countess of Huntingdon*, London, 1840, vol I, p. 368.
4.   *Justification by Faith Alone, Works*, pp. 350-51.
5.   *Christian World Unmasked*, p. 6.
6.   *Ibid.*, pp. 37-8.
7.   Sermon Outlines, *Works*, p. 556.
8.   *Evangelical Magazine 1793*,  p. 11.
9.   *Arminian Magazine 1797*, vol. XX, pp. 612-3.
10.  *Arminian Magazine 1780*, p. 105.
11.  *Justification by Faith Alone, Works*, p. 351.
12.  *Ibid.*
13.  *Memoir of the Life and Labours of the late Septimus Sears*, London, 1880, p. 2.
14.  *Works*, p.xxv.
15.  *Ibid.*, p.xv.
16.  Letter to Rev. D. Simpson, 8 August 1775, *Works*, pp. 529-30.
17.  *Gospel Gems*, Preface.
18.  Letter to Rev. D. Simpson, 8 August 1775, *Works*, p. 529.
19.  *Arminian Magazine 1797*,  vol. XX, pp. 612-3.
20.  *Arminian Magazine 1780*, p. 105.
21.  Letter to Rowland Hill, 31 October 1770,  *Congregational Magazine 1841*, p. 601.
22.  *Journal of John Wesley*, vol. IV, p. 321.
23.  *Ibid.*
24.  Published to be read in his hymn collection of early 1760.*Works*, pp.327-8.
25.  *Collection of Letters of George Whitefield*,  London, 1772, vol III, p. 238.
26.  Letter to B. Mills, 1 November 1786. *Works*, p. 434.
27.  *Journal of John Wesley*, vol. IV, p. 291.
28.  *Ibid.*
29.  *Ibid.*, p. 295.
30   *Works*, p. xxvi.

**Chapter 6**
1.   'An Interview with the late Mr Berridge,' *Evangelical Magazine 1794*, pp.73-76.
2.   *Ibid.*, p. 73.
3.   *Ibid.*, pp. 73-4.
4.   *Gospel Gems*, p. iv.
5.   *Evangelical Magazine 1794*, p. 74.
6.   Letter to David Simpson, 8 August 1775, *Works*, p. 530.
7.   *Evangelical Magazine 1794*, p. 74.
8.   *Ibid.*
9.   *Ibid.*, p. 75.
10. Hymn 159, *Works*, p. 256.
11. *Evangelical Magazine 1794*, p. 75.
12. *Ibid.*, p. 76.

**Chapter 7**
1.   *Journal of John Wesley*, vol. IV, p. 300.
2.   Seymour, *Life of Countess of Huntingdon*, vol. I, pp. 398-9.
3.   *Ibid.*, p. 399.
4.   *Journal of John Wesley*, vol. IV, p. 321.
5.   *Ibid.*
6.   *Ibid.*, p. 322.
7.   *Ibid.*, p. 317.
8.   *Ibid.*, p. 318.
9.   *Ibid.*, p. 319.
10. *Ibid.*, p. 321.
11. *Ibid.*, p. 318.
12. *Ibid.*
13. *Ibid.*
14. *Ibid.*, p. 319.
15. *Ibid.*
16. *Ibid.*
17. *Ibid.*
18. *Ibid.*, p. 320.
19. *Ibid.*, p. 322.
20. *Ibid.*
21. *Arminian Magazine 1780*, vol. 3, p. 611.
22. *Ibid.*, p. 612.
23. *Ibid.*
24. *Ibid.*, pp. 612-3.
25. *Journal of John Wesley*, vol. IV, p. 334.
26. *Ibid.*
27. *Ibid.*
28. Seymour, *Life of Countess of Huntingdon*, vol. I, p. 398.
29. *Journal of John Wesley*, vol. IV, p. 336.
30. *Ibid.*
31. *Ibid.*
32. *Ibid.*, p. 337.
33. *Ibid.*, p. 338.

34. *Ibid.*, pp. 338-9.
35. *Ibid.*, p. 340.
36. *Ibid.*, p. 341.
37. *Ibid.*, pp. 340-41.
38. *Ibid.*, p. 341.
39. *Ibid.*
40. *Ibid.*, p. 342.
41. *Ibid.*, p. 345.
42. *Ibid.*, p. 347.
43. *Ibid.*
44. *Ibid.*, p. 350.

**Chapter 8**
1. Green, *Principles and Practices of the Methodists*, pp. 28,29.
2. *Ibid.*, p. 75.
3. *Journal of John Wesley*, vol. IV, p. 360.
4. *Ibid.*, p. 359.
5. *Ibid.*
6. *Ibid.*, p. 360.
7. *Ibid.*, p. 347.
8. *Ibid.*, p. 359.
9. *Ibid.*, p. 360.
10. *Ibid.*, p. 434.
11. *Ibid.*, p, 433.
12. Ibid., p. 483.
13. Green, *Principles and Practices of the Methodists*, p. 28.
14. *Journal of John Wesley*, vol. IV, pp. 347-348.
15. Letter to Lady Huntingdon, 23 March 1770. *Works*, p. 507.
16. Ryle, *Five Christian Leaders*, p. 127.
17. Skevington Wood, 'John Berridge and the Everton Revival', p. 3.
18. Loane, *Cambridge and the Evangelical Succession*, pp. 77-78. S. Carpenter, *Eighteenth Century Church and People*, London, 1959, p. 231.
19. A Dallimore, *George Whitefield*, Banner of Truth, London, 1980, vol. 2, p. 183.
20. Letter to an unknown friend, 20 April 1770, Manuscript , Rylands Library.
21. *Journal of John Wesley*, vol. IV, p. 484.
22. C.E. Vulliamy, *John Wesley*, Geoffrey Bles, London, 1933, p. 278.
23. Abbey & Overton, *English Church in the Eighteenth Century*, vol. 2, p.178.
24. G.M. Trevelyan, *Illustrated English Social History*, Longmans, London 1951, vol. 3, p. 64.
25. E. Walker, 'John Berridge of Everton', *Bedfordshire Magazine*, vol. IV, no.30, 1954, p. 247.
26. W. Sargant, *Battle for the Mind*, Pan Book with Heinemann, London, 1959, p. 88.

**Chapter 9**
1. *A Fragment of the True Religion*, p. iii
2. Green, *Principles and Practices of the Methodists*, p. 2.

3. *A Fragment of the True Religion*, p. vi.
4. Preface to *Justification by Faith Alone, Works*, p. 342.
5. *A Fragment of the True Religion*, p. iv.
6. *Ibid.*, p. v.
7. *Ibid.*, p. 24.
8. *Justification by Faith Alone, Works*, p. 357.
9. Green, *Principles and Practices of the Methodists*, p. 4.
10. *Ibid.*, p. 20.
11. *A Fragment of the True Religion*, p. 3.
12. *Ibid.*, pp. 15,16.
13. Green, *Principles and Practices of the Methodists*, p. 23.
14. *Ibid.*, p. 24.
15. *Ibid.*, p. 26.
16. *Ibid.*, p. 27.
17. *Ibid.*, p. 26.
18. *Ibid.*, p. 27.
19. *Ibid.*, p. 26.
20. *Ibid.*, p. 39.
21. *Ibid.*, p. 49.
22. *Ibid.*, p. 51.
23. *Ibid.*, p. 65

**Chapter 10**
1. Letter to John Thornton, 3 May 1773, *Congregational Magazine 1842*, p.221.
2. Dyer, *Memoirs of Robert Robinson*, p. 54.
3. Letter to Lady Huntingdon, *Works*, p. 503.
4. Seymour, *Life of Countess of Huntingdon*, vol. II, p. 28.
5. Sermon Notes, *Works*, p. 563.
6. E. Smith, *Two Centuries of Grace. History of Baptist Church*, Waterbeach, 1903, p.8.
7. *The Bletchley Diary of the Rev. William Cole*, 1765-67, ed. F.G. Stokes, 1935, p.249.
8. *Ibid.*, p. 298.
9. Letter to Mrs Barton, Carpenter, *Eighteenth Century Church and People*, John Murray, p. 181.
10. Baker, *History of St John's College*, ed. J.E. Major, 1869, p. 1046, quoted in Hunt, *David Simpson and the Eighteenth-Century Revival*, p. 115.
11. *Congregational Magazine 1819*, p. 697.
12. *Ibid.*, p. 437.
13. *Ibid.*, p. 502.
14. *Ibid.*, p. 630.
15. D.C. Williams, *Duxford Congregational Church, a Short History*, (no details).
16. *Congregational Magazine 1819*, p. 375.
17. *Congregational Magazine 1820*, p. 58.
18. Smyth, *Simeon and Church Order*, p. 267.
19. *Works*, p. 352.
20. *Works*, p. 353.

21. Letter to Lady Huntingdon, 8 June 1791, *Works,* p. 512.
22. T. Beynon, *Howell Harris, Reformer and Soldier,* 1714-1773, Calvinistic Methodist Bookroom, Caernarvon, 1958, p. 76.
23. Hymn 34, *Works,* pp. 214-5.
24. Letter to John Thornton, 3 May 1773, *Congregational Magazine 1842,* p.221.
25. Beynon, *Howell Harris,* p. 204.
26. Letter to Lady Huntingdon, 26 April 1777, *Works,* p. 516.
27. Letter to John Thornton, 3 May 1773, *Congregational Magazine 1842,* p.221.
28. B.Butler, *The Story of the Cambridge Baptists,* Cambridge, 1912, p. 69.

**Chapter 11**
1. L. Tyerman, *Wesley's Designated Successor,* London 1882, p. 51.
2. Seymour, *Life of Countess of Huntingdon,* p. 400.
3. *Ibid.*
4. *Works of George Whitefield,* vol. III, 1772, p. 264.
5. *Ibid.,* p. 265.
6. L.Tyerman, *The Life of Whitefield,* vol. II, London, 1890.
7. *Journal of John Wesley,* vol. IV, pp. 482-483.
8. *Works,* p. xxxi.
9. Farewell Sermon, *Works,* p. 613.
10. Letter to Lady Huntingdon, 16 November 1762, *Works,* p.445.
11. Letter to Lady Huntingdon, 23 June 1763, *Works,* pp. 446-447.
12. Letter to Lady Huntingdon, 27 June 1763, *Works,* p. 447.
13. Letter to Mr Reynolds, 23 September 1763, Manuscript, Rylands Library.
14. Beynon, *Howell Harris,* p. 139.
15. *Ibid.,* p. 204.
16. *Ibid.*
17. *Ibid.*
18. *Ibid.,* p. 205.
19. Flyleaf of his Study Bible, *Gospel Gems.* Also *Notes of the Masters, Fellows, Scholars, Exhibitioners of Clare College,* Harrison, Cambridge 1953, notes that Berridge was an Exeter Fellow in 1740, Diggons Fellow in 1743 and Clare Fellow 1748-64.
20. Letter to Rowland Hill, 18 December 1764, *Works,* p. 449.
21. E.Sidney, *The Life of the Rev. Rowland Hill,* London 1834, p. 22.
22. *Ibid.*
23. *Congregational Magazine 1841,* p. 400.
24. Sherman, *Life of Rowland Hill,* p. 48, quoted in Hunt, *David Simpson and the Evangelical Revival,* p. 111.
25. *Works,* pp. 533-4.
26. Letter to Lady Huntingdon, 26 December 1767, *Works,* pp. 502-3.

**Chapter 12**
1. Wesley, *Letters,* vol. IV, p. 58.
2. Letter to John Newton, 13 March 1773, *Works,* p. 363.
3. *Works,* pp. lii-liii.
4. *Collection of Divine Songs,* p. v.

5.  Wesley, *Letters*, vol. VII, p. 23.
6.  *Arminian Magazine 1780*, p. 499
7.  *Methodist Magazine 1797*, p. 305.
8.  Preface to *Collection of Divine Songs, Works*, p. xxxiv.
9.  Beynon, *Howell Harris*, p. 204.
10. Wesley, *Letters*, vol. V, p. 38.
11. Letter to Lady Huntingdon, 26 March 1763, Tyerman, *Life of John Wesley*, vol.II, p.463.
12. R. Knox, *Enthusiasm*, Clarendon Press, Oxford, 1950, p. 543.
13. *Works*, p. li.
14. *Ibid.*, pp. li-lii.
15. Letter to Rev. A. Coates, 22 April 1761, *Works*, p. 362.
16. *Arminian Magazine*, vol. 6, 1783, p. 616.
17. R. Tuttle, *John Wesley, His Life and Theology*, Paternoster Press, 1979, p.335.
18. *Ibid.*, p. 336.
19. Letter of 20 March 1768 in Seymour, *Life of Countess of Huntingdon*, vol.II, p. 234.
20. Letter to John Thornton, 10 November 1773, *Works*, pp. 381-382.
21. *Christian World Unmasked*, p. 9.
22. *Ibid.*, p. 10.
23. *Life and Letters of Henry Venn*, p. 218.
24. Letter of 15 January 1774, J. Gadsby, *Memoirs of the Principal Hymn-Writers and Compilers of the 17th, 18th and 19th Centuries*, London, 1882, p.34.
25. *Ibid.*, p. 35.
26. Cheerful Piety, *Works*, pp. 343-4.
27. *Journal of John Wesley*, vol. V, pp. 471-2.

**Chapter 13**
1.  Letter to S. Lucas, 23 October 1775, *Works*, p. 396.
2.  Ryle, *Five Christian Leaders*, p. 131.
3.  Letter to B. Mills, 4 November 1785, *Works*, p. 432.
4.  Letter to John Thornton, 4 November 1785, *Works*, p. 411.
5.  For an example of the use of the word in another context, Berridge writes to Thornton about a paper he had written: 'Your comment on Deuteronomy 33:26 is nervous, and your reflections are pertinent; but an application at the close seemeth wanting, to give the comment proper length, and full weight.' *Works*, p. 369. Toplady speaks of 'Dr Gill's excellent and nervous trait on predestination' (A. Toplady, *Works*, vol. IV, p. 17).
6.  Letter to Mr Adams, 3 June 1771, *Works*, p. 527.
7.  Letter of 31 October 1770, *New Methodist Magazine 1817*, vol. XX, p.301.
8.  Letter to John Newton, 10 June 1771, *Works*, p. 366.
9.  *Ibid.*
10. Letter to Mr Adams, 3 June 1771, *Works*, p. 527.
11. Letter to Rowland Hill, 19 January 1770, *Congregational Magazine 1841*, p. 601.
12. *Works*, p. xvi.

13. Letter to Lady Huntingdon, 30 December 1768, *Works*, p. 504.
14. *Ibid*.
15. Letter to George Whitefield, 22 May 1769, *Works*, p. 443.
16. Letter to John Thornton, 29 September 1772, *Congregational Magazine*, vol. VI, p.218.
17. Letter of 22 November 1771, *Life and Letters of Henry Venn*, p. 178.
18. Hymn 263, *Works*, p. 296.
19. Letter to Lady Huntingdon, 23 March 1770, *Works*, p. 507.
20. Letter to Lady Huntingdon, 8 June 1771, *Works*, p. 512.
21. Hymn 286, *Works*, p. 310.
22. Letter to John Thornton, 18 August 1773, *Works*, p. 371.
23. Letter to John Newton, 20 September 1773, *Works*, p. 377.
24. Letter to John Thornton, 3 May 1773, *Congregational Magazine 1842*, p.221.
25. Letter to Mrs Elizabeth H., 31 March 1780, *Works*, p. 398.
26. Letter to R.S. Lucas, 23 October 1775, *Works*, p. 397.
27. Letter to John Newton, 20 September 1773, *Works*, p. 377.

**Chapter 14**
1. Hymn 289, *Works*, p. 312.
2. Letter to Lady Huntingdon, 23 March 1770, *Works*, p. 508.
3. *Works*, p. liv.
4. Letter to Lady Huntingdon, 23 March 1770, *Works*, pp. 507-508.
5. Letter to Rowland Hill, 31 October 1770, *Congregational Magazine 1841*, p. 602.
6. *Congregational Magazine 1841*, p. 869.
7. *Ibid.*, p. 870.
8. Letter to Mr Lee, 7 September 1767, *Works*, p. 451.
9. Letter to B. Mills, 24 September 1782, *Congregational Magazine 1845*, p.273.
10. Letter to Mr Adams, 21 August 1765, *Works*, p. 526.
11. Letter to John Newton, 18 October 1771, *Works*, p. 368.
12. Letter to John Thornton, 24 November 1781, *Works*, p. 404.
13. *Ibid*.
14. Letter to Miss L., 27 April 1786, *Works*, p. 419.
15. Letter to Lady Huntingdon, 23 March 1770, *Works*, p. 508.
16. *Works of John Wesley*, 1830, vol. XI, p. 459.
17. *Journal of John Wesley*, entry for 27 March 1751, quoted in S. Ayling, John Wesley, Collins, London, 1979, p. 217.
18. W. Fitchett, *Wesley and His Century*, London, 1906, p. 471.

**Chapter 15**
1. *Works*, p. xxii.
2. Hymn 57, *Works*, p. 222.
3. *Works*, p. xxi.
4. *Collection of Divine Songs*, p. xxi.
5. Hymn 57, *Works*, p. 222.
6. 1 January 1768, *Arminian Magazine*, vol.6, 1783, p. 616.
7. 13 March 1771, *Works*, p. 364.

8. Letter to Lady Huntingdon, 9 January 1770, *Works,* p. 507.
9. Hymn 87, *Works,* p. 232.
10. Letter to John Thornton, 11 February 1779, *Works,* p. 395.
11. Letter to John Thornton, 1 October 1784, *Works,* p. 412.
12. Letter to B.Mills, 23 November 1790, *Works,* p. 436.
13. Letter to John Thornton, 31 August 1773, *Works,* p. 375.
14. Letter to B.Mills, 22 September 1776, *Congregational Magazine 1845,* p.272.
15. Letter to John Thornton, 20 September 1776, *Congregational Magazine 1845,* pp. 274-5.
16. *Christian World Unmasked,* p. 198.
17. Letter to John Thornton, 25 September 1773, *Works,* p. 378.
18. *Works,* p. xviii.
19. *Ibid.*
20. Letter to John Newton, 18 October 1771, *Works,* p. 367.
21. Letter to John Thornton, 3 May 1773, *Congregational Magazine 1842,* p.223.
22. Letter to Rowland Hill, 3 September 1773, *Works,* p. 513.
23. Abbey & Overton, *English Church in the Eighteenth Century,* vol. II, p.178.
24. J.H. Overton and F. Relton, *The English Church from the Accession of George I to the end of the Eighteenth Century, 1714-1800,* London 1906, p.176.
25. E.J. Poole-Connor, *Evangelicalism in England,* Fellowship of Independent Evangelical Churches, 1965, p. 186.
26. J. Overton, *The Evangelical Revival in the Eighteenth Century,* London, 1907, p. 62.
27. Smyth, *Simeon and Church Order,* p. 186.
28. *Ibid.,* p. 186.
29. Tyerman, *Life of John Wesley,* vol. III, p. 158.
30. R. Butterworth, 'The Rev. John Berridge and his Hymn Book 1760-1785' in *Proceedings of the Wesley Historical Society,* vol. XI, 1918, p. 171.
31. *Works,* p. 60.
32. *Christian World Unmasked,* pp. 2-3.
33. *Works,* p. xvii.
34. *Christian World Unmasked,* pp. 179-80.
35. E. Sidney, *Life of Rev. Rowland Hill,* London, 1854, p. 430.

**Chapter 16**
1. T. Guthrie, *Introduction to Christian World Unmasked,* p. xviii.
2. *Christian World Unmasked,* p. 212.
3. *Ibid.,* p. 4.
4. *Ibid.,* p. 67.
5. *Ibid.,* p. 95.
6. *Ibid.,* p. 5.
7. *Ibid.,* p. 47.
8. *Ibid.,* p. 210.
9. *Ibid.,* p. 212.
10. *Ibid.,* p. 40.

11. *Ibid.*, p. 96.
12. *Ibid.*
13. *Ibid.*, pp. 104-5.
14. *Ibid.*, p. 151.
15. *Ibid.*, p. 152.
16. *Ibid.*, p. 55.
17. *Ibid.*, p. 166.
18. *Ibid.*, p. 172.
19. *Ibid.*, p. 80.
20. *Ibid.*, p. 83.
21. *Ibid.*, pp. 184-185.
22. *Ibid.*, p. 210.
23. *Ibid.*, p. 169.
24. *Ibid.*, p. 159.
25. *Ibid.*
26. *Ibid.*, p. 121.
27. *Ibid.*, p. 163.
28. *Ibid.*
29. *Ibid.*, p. 179.
30. *Ibid.*, p. 182.
31. *Ibid.*, p. 188.
32. *Ibid.*
33. *Ibid.*, p. 194.
34. *Ibid.*, p. 193.
35. *Ibid.*, p. 148.
36. *Ibid.*, p. 149.
37. *Ibid.*, p. 150.
38. *Ibid.*, p. 151.
39. *Ibid.*, pp. 201-3.
40. *Ibid.*, p. 203.
41. Letter to John Newton, 20 September 1773, *Works*, p. 377.
42. Letter to John Thornton, 25 September 1773, *Works*, pp. 378-9.
43. *Ibid.*, p. 379.
44. *Ibid.*, p. 378.

**Chapter 17**
1.    C.E. Vulliamy, *John Wesley*, London, 1933, from a letter to Lady Huntingdon, p.300.
2.    Abbey & Overton, *English Church in the Eighteenth Century*, p. 364.
3.    Tyerman, *Wesley's Designated Successor*, p. 296.
4.    Letter to John Thornton, 18 August 1773,*Works*, p. 373,
5.    Letter to John Thornton, 31 August 1773, *Works*, pp. 374-5.
6.    Letter to John Thornton, 25 September 1773, *Works*, p. 378.
7.    *Ibid.*
8.    B.Semmel, *The Methodist Revolution*, Heinemann, London, 1973, p. 51.
9.    See Fletcher, *Works*, vol. I, p. 405.
10.   *Christian World Unmasked*, p. 177.
11.   Fletcher, *Works*, vol.I, p. 403.
12.   *Ibid.*, p. 425.

13. *Ibid.*, p. 427.
14. *Ibid.*, p. 432.
15. *Christian World Unmasked*, 1851, new edition carefully compared with third edition, p. 23.
16. *Christian World Unmasked*, p. 26.
17. Tyerman, *Wesley's Designated Successor*, p. 297.
18. *Ibid.*
19. *Ibid.*
20. See Appendix III for Berridge on sincere obedience and Fletcher's criticism.
21. Fletcher, *Works*, vol. I, p. 444.
22. *Ibid.*, p. 445.
23. *Works*, p. xliv.
24. *Ibid.*
25. *Ibid.*
26. Letter to unknown friend, 20 September 1776, *Congregational Magazine 1845*, p.272.

**Chapter 18**
1. Ryle, *Five Christian Leaders*, p. 135.
2. *Christian World Unmasked*, p. 8.
3. John Thornton to Berridge, 13 October 1775, *Works*, p. 522.
4. L. E. Elliot-Binns, *The Early Evangelicals, a Religious and Social Study*, Lutterworth, London, 1953, p. 28.
5. Letter to John Thornton, 22 October 1775, *Works*, p. 525.
6. *Ibid.*
7. John Thornton to Berridge, 17 October 1775, *Works*, pp. 522-4.
8. Letter to John Thornton, 22 October 1775, *Works*, pp. 524-6.
9. *Works*, p. xi
10. Smyth, *Simeon and Church Order*, p. 182.
11. Balleine, *History of the Evangelical Party in the Church of England*, p. 99.
12. Ryle, *Five Christian Leaders*, p. 134.
13. Seymour, *Life of Countess of Huntingdon*, vol. I, p. 368.
14. A.H. New, *Coronet and the Cross*, London, 1858, p. 141.
15. *Gospel Magazine 1794*, p. 14.
16. Hymn 141, *Works*, p. 250.
17. E. Vaughan, *Some Account of Rev. T. Robinson*, London, 1815, p. 251.
18. Letter to John Thornton, 11 April 1775, *Works*, p. 389.
19. *Ibid.*
20. *Ibid.*, p.390.
21. Hymn 48, *Works*, p. 219.
22. Ryle, *Five Christian Leaders*, p. 133.
23. *Works*, p. liii.
24. *Ibid.*
25. *Ibid.*
26. *Ibid.*
27. Hymn 74, *Works*, p. 227.
28. Letter to John Newton, 17 September 1782, *Works*, p. 408.
29. *Christian World Unmasked*, p. 13.
30. *Ibid.*, p. 131.

31. *Ibid.*, p. 83.
32. Fletcher, *Works*, vol. I, p. 445.

**Chapter 19**
1. Letter to John Thornton, 20 February 1787, *Works*, p. 424.
2.    Letter to Rowland Hill, 7 June 1776, *Congregational Magazine 1841*, p.871.
3. *Life and Letters of Henry Venn*, p. 217.
4. Letter to Mrs Elizabeth H., 31 March 1780, *Works*, p. 398.
5. Letter to John Thornton, 10 August 1774, *Works*, p. 384.
6.    Letter to Rowland Hill, 7 June 1776, *Congregational Magazine 1845*, p.871.
7. Letter to John Thornton, 21 September 1788, *Works*, p. 521.
8. Letter to John Thornton, 13 July 1785, *Works*, p. 415.
9. Letter to B. Mills, 4 November 1785, *Works*, p. 432.
10. Letter to John Newton, 12 December 1780, *Works*, p. 402.
11. Letter to John Newton, 17 September 1782, *Works*, p .408.
12. Letter to B. Mills, 24 September 1782,   *Congregational Magazine 1845*, p.273.
13. Letter to John Thornton, 13 July 1785, *Works*, p. 415.
14. Letter to John Newton, 17 December 1780, *Works*, p. 402.
15. Letter to John Thornton, 30 December 1788, *Works*, p. 429.
16. Letter to John Thornton, 20 October 1780, *Works*, p. 400.
17. Letter to B. Mills, 1 November 1786, *Works*, p. 422.
18. *Life and Letters of Henry Venn*, p. 432.
19. Letter to John Thornton, 21 September 1788, *Works*, p. 520.
20. Letter to John Thornton, 11 October 1786, *Works*, p. 422.
21. Letter to John Berridge (nephew), 30 May 1780, *Works*, p. 401.
22. Letter to B. Mills, 3 October 1783, *Works*, p. 431.
23. Letter to John Thornton, 2 July 1785, *Works*, pp. 413-4.
24. Letter to John Thornton, 13 July 1785, *Works*, p. 415.
25. Letter to John Newton, 13 April 1782, *Works*, p. 405.
26. *Ibid*.
27. Letter to John Newton, 17 September 1782, *Works*, p. 408.
28. Letter to John Newton, 12 November 1785, *Works*, p. 417.
29. Letter to John Newton, 14 June 1786, *Works*,  p. 420.
30. *Ibid.*, p. 421.
31. Bogatzky, *Golden Treasury*, p. xv.

**Chapter 20**
1.    A. Brown, *Recollections of the Conversation Parties of the Rev. Charles Simeon*, London, 1863, pp. 200-202.
         Brown, a curate of Simeon's, relates conversation by Simeon twenty-seven years after Simeon's death and seventy years after Berridge's death. He gets Berridge's college wrong and a story about a visit by Simeon, the Robinsons and Fletcher does not fit the evidence given by Gorham about Berridge's last meeting with Fletcher. He says, 'Mr Berridge in his late years became hypochondriac, and fancied that he was made of glass, or that he was swollen to an enormous size, etc., etc. Once, in very cold weather, when visiting with

other clergymen at a friend's house, he slipped out of the parlour in the evening, and went up to his bedroom to pray as was his wont. After a while the assembled party were alarmed by frightful groans from upstairs, and rushed to Berridge's room, whence the groans proceeded. The old man was sitting, buttoned up in a greatcoat, evidently not his own, groaning; and when asked what was the matter, said, "Matter? Don't you see how I am swelling up? I shall burst into shivers presently. See how my greatcoat has suddenly grown too tight for my arms and shoulders and waist!" The host replied, "Why, Mr Berridge, you have put on a very small greatcoat in the hall instead of your own; I wonder how you ever drew it on." The old man looked at it and said, "So I have; it is all right."' (pp. 202-3).

2.   Letter to John Thornton, 10 January 1789, *Congregational Magazine 1845*, p. 741.
3.   *Ibid.*
4.   *Torrington Diaries,* vol. IV, p. 105.
5.   Letter to B. Mills, 23 November 1790, *Works*, p. 435.
6.   *Works*, p. xlvii.
7.   *Life and Letters of Henry Venn*, p. 469.
8.   *Diary of the Rev. B. Gilpin,* Extract published in *Bedfordshire Magazine*, vol. 18, no. 137, 1981, p. 25.
9.   Farewell Sermon, *Works*, p. 612.
10.  *Ibid.*, p. 613.
11.  Letter to Miss L., 6 May 1792, *Works*, pp. 436-7.
12.  Letter to Mrs E., August 1792, *Works*, pp. 437-8.
13.  *Cheerful Piety, Works*, p. 340.
14.  *Ibid.*
15.  *Ibid.*, p. 353.
16.  *Ibid.*
17.  *Life and Letters of Henry Venn*, p. 489.
18.  *Works*, p. xlvi.
19.  Letter of 22 January 1793, *Works*, p. 614.

## Chapter 21

1.   Smyth, *Simeon and Church Order*,  p. 182.
2.   Ryle, *Five Christian Leaders*, p. 116.
3.   *Works*, p.556.
4.   Sermon Notes XVIII, *Works*, p. 563.
5.   Hymn 33, *Works*, p. 214.
6.   Letter to Lady Huntingdon, *Works*, pp. 449-450.
7.   Farewell Sermon, *Works*, p. 612.
8.   *Private Correspondence of William Cowper*,  vol. II, London, 1824, pp.262-3.
9.   Sidney, *Life of Rowland Hill*, p. 51.
10.  *Christian World Unmasked*, p. 54.
11.  Letter to Rowland Hill, 3 September 1774, *Congregational Magazine 1841*, p. 870.
12.  Letter to S. Lucas, 23 October 1775, *Works*, p. 397.
13.  *Works*, p. 439.
14.  Hymn 225, *Works*, p. 279.

15. *Works*, p. xx.
16. *Life and Letters of Henry Venn*, p. 176.
17. *Works*, p. xlvii.
18. *Ibid.*
19. Letter to John Thornton, 27 July 1775, *Works*, p. 395.
20. Bogatzky, *Golden Treasury*, p. 12.
21. *Ibid.*, comment for 8 June.
22. *Ibid.*
23. Letter to B. Mills, 4 November 1785, *Works*, p. 432.
24. Letter to Mr Edwards, 26 March 1771, *Works*, p. 365.
25. Letter to John Thornton, 3 April 1773, *Works*, pp. 369-70.
26. Letter to John Thornton, 17 October 1775, *Works*, p. 522.
27. Seymour, *Life of Countess of Huntingdon*, vol.1, p. 368.
28. *Works*, pp. xxiii-xxiv.
29. Sermon Outline, *Works*, p. 562.
30. *Ibid.*, p. 577.
31. See Appendix 2, Farewell Sermon.
32. Hymn 47, *Works*, p. 219.
33. Hymn 215, *Works*, p. 275.
34. *Christian World Unmasked*, p. 41.
35. Farewell Sermon, *Works*, p. 611.
36. *Christian World Unmasked*, p. 83.
37. Hymn 236, *Works*, p. 284.
38. Hymn 282, *Works*, p. 308.
39. *Christian World Unmasked*, p. 42.
40. Sermon Notes, *Works*, p. 550.
41. *Christian World Unmasked*, p. 218.
42. *Ibid.*, p. 6.
43. Sermon Outlines, *Works*, p. 544.
44. Letter to C. Simeon, *Works*, pp. 439-40.
45. Hymn 235, *Works*, p. 283.
46. Letter, 14 July 1759, *Congregational Magazine 1780*.
47. *Works*, p. 631.
48. Letter to Simeon, *Works*, p. 44.
49. Letter to Rowland Hill, 8 May 1771, *Works*, p. 511.
50. Letter to John Thornton, 2 July 1785, *Works*, p. 413.
51. Letter to John Thornton, 1 October 1784, *Works*, p. 413.

**Chapter 22**
1. Dyer, *Memoirs of R. Robinson*, p. 54.
2. Overton & Relton, *English Church 1714-1800*, p. 150.
3. Dyer, *Memoirs of R. Robinson*, p. 54.
4. *Justification by Faith Alone, Works*, p. 352.
5. Letter to Miss L., 6 May 1782, *Works*, p. 436.
6. *Christian World Unmasked*, p. 72.
7. *Ibid.*, p. 70.
8. *Ibid.*, p. 71.
9. *Ibid.*, p. 70
10. *Ibid.*, p. 72.

11. Letter to John Newton, 13 March 1771, *Works*, p. 364.
12. Letter to S. Wilks, 16 August 1774, *Works*, p. 387.
13. Fletcher often combines reason and Scripture as a basis for his approach.
14. *Christian World Unmasked*, p. 29.
15. *Ibid.*, p. 64.
16. Tyerman, *Life of John Wesley*, vol. II, p. 491.
17. Dyer, *Memoirs of R. Robinson*, p. 55.
18. Letter to John Thornton, 20 October 1780, *Works*, p. 400.
19. *Christian World Unmasked*, p. 71.
20. Letter to Rowland Hill, 8 May 1771, *Works*, p. 511.
21. Hymn 22, *Works*, p. 209.
22. *Christian World Unmasked*, p. 3.
23. Hymn 171, *Works*, p. 260.
24. *Christian World Unmasked*, p. 47,
25. *Ibid.*, p. 61.
26. *Ibid.*, p. 73.
27. *Ibid.*, p. 138.
28. Sermon Outlines, *Works*, p. 539.
29. Hymn 232, *Works*, p. 282.
30. *Gospel Gems*, p. 15.
31. Nor on the earth, nor in myself,
    I find a single meal of good;
    Then reach my Bible from the shelf,
    For there I find substantial food
        (Hymn 166, *Works*, p. 258).
32. Sermon Outlines, *Works*, pp. 576-7.
33. *Christian World Unmasked*, p. 128.
34. Hymn 151, *Works*, p. 253.
35. Letter to John Thornton, 14 January 1774, *Congregational Magazine 1845*, p. 27.
36. Hymn 4, *Works*, p. 202.
37. *Christian World Unmasked*, pp. 224-5.
38. *Ibid.*, p. 19.
39. Hymn 276, *Works*, p. 304.
40. Hymn 319, *Works*, p. 321.
41. *Christian World Unmasked*, pp. 57-8.
42. *Ibid.*, pp. 105-6.
43. Letter to John Thornton, 3 April 1773, *Works*, p. 370.
44. Sermon Outlines XIII, *Works*, pp. 555-6.
45. Hymn 308, *Works*, p. 318.
46. Hymn 47, *Works*, p. 219.
47. Sermon Outlines, *Works*, p. 571.
48. *Works*, p. 349.
49. Hymn 148, *Works*, p. 252.

**Chapter 23**
1. Hymn 258, *Works*, p. 293.
2. Letter to Lady Huntingdon, 9 January 1770, *Works*, pp. 506-7.
3. *Christian World Unmasked*, p. 207.

4.   *Ibid.*
5.   Letter to Lady Huntingdon, 26 April 1777, *Works*, p. 515.
6.   Letter to John Thornton, 17 November 1784, *Congregational Magazine 1784*, p. 275.
7.   *Christian World Unmasked*, p. 87.
8.   *Justification by Faith Alone, Works*, pp. 353-4.
9.   H. Tibbut, 'Joshua Symonds Diarist', *Bedfordshire Magazine*, vol. 4, 1955, no. 32, p. 339.
10.  Letter to Lady Huntingdon, 26 April 1777, *Works*, p. 515.
11.  *Works*, p. 517.
12.  *Ibid.*, p. 515.
13.  F.C. Hamlym, *History of the Parish Church of St Mary Everton-Tetworth*, St Neots, 1947, p. 14.
14.  Letter to B. Mills, 20 November 1784, *Congregational Magazine 1838*, pp.163-4.
15.  Smyth, *Simeon and Church Order*, p. 253.
16.  Letter to Lady Huntingdon, 26 April 1777, *Works*, p. 515.
17.  Letter to John Newton, 14 June 1786, *Works*, p. 421.
18.  *Christian World Unmasked*, p. 203.
19.  *Ibid.* pp. 221-3.
20.  Hymn 308, *Works*, p. 317.
21.  Letter to John Thornton, 27 October 1787, *Works*, p. 425.
22.  Smyth, *Simeon and Church Order*, p. 250.
23.  Brown, *Recollections of Conversation Parties*, p. 200.
24.  Bateman, *Life of Daniel Wilson*, p.40, quoted in Elliot-Binns, *The Early Evangelicals*.
25.  Letter to John Thornton, 2 July 1785, *Works*, p. 414.
26.  Letter to D.Simpson, 8 August 1775, *Works*, p. 530.
27.  Letter to C. Simeon, *Works*, p. 441.
28.  Letter to Rowland Hill, 7 June 1776, *Congregational Magazine 1841*, p.870
29.  Letter to John Thornton, 10 August 1774, *Works*, p. 385.
30.  *Christian World Unmasked*, p. 85.
31.  *Ibid.*, p. 78.
32.  Letter to C. Simeon, *Works*, p. 439.

**Chapter 24**
1.   *A Collection of Divine Songs*, p. vii.
2.   Letter to Rev.S. Lucas, 23 October 1775, *Works*, pp. 397-8.
3.   Letter to John Thornton, 13 July 1785, *Works*, p. 416.
4.   Jay, *Memoirs of Cornelius Winter*, p. 85.
5.   Sermon Outlines, *Works*, p. 585.
6.   *Ibid.*
7.   Ryle, *Five Christian Leaders*, p. 147.
8.   Letter to Mrs Hilliar, 10 April 1778, Manuscript, Rylands Library.
9.   Farewell Sermon, *Works*, p. 612.
10.  *Christian World Unmasked*, p. 56.
11.  Letter to Mrs E.H., 31 March 1780, *Works*, p. 398.
12.  Letter to S. Wilks, 16 August 1774, *Works*, p. 398.

13. Letter to R. Woodgate, 21 April 1775, Rylands Mansucript.
14. Hymn 310, *Works*, p. 318.
15. Hymn 311, *Works*, p. 318.
16. Letter to Mrs E., 2 August 1792, *Works*, p. 438.
17. Letter of 9 October 1788, *Works*, p. 427.
18. Hymn 316, *Works*, p. 320.
19. Hymn 314, *Works*, p. 313.
20. Letter to John Thornton, 15 November 1785, *Works*, pp. 410-411.
21. Letter to John Newton, 12 November 1785, *Works*, p. 416.
22. Letter to Lady Huntingdon, 9 July 1763, *Works*, p. 448.
23. Letter to George Whitefield, 22 May 1769, *Works*, p .444.
24. Letter of 26 April 1776, *New Methodist Magazine 1818*, p. 255.
25. Letter to Rowland Hill, 7 June 1776, *Congregational Magazine 1841*, p.871.
26. Letter to Rev. Mr Lee, 7 September 1767, *Works*, p. 451.
27. Letter to John Newton, 10 June 1771, *Works*, p. 367.
28. Letter to John Newton, 12 November 1785, *Works*, p. 417.
29. Letter to John Newton, 12 December 1780, *Works*, p. 402.
30. Letter to John Thornton, 23 January 1783, *Works*, p. 409.
31. Letter to John Thornton, 13 July 1785, *Works*, p. 415.
32. Letter to Adams (not to Housman, Adams' son-in-law, as stated in *Works*), 21 August 1765, *Works*, pp. 526-7.
33. Letter to Samuel Wilks, 8 April 1774, *Works*, p. 383.

**Chapter 25**
1. *A Collection of Divine Songs.*
2. See note, 'Early Evangelicals and their Hymn Books' at the end of Butterworth, 'The Rev. John Berridge and his Hymn Book', pp. 169-174.
3. Preface, *Sion's Songs or Hymns 1785*, pp. iii and iv.
4. *Ibid.*, p. vii.
5. Letter to John Thornton, 27 July 1775, *Works*, p. 395.
6. *A Collection of Divine Songs*, p. x.
7. *Sion's Songs*, p. iii.
8. *Ibid.*, p. vii.
9. *Ibid.*, p. viii.
10. *Ibid.*
11. T. Wright, *Toplady and Contemporary Hymn-Writers*, London, 1911, p.258.
12. *Sion's Songs*, p. vi.
13. *Works*, p. v.
14. J.C. Philpot, *Preface to Zion's Songs or Hymns*, new edition 1842, p. xiv.
15. Gadsby, *Memoirs of the Principal Hymn-Writers*, p. 153.
16. Butterworth, 'Rev. John Berridge and his Hymn-Book', p. 170.
17. Ryle, *Five Christian Leaders*, p. 136.
18. Philpot, *Preface to Zion's Songs*, p. xi.
19. Wright, *Life of Toplady*, p. 258.
20. *Sion's Songs*, p. v.
21. Philpot, *Preface to Zion's Songs*, p. iv.
22. Hymn 210, *Works*, p. 273.

23. *Sion's Songs*, p. iv.
24. Bogatzky, *Golden Treasury*, comment on 24 February.
25. *Ibid.*, comment on 1 November.
26. Philpot, *Preface to Zion's Songs*, p. v.
27. Hymn 320, *Works*, p. 322
28. Hymn 226, *Works*, p. 279.
29. Hymn 63, *Works*, p. 224.
30. Hymn 94, *Works*, p. 234.
31. Hymn 47, *Works*, p. 219.
32. *Sion's Songs*, p. iv.
33. Hymn 77, *Works*, p. 228.
34. Hymn 117, *Works*, p. 241.
35. Hymn 75, *Works*, p. 228.
36. Philpot, *Preface to Zion's Songs*, p. ix.
37. Hymn 38, *Works*, p. 216.
38. Hymn 13, *Works*, p. 206.
39. Hymn 2, *Works*, p. 201.
40. Hymn 83, *Works*, p. 233.
41. Bogatzky, *Golden Treasury*, comment on 24 January.
42. *Ibid.*, comment on 18 November.
43. *Ibid.*, comment on 25 January.
44. *Ibid.*
45. *Ibid.*
46. *Ibid.*, comment on 4 February.

**Chapter 26**
1.  Hymn 159, *Works*, p. 255.
2.  *Works*, pp. xxx-xxxi.
3.  The Christian's Warfare and Crown. A sermon occasioned by the death of the Rev. John Berridge by the Rev. W. Holland', *Works*, p. 631.
4.  Sermon Outline XXVI, *Works*, p. 576.
5.  Hymn 203, *Works*, p. 271.
6.  Hymn 248, *Works*, p. 288.
7.  Hymn 137, *Works*, p. 248.
8.  Letter to John Thornton, 21 February 1788, *Works*, p. 426.
9.  Jay, *Memoirs of Cornelius Winter*, p. 86.
10. *Cheerful Piety*, *Works*, p. 358.
11. Hymn 224, *Works*, p. 278.
12. *Works*, p. xxix.
13. Letter to S. Wilks, 11 April 1775, *Works*, p. 387.
14. Hymn 104, *Works*, p. 237.
15. *Works*, p. xxii.
16. *Ibid.*
17. Ryle, *Five Christian Leaders*, p. 144.
18. Hymn 234, *Works*, p. 283.
19. *Churchman's Monthly Penny Magazine 1852*, quoted in Ryle, *Five Christian Leaders*, pp. 144-5.
20. *Cheerful Piety*, *Works*, p. 349.
21. Letter to John Thornton, 23 September 1788, *Works*, p. 519.

22. Hymn 216, *Works*, p. 276.
23. Letter to Lady Ingham, 28 January 1766, Gadsby, *Memoirs of the Principal Hymn-Writers*, p. 34.
24. Hymn 196, *Works*, p. 268.
25. *Works*, p. xxv.
26. *Ibid.*, p. xxx.
27. Hymn 31, *Works*, p. 213.
28. Letter to B. Mills, 2 September 1782, *Congregational Magazine 1845*, p.273.
29. Letter to John Thornton, 3 May 1773, *Congregational Magazine 1842*, p.221.
30. Letter to John Thornton, 31 August 1773, *Works*, p. 375.
31. *Works*, p. 533.
32. Letter to John Thornton, 3 May 1773, *Congregational Magazine 1842*, p.221.
33. Works, p. xxvii.
34. Letter to John Thornton, 3 May 1773, *Congregational Magazine 1842*, p.221.
35. Letter to John Thornton, 27 October 1778, *Works*, p. 393.
36. Letter to John Thornton, 31 August 1773, *Works*, p. 276.
37. Letter to Lady Huntingdon, 23 March 1770, *Works*, pp. 508-9.
38. *Gospel Gems*, p. iv.
39. Letter to John Thornton, 10 August 1774, *Works*, p. 384.
40. Jay, *Memoirs of Cornelius Winter*, p. 85.
41. Letter to Lady Huntingdon, 26 April 1777, *Works*, p. 516.
42. Letter to Rowland Hill, 16 January 1770, *Congregational Magazine 1841*, p. 600.
43. J.H. Overton, *The Evangelical Revival in the Eighteenth Century*, London, 1886, p.64.

# Index